I0881402

A HISTORY OF ALCOHOLIC SPIRITS

A HISTORY OF ALCOHOLIC SPIRITS

How Our Favourite Tipples Changed The World

Jamie Ryder

PEN & SWORD
HISTORY
AN IMPRINT OF PEN & SWORD BOOKS LTD.
YORKSHIRE – PHILADELPHIA

First published in Great Britain in 2025 by
PEN AND SWORD HISTORY
An imprint of
Pen & Sword Books Ltd
Yorkshire – Philadelphia

ISBN 978 1 03612 205 8

A CIP catalogue record for this book is available from the British Library.

Typeset in Times New Roman 11.5/14 by
SJmagic DESIGN SERVICES, India.
Printed and bound in the UK by CPI Group (UK) Ltd.

The Publisher's authorised representative in the EU for product safety is Authorised Rep Compliance Ltd., Ground Floor, 71 Lower Baggot Street, Dublin D02 P593, Ireland.
www.arccompliance.com

For a complete list of Pen & Sword titles please contact
PEN & SWORD BOOKS LIMITED
George House, Units 12 & 13, Beevor Street, Off Pontefract Road,
Barnsley, South Yorkshire, S71 1HN, England
E-mail: enquiries@pen-and-sword.co.uk
Website: www.pen-and-sword.co.uk

or

PEN AND SWORD BOOKS
1950 Lawrence Rd, Havertown, PA 19083, USA
E-mail: uspen-and-sword@casematepublishers.com
Website: www.penandswordbooks.com

MIX
Paper | Supporting responsible forestry
FSC® C013604

Contents

Introduction

To understand the history of the world is to understand the history of alcoholic spirits. I know that's a bold claim to make and as you reach across the bar for a pint or glass of your favourite booze, you might need to take more than one or two sips to put yourself in the kind of philosophical mood needed to think about that claim in depth. (I've always found pubs to be an excellent place to be philosophical and to set the world to rights.)

As you take a sip, and then the next, your eyes and mind may wander. You see bartenders pouring Scotch whisky for blokes who look like they drink nothing but the stuff. Stag and hen parties slamming tequila and vodka shots. You hear families and friends talking about the state of the country over glasses of rum and coke. The sloshing, rapid-fire mixing of cocktails makes you wonder what kind of drinks are being made and the rainbow of bottles and brands on the back bar blend in some wonderful, confusing kaleidoscope of marketing madness.

Once you think about my claim in those terms, hopefully it starts to make a little more sense. Because for as long as people have been around, we've been making and using alcoholic spirits to push our world forward.

Western spirits like gin, rum and whisky have been at the centre of vast societal changes, from the court of kings and queens, into the shadowy cabinets of parliaments and governments, down to the streets where everyday people drink and dream. Eastern spirits like Japanese shochu, Okinawan awamori and Chinese baijiu have fuelled armies and empires. They've been used as a social lubricant, currency, medicine, gateway to the other side and tool of self-destruction.

Spirits have been used to tell stories and that is what this book is about. *A History Of Alcoholic Spirits: How Our Favourite Tipples Changed*

The World is about the stories of different categories and the cultural crossovers and exchanges that have linked major historical events.

It's a book about distillers, bartenders, outlaws, politicians, kings, queens and every social class in between that had a hand in building categories like tequila, mezcal, bourbon and Scotch into what they are today. It's about the people who shaped these industries for better and for worse, as much as the people who tried to tear them down and destroy them completely.

What this book isn't, is a complete and expansive history of every category that's featured in the pages. That goes beyond the scope of the subject. For deep academic dives into specific categories, I'll refer you to the bibliography, where you can discover resources that have been vital research material and written by specialists who can probably tell you about the exact measurements of distillates, flavour compounds and specifications. I recommend following the work of any author covered in the bibliography because they know a lot more about those technical details than I do.

A History Of Alcoholic Spirits is suited to casual drinkers and students of history who're looking for more context about the booze they're sipping. Drinkers who enjoy hearing wild, outlandish stories cut from the cloth of a Mark Twain aphorism like 'why shouldn't truth be stranger than fiction? Fiction, after all, has to make sense.'[1] (You'd assume that an all-American literary hero like Twain would choose bourbon as his spirit of choice, right? Nope. He was a Scotch man through and through.[2])

The book is also suited for bartenders and drink professionals who're interested in learning about the history behind famous distilleries and brands so they can improve their own storytelling skills to educate consumers.

When conducting research into brands, I've chosen to dig beneath the marketing rhetoric that's presented to the public by the companies that sell them where possible. I've looked at independent writers and academics with no brand affiliation, historical texts and sources to try and root the products in the context of their time.

This research has been done to provide a balanced viewpoint and the stories I've included about distilleries, brands and products stem from a personal curiosity about them and are not a personal endorsement to buy them. Every product I've reviewed has been paid for out of my pocket and all opinions are my own.

I'd also like to mention that *A History Of Alcoholic Spirits* isn't written as a chronological narrative, because the cross-culture exchanges of alcoholic beverages has no structured order to it. Better you treat the book as a kind of literary museum of spirits – you can leisurely explore a category at your own pace by flipping between chapters. Every chapter is arranged around one category and you can start at whichever drink you most enjoy or are curious about.

So, here's to you, dear reader. Cheers, sláinte, salute, prost, nostrovia, skoll, ganbei, kanpai, however the hell you toast with your favourite tipple in hand. Enjoy your journey through *A History Of Alcoholic Spirits*.

Once you get to the end, you can tell me your thoughts over at my drinks newsletter drinktothat.substack.com. Or you can leave an honest review on Amazon or wherever else you feel comfortable writing a review.

Now, before you begin this spirit-fuelled odyssey across the globe, it's worth knowing about the process of distillation and how it's impacted the transmission of the spirits you'll learn about.

An Overview of the Distillation of Alcoholic Spirits

The origins of distillation, i.e. the separation of liquid by evaporation and condensation, are as murky as the origins of every spirit developed out of this process. As early as the fourth century BC, the Greek philosopher Aristotle wrote instructions on the distillation of non-alcoholic and alcoholic beverages: 'Seawater can be made potable by distillation as well as wine and other liquids can be submitted to the same process.'[1]

For a time, it was thought that the Greeks invented distillation, but it's now generally assumed that distillation technologies can be traced to China and the East. In her book, *Soju: A Global History*, Hyunhee Park writes:

> we now know distillation technology, at first used to purify mercury, not alcohol, is older in China than it is in the West, and given inherent differences in the two general methods, most likely developed independently. The Chinese never used worm tubs, a standard component of a classic pot still popular in the West, through which distillates were condensed and collected.[2]

As far as the invention of the first alembic device to distil liquids goes, this is generally attributed to a woman called Maria the Jewess from Alexandria, in the first or third centuries ad. (Different types of distillation technologies and how they influence spirits will be explored in more depth throughout the coming chapters.)

Of course, this is only one Western viewpoint and opinions continue to differ. Several attempts have been made by scholars and academics to trace the exact geographical location and time of distillation's dawn.

Some believe that the process began in Egypt or Mesopotamia for medicinal purposes around 2000 bc. There's a story of 1810 bc when the king of Mesopotamia, King Zimrilim, used distillation to make hundreds of litres of balms from ginger, myrrh, cedar and cypress, each month that were used for embalming rituals.[3]

The distillation of alcohol must also be appreciated alongside the art of alchemy – the practice of trying to convert base metals into gold and the pursuit of the 'elixir of life'. Alchemists were the first distillers and chemists, attempting to create substances like The Philosopher's Stone à la Harry Potter.

In this vein, we see another story about the possible creation of the first alembic from Jabir Ibn Hayyan, a ninth-century alchemist credited as being the Father of Chemistry and the inventor of several other scientific processes like evaporation, crystallisation and calcination.[4]

To say that alchemy was a 'direct' precursor to alcoholic distillation is an oversimplification because the crude distillation of alcohol was already happening in other parts of the world. And many cultures have their own origin stories in terms of the evolution of distilled alcohol.

In 800 bc, the Chinese were distilling a beverage from rice beer. The Romans produced a distilled drink, although no written references have been found before 100 ad. Poitin, the oldest of Irish spirits, was being made in Ireland from the sixth century onwards. Arak, a Levantine and Arabic spirit made from fermented grapes and aniseed, was distilled in the ninth century alongside the development of alembic technology.

Into the Later Middle Ages, the first documented evidence of distillation in the Western world was recorded in ad 1150 in Salerno, Italy. This story also has its origins in the ancient past, when a Greek pilgrim named Pontus stopped in Salerno and sheltered from a thunderstorm under an aqueduct.

An Italian wanderer, Salernus, sheltered in the same place and depending on the sources, either one of them had been hurt. Two other travellers, a Jewish man Helinus and an Arab man Abdela, escaped the thunderstorm and applied their knowledge to the wounds of the Italian or Greek. Later, all four discovered they were doctors and they decided to create the Medical School of Salerno, the oldest medical school in the West that brought the knowledge of multiple cultures together.

Perhaps at the school is where our 1150 anecdote comes from, for a man identified only as the 'Master of Salerno' wrote an introduction on the distillation of wine in a manuscript that contained recipes on a variety of craft techniques on glass, metals and dyes.

The rough translation from Latin for this distillation technique is 'a mixture of pure and very strong XKNK with three QBSUF TBMKT cooked in the usual vessel make a water, which will flame up when set on fire but leave the material unburnt.'[5]

Apparently the capitalised words are word puzzles that feature a mistake. They're formed by substituting the correct letter in Latin, the letter that follows it in the alphabet. So, XHNK means VINI (wines), QBSUF is PARTE (part) and TBMKT is SALIS (salt). The mistake may be in the XHNK – the 'n' should have been an 'o'.[6]

Into the 1800s, as countries like England, France, Spain and Scotland marched towards industrialisation, new ways of distilling spirits on a mass scale were invented. In France particularly, there was a push for creating efficient stills that could operate continuously to produce industrial alcohol and spirits.

During an age described as an 'avalanche of patents', Jean-Baptiste Cellier-Blumenthal invented the first continuous still in 1808 and patented the design in 1813. Over a decade later in 1824, Jean-Jacques Saint Marc from the Belmont Distillery in Vauxhall, London, got an early patent for a single-distillation still. This would be a precursor to the twentieth-century Lomond still, a pot still with a rectifying head used to distil potato spirit.

Meanwhile, in the Scottish Highlands and Lowlands, new designs were being worked on by the Steins, a famous Scotch whisky family. Robert Stein got his first continuous distillation patent in 1827 and while it was being tested an Irishman known as Aeneas Coffey also threw his hat into the ring with a patent in 1830 that became known as the Coffey still. The Irishman's still became a commercially successful continuous distillation method and the bedrock of Scotch whisky production.

The eternal truth of all these legends, stories and inventions is that alcoholic spirits are never static. That one single moment, conversation or decision can't be pinpointed as the source of separating alcohol from water using evaporation and condensation.

These spirits of the age you'll learn about are products of countless cultural exchanges, political upheavals, transatlantic explorations and human ingenuity in equal parts madness, brilliance and business sense.

Chapter 1
Gin

To the Mortal Memory of
Madam Geneva.
Who died Sept 29. 1736
Her Weeping Servants &
Loving Friends consecrate
This Tomb.

This epitaph, scrawled onto a distiller's apron doubling as a banner, decorates a funeral monument surrounded by mourners of all shapes and sizes. An elderly woman in rags, toothless, befuddled and in the process of losing her slipper, lies back against a barrel with an empty glass in one hand. Her other hand points to the bottom of the monument where the image of the sun being eclipsed in darkness overshadows the words 'cease to drop distil no more'.

Beside her, two urchins hold up an empty barrel, while a pregnant fishwife to the left of the old woman is inconsolable on top of the barrel on which she stands. She's so lost in her lamentations that she ignores her child who tugs at her clothes.

On the right side of the monument, a male distiller moodily leans on the worm of his still, mourning the loss of his livelihood. Atop the sepulchre, a grenadier points forlornly down at a central barrel fixed onto a tall, wooden pedestal as the symbolic death knell of an industry that's caused naught but death and ruin in the cities, towns and villages of England.[1]

The Dark Days of Genever and Gin

The scene I've described is a satirical illustration in the wake of the Gin Act of 1736, which attempted to curb excessive gin consumption among the English. The Act, which was the third of its kind, brought in heavy excise duties on gin production, making life more expensive for distillers and retailers. Sellers were restricted to a two-gallon minimum unit of sale with swingeing duties of £1 per gallon. They were also required by law to buy a £50 annual licence, which amounted to fourteen months' wages[2] for a competent craftsman.

Instead of slowing down gin drinking, the act sparked rebellion and protests, driving gin-making underground and reinforcing the crime and poverty that the British Parliament was trying to put a stop to.

Between 1720, nine years before the first Gin Act was passed, and the last Act of 1751, an era of hysteria – the perceived breakdown of moral order between social classes, sickness, smuggling and awakening to the damaging effects of alcohol – gripped Great Britain. All of it was concentrated into a single spirit cast in the role of a nightmarish fuel for the worst impulses of humanity and a social decay lubricant that brought ruin to mothers, respectable men and children alike.

The Gin Craze as it was known became the first social phenomenon of its kind to show the world the consequences of alcohol abuse. The conditions for it were created decades before with the arrival of a Dutch beverage that captured the imagination of the English aristocracy – genever.

The Court of Genever

This distinctive spirit is a botanically infused clear liquid made from a neutral spirit and malt grain that retains a certain flavour. As of 2008, genever has an official AOC (appellation d'origine contrôlée) stating that it can only be made in the Netherlands and Belgium and specific areas of Germany and France. As will become clear with every spirit discussed, no origin story is the same. But it *does* make for a riveting debate among category purists and casual drinkers.

In genever's case, one popular story is that it was invented by an alchemist called Sylvius de Bouve who had a knack for distilling medicines with juniper berry oil at the University of Leiden in the seventeenth century. Yet none of his records contain any mention of genever and historically, he wasn't the first juniper distiller. References to genever date back as far as the thirteenth century to Thomas of

Cantimpré's *The Nature of Things,* an adaptation of even earlier Greek and Roman sources.

As for how genever came to England, it wasn't some overnight sensation bolstered by slick marketing campaigns or well-placed ads. It was likely a gradual cross-border exchange of information and distilling traditions between monks in the 1500s who were displaced by Henry VIII's Dissolution of the Monasteries in the aftermath of the Reformation and forced to make a living as distillers. Into the 1600s, English soldiers and sailors may have brought genever back to Britain during the wars they fought under the reign of Elizabeth I.

But it was two different royals that established genever as a drink of the English and set in motion its transformation into gin, the drink of the destitute. They were William of Orange and his wife Mary, who came to power after the English Civil War.

And as Wayne Curtis points out in *And A Bottle Of Rum*: *A History Of The New World In Ten Cocktails*, war is one of the surest ways for nations to change their drinking habits with any spirit. 'Soldiers abroad find new and appealing means of intoxication and seek to recreate them when they return; at home, consumers adapt to shortages of old favourites by developing a preference for something more available. Such a shift might start begrudgingly and evolve into genuine enthusiasm.'[3]

The English wars against Holland and at home brought gin to the masses. By the time William and Mary took the throne in 1689, the people were eager to drink in honour of their Dutch king who enjoyed copious amounts of genever.

William didn't waste time renewing the cycle of creating new drinking habits with war. One of his first acts was to declare war on France and a ban on the imports of French brandy. This led to a liberal distilling culture, where anyone could make spirits from British grain because of the lowered taxes on corn and the ease with which they could distil, so long as they paid a token custom fee and gave ten days' notice.

Landowners and farmers cashed in together, creating inexpensive distilleries for the drink that would become gin. It was lower in quality than genever, cheaper to make and easier to earn a quick profit on because it could be sold on the mass market.

Thus, genever remained an imported luxury for the wealthy, while gin, at the dawn of the 1700s, became an intoxicant for the poor and a ravaging blight that would destroy countless lives over the next half-century. And over that time, two camps drew a line in the sand between sobriety and heavy drinking.

We'll call the first camp the Gin Opposition, made up of the politicians and reformers who fought to curb gin consumption. The second camp we'll call the Gin Radicals, formed by the distillers, smugglers and bon vivants who were here for a good time and a long time.

The Gin Opposition

> The drunkenness I here intended is that acquired by the strongest intoxicating liquors, and particularly by that poison called gin which is … the principle sustenance … of more than a hundred thousand people in this metropolis … the dreadful effects of which I have had the misfortune every day to see and to smell to.[4]

This observation was written by the respected novelist, playwright and magistrate Henry Fielding, to describe the destructive force that was gin in the streets of London. Fielding was one of the most vocal members of the Gin Opposition, decrying the epidemic of cheap gin being flogged in the back alleys and gin shops that powered an alcohol-washed crimewave, unnoticed until it was pointed out by people with the power to make others listen and to make decisions:

> Many instances of this I see daily; wretches are often brought before me, charged with theft and robbery, whom I am forced to confine before they are in a condition to be examined; and when they have afterwards become sober, I have plainly perceived … that gin alone was the cause of the transgression.[5]

Fielding's hard line against gin is thought to have come from a humanitarian perspective, as in his magisterial career he was known for his impartial judgements, refusing to take money from the poor and his development of perhaps London's first police force, the Bow Street Runners, with his half-brother John in 1749.

But what's interesting is that in another life, he could have stood across the picket line with the gin rebels and distillers, as he was no stranger to skewering prohibition and censorship. Fielding had begun his career as a writer of political satire, putting on plays that poked fun at the status quo of the government at the Little Theatre in Haymarket.

In 1737, the Theatre Licensing Act was passed, essentially putting a stop to any political satire. Fielding's plays had set the tone and his work was one of the major reasons why the Act was passed in the first place. The Act put a stop to Fielding's career as a playwright and so he turned to writing satirical novels and news articles.

In his role as the main writer and editor of the satirical paper *The Champion* between 1739–40, he wrote scathing attacks on the Richard Walpole-led Tory government. He aimed to avoid libel charges by making his writing so funny and embarrassing for his victims that to go through a publicised court case would make the situation seem even worse. Fielding also found some success with his novel *The History of Tom Jones, a Foundling* (1749) though Fielding had a habit of falling on hard times and hard drinking.

Fielding's beloved wife Charlotte died in 1744 and he became depressed, in debt and generally discontented with his lot. With his good friend and fellow creative William Hogarth, he frequented the Bedford Arms pub, running a card game and drowning his sorrows. As the poet Edward More reported in 1749, 'Fielding continues to be visited for his sins so as to be wheeled about from room to room … His disorder is the gout and intemperance the cause.'[6] While Fielding lobbied against gin through his writing of texts like *Enquiry into the Causes of the late Increase of Robbers,* his friend Hogarth did so through art.

As passionate about the repeal of gin sales as Fielding, Hogarth's most enduring works of this period are *Gin Lane* and *Beer Street.* Both paintings stand as opposites to each other – gin is depicted as tearing society apart at the seams, while beer is positioned as the brew of the people, contributing to a healthier, industrial society.

The paintings have been widely discussed in the discourse of the Gin Craze and there are plenty of articles online that discuss their depictions in depth. I think what's more useful is to examine Hogarth's motivations in creating early propaganda, in a similar way that the brands in the Gin Radicals' camp would later use to promote their products.

Since his boyhood days, Hogarth had felt the damaging effects that crime and punishment can wreak on a family. His father, Richard, fell into debt after opening a failed coffee shop and being confined to Fleet prison. The young Hogarth lived within the jurisdiction of the prison, fending for himself and being constrained by his upbringing.

Unable to climb any higher than as an apprentice to a silver engraver, Hogarth used his experiences to paint and print gritty, satirical scenes as a critique of moral bankruptcy and social disorder. He won fame through his scathing depiction of the South Sea Bubble Scheme of 1720, which became the world's first financial crash, along with his moralising tableaus such *A Harlot's Progress* and *A Rake's Progress.*

Like Fielding, Hogarth was a humanitarian who had altruistic intentions when he created *Gin Lane.* According to Fiona Haslam, a clinical assistant in Obstetrics and Gynaecology at Bolton General Hospital, Hogarth,

> wished to draw attention to various social and moral issues in society. He would have had nothing to gain and much to lose by misrepresentation of facts with regard to these issues ... By coordinating his graphic images with those images provided by his literary contemporaries and in medical writings of the time ... Hogarth offers a well-informed layman's view of the world of medicine as it impinged on the society that he portrayed. Alcohol abuse is just one example.[7]

Hogarth and Fielding were joined in the Gin Opposition by several other strong voices, both male and female. Isaac Maddox, a former Lord Bishop of Worcester, published a pamphlet called *Expediency of Preventative Wisdom.* His main argument was that excessive gin drinking robbed the nation of its labour force, thus destroying businesses and the future of England's wealth.

The writer and actress Eliza Haywood was horrified by the cautionary tales of women being ruined by gin and the effect it had on home life in the case of spousal abuse. She wrote a pamphlet called *A Present for Women Addicted to Drinking Adapted to all the different Stations of Life, from a Lady of Quality to a Common Servant.* Her critique of 'you will ... look upon a Dram Glass, as a more dangerous Instrument than a

Blunderbuss',[8] found favour with the powers that be, as did the swell of outrage from all members of the Gin Opposition.

In 1751, a Gin Act was passed that finally made a difference. It enforced licensing requirements, increased the duty tax on spirits and made it illegal for gin to be sold in chandler and grocery shops, a common practice for so many years prior, where gin was sold alongside bread, small beer and cheese. The cheap fare people could order at these establishments meant breakfast was likely to be ordered with a side of gin to wash it down.

The new laws stopped this from happening and gin sales steadily declined. By 1760, parliament decided to increase the duty tax because they thought 'the high price of spirits hath greatly contributed to the health, sobriety and industry of the common people'.[9]

That didn't stop people from drinking gin, though. It made the movers and shakers of the Gin Radicals more creative and contributed to the underground reputation that gin and many other spirits would go through as they evolved from poor man's concoctions to the tipple of the rich, the curious, the hipsters and everything in between.

The Gin Radicals

As politicians and reformers were looking for ways to demonise gin, distillers, smugglers and businessmen were looking for loopholes to exploit and ideas to legitimise. One of the earliest people to take advantage of loopholes in the system was the Irish adventurer and con artist Captain Dudley Bradstreet.

A savvy showman and wheeler-dealer, Bradstreet never met a get-rich-quick scheme he didn't like. Raised by a foster family in Co. Tipperary, Bradstreet blamed his reckless attitude and criminal activity on the high living of his adoptive father. No matter what occupation he had through the years – brewer, card sharp, linen manufacturer, soldier, secret government agent – Bradstreet identified himself as a fortune hunter first.

A claim to fame he would be proud to talk anyone's ear off about was how, after saving a doctor from blackmail in 1744, he was encouraged to become a government spy. He infiltrated Irish political groups and exaggerated his own importance in stopping Jacobite plots that were rampant at the time.

Another claim to fame was his invention of a unique gin-selling system. At the height of the Gin Craze, parliament encouraged the act of informing so justices of the peace could find and crack down on properties where gin was being sold illegally. Bradstreet cottoned on to a legal loophole that stated informers had to know the name of the person renting the property from where gin was being sold. Without that knowledge, the authorities couldn't break into properties and make an arrest.

In Bradstreet's autobiography, *The Life and Uncommon Adventures of Captain Dudley Bradstreet*, he claimed he worked out a scheme where his friend rented a house in the City of London on Blue Anchor Alley. He also bought a sign with a cat and nailed it to a window in the street. Bradstreet then spent his last £13 on Langsdale Brewery gin from Holborn and told everyone in the area that gin was going to be sold at the sign of the cat the next day and then barricaded himself into the house with all the wild and reckless enthusiasm of a drunk at a lock-in.

While Bradstreet waited, he hooked up a lead pipe with a funnel beneath the cat sign. He kept on waiting until,

> I heard the Chink of Money, and a comfortable Voice say, 'Puss, give me two Pennyworth of Gin.' I instantly put my Mouth to the Tube and bid them receive it from the Pipe under her Paw, and then measured and poured it into the Funnel, from whence they soon received it.[10]

Bradstreet's Puss and Mew System caught on and was quickly copied throughout London.

The Big Smoke wasn't the only stomping ground of gin smugglers. The north of England had its fair share of bootleggers with lives as colourful as Bradstreet's. The Yorkshire village of Robin Hood's Bay was an epicentre of illegal gin activity in the late eighteenth and early nineteenth centuries, with it essentially being an entire village operation of contraband being smuggled from the bottom of the village to the top, without the contraband ever seeing the light of day.

George 'Stoney' Fagg was one of Robin Hood's Bay's most prominent smugglers, swanning up and down the coast of Whitby to Scarborough in his schooner, *The Kent*, armed with powerful swivel guns. Like everyone in his trade, Fagg was in opposition with the excise men who patrolled the waters looking to collect excise tax and prevent smuggling.

A devil-may-care sort of bloke at the best of times, Fagg was feeling particularly ballsy one day in 1777 when he invited an excise crew onto *The Kent* while he was trading with ships in Bridlington Bay. When he found out that gin supplies were low on the rival ship, he invited them on board for a drink and even sent them back with a free gin sample. The excise men returned the favour a few weeks later by cornering Fagg with an armada of ships at Filey.

'Fire away you buggers and be damned with you!' Fagg cried at the order from his former drinking partners to 'heave to or we fire'. A battle commenced and Fagg was eventually forced to surrender, leading to 200 tonnes of illegal merchandise being confiscated from *The Kent.*[11]

Another smuggler who was never able to kick the habit was Joss Bay, a man active in the south-east of England in the same period as Fagg. Living to the ripe old age of 96, Bay had several brushes with the law and carried on in his twilight years, being fined £100 for smuggling when he was 89. He set this example for his son and grandson who followed him into the family business and when a young Queen Victoria visited Broadstairs, Bay was presented to her as 'the famous smuggler'.[12]

Criminals weren't the only people with an interest in gin. Many business magnates went on to start empires, with brands that are commercially successful in the modern era. The story of a quintessential British gin started in 1769 with a man called Alexander Gordon.

A Scottish brewer, Gordon started his booze career at the age of 18 by being put in charge of an Aberdeen-based brewery and later moved to London, where he started a distillery in Southwark. His gin recipe seemed to be enjoyable for the standards of the time and the Gordon family history would become intertwined with the iconic green bottle and wild boar logo of Gordon's Dry Gin. (Even after the Gordon family ceased to have any connections with the brand after 1899 when the last owner Charles Gordon died.)

As the legend goes, a member of the Scottish Clan Gordon saved the King of Scotland from a boar attack while the king was hunting, lending a masculine image to the gin that has since evolved through the decades with glitzy advertising campaigns that have positioned Gordon's Gin as a tipple for all types of drinkers. A stalwart bottle on the shelves of supermarkets and back bars, Gordon's has remained a standard base for gin and tonics across the world.

In 1898, Gordon and Co. merged with another future gin giant called Charles Tanqueray & Co. One of the most elusive figures in the history of gin, Charles Tanqueray came from a French family with an eye for business and success at everything they turned their hands to. Tanqueray's great-great-grandfather was renowned for his gold and silversmithing skills, receiving royal recognition as the 'Subordinate Goldsmith' to King George II.

Born the sixth of fourteen children, Charles followed in his family's footsteps as an entrepreneur. Always inventing, Tanqueray could rarely sit still and he set his sights on the gin market and competing with contemporaries Felix Booth and Alexander Gordon to make a better gin.

He developed several recipes, the winner being his London Dry recipe which remains a closely guarded secret today. According to Tom Nichol, Tanqueray's current Master Distiller:

> Charles won the lottery with that one. He wasn't the genius recluse like we sometimes see today, but I think he was a genius who told everyone he was a genius. From his proud stature to his knee-length frock coat, to his stately moustache and beard, Charles Tanqueray liked to show off his success.[13]

The products of these early pioneers may have found their way into the gin dens and palaces that popped up in London like gaudy, magnificent mushrooms for people looking for quick drams and liaisons. The latter began to appear in the 1820s and as one observer described the typical gin palace was:

> a splendid edifice, the front ornamental with pilasters supporting a handsome cornice and entablature and balustrades, and the whole elevation remarkably striking and handsome … the doors and windows glazed with very large squares of plate glass, and the gas fittings of the most costly description … the street became almost impassable from the number of people collected.[14]

It was in these gin palaces that the notion of branding and marketing began to take off with different gins being labelled to distinguish them, and likely to make them more appealing to customers who only came inside to choose swiftly and be out the door so the next patron could take their place. Many barrels were labelled with names like Best Cordial Gin, Cream of the Valley and Knock Me Down, Old Tom 549 and Young Tom 360.

Through seeing the positive and negative associations of gin in its early history, we can now appreciate how the scene would be set for the modern gin boom that began at the dawn of the twenty-first century, from the delayed fuse that first ignited in the 2010s.

The Gin-plosion

Women, as much as men, have had a major hand in the evolution of gin and one of the key moments in the resurgence of gin was down to a scientist who was willing to take risks at a time when not many people saw an opportunity for a new kind of gin. Her name is Lesley Gracie, Master Distiller of Hendrick's Gin.

A native of Yorkshire, Gracie came from a background of flavour testing and making medicinal drugs more palatable. This penchant for experimentation led her to join William Grant & Sons, a Scottish whisky distiller in 1988.

Starting in the whisky department, she got involved with a daring new product when the chairman of William Grant, Charlie Gordon, wanted to launch a gin that had never been seen on the market before. Tasked with trying new ingredients, Gracie distilled with two old stills that had been bought in London in the 1960s, an antique Bennett pot still from 1860 and a 1948 Carterhead.

Of all the ingredients tried out, rose and cucumber were the two winners. Only Gracie discovered that the cucumber couldn't be put into the stills because it went black and smelled like old cabbage. Based on her keen sense of smell, Gracie agreed with Gordon that the rose and cucumber should be added to the gin after distillation. This decision led to arguably the UK's original artisanal gin and Hendrick's sales grew steadily, buoyed by the unique flavour profile, word-of-mouth reviews and the growing cocktail culture throughout the 1990s.[15]

A decade later, a man called Sam Galsworthy couldn't understand why the market for gin wasn't expanding quickly like it was in America. After all, wasn't gin known as 'the Spirit of London?'

There weren't any craft gin distillers in the capital and after doing some digging, Galsworthy discovered something extraordinary – the Gin Act of 1751 had stopped small-scale distilleries from operating in London. For two years, Galsworthy battled with HMRC, MPs and trade organisations to repeal the 250-year-old Act. In the end, he won. In 2009, he set up London's first craft gin distillery since 1820 – Sipsmith.

This was the moment that opened the floodgates for the gin renaissance, as craft distillers appeared all over the UK and beyond. Brands have tapped into the full spectrum of gin's past to define its future, with words like 'bathtub gin' coined in the Prohibition era, and Victorian imagery being common motifs within marketing collateral and labels.

A company called Bathtub Gin set up in 2011, touting the historical narrative of gin being distilled in the aforementioned bathroom fixture. Hawkridge Gin, based in Compton, Berkshire, has a 'Victorian Aphrodisiac' blend inspired by the spirit once being prized for its supposed medicinal qualities and cure for impotency.

Further afield, gin has taken on the botanicals and flavours of the countries in which it is made. In 2016, two whisky men, David Kroll and Marcin Miller, joined forces to set up the Kyoto Distillery, Japan's first dedicated gin distillery.

Kroll, his wife Noriko, and Miller had been introducing single malt whiskies into the Japanese market for twenty years and wanted to create a gin with a distinctively Japanese flavour. Mixing the legendary water of the Fushimi region used in sake brewing for centuries with eleven Japanese botanicals arranged into six elements, the trio created KI NO BI gin, which translates to 'the beauty of the seasons'. Marketed as an 'ultra-premium' gin, KI NO BI was the first Japanese gin to make a splash and created the blueprint for brands like Roku and Etsu that came after it.[16]

In Australia, unusual gin botanicals are the name of the game. Angry Ant Gin from the Bass & Flinders Distillery is made with a type of Australian ant that releases a specific kind of pheromone to give the gin its flavour.

Sacha La Forgia from the Adelaide Hills Distillery decided to experiment with green ants and vapour infusion as part of an initiative to use Aboriginal ingredients. She left a few green ants in the liquid she created and after tasting it discovered 'it was limey, coriander with herbaceous notes'.[17]

These gins are a microcosm of the varieties that are out there in the wild for you to try. From the dark days of the Gin Craze to the gin renaissance of the last decade, the spirit once called Mother's Ruin has come a long way.

Despite the challenges of a pandemic, the rise of spirits like rum (discussed in Chapter 3) and an interest in the no- and low-alcohol category, gin remains a resilient drink. Madam Geneva was put to rest once and resurrected herself, and she's carried on doing that with every new product and botanical.

As the philosophical writer Albert Camus observed in *The Fall*, about the human penchant for seeking value and meaning in an absurd world, 'There is gin, the sole glimmer in this darkness. Do you feel the golden, copper-coloured light it kindles in you? I like walking through the city of an evening in the warmth of gin.'[18]

So long as people search for that feeling of excitement and intrigue, gin will remain one of their chosen companions.

Chapter 2

Scotch

Gie him strong drink until he wink,
That's sinking in despair;
An' liquor guid to fire his bluid,
That's prest wi' grief and care:
There let him bowse, an' deep carouse,
Wi' bumpers flowing o'er,
Till he forgets his loves or debts,
An' minds his griefs no more.[1]

This stanza is the opening salvo of the poem *Scotch Drink* from Robert Burns. In the poem, Burns waxes lyrical about how the spirit of his homeland is also its lifeblood. To him, it was the dram of the ordinary man, the fuel of industry and festival celebrations.

A lover of Scotch, freedom and independence, Burns was as vocal about whisky as he was about everything else to do with Scottish traditions and heritage.

He wrote *Scotch Drink* in either 1785 or 1786 in response to the passing of the Wash Act, a tax law imposed by the British government he felt was a slap in the face to the distillers of Scotland, which made it harder for them to do business in England.

Another source of controversy was the tribalism it caused between Lowland and Highland distillers. Under the Act, Lowland distillers were taxed per gallon in the wash, while Highland distillers were taxed due to the size of their still.

It wasn't the first whisky taxation act and it wouldn't be the last in the weird and wonderful history of Scotch and Burns wouldn't be the only defender of the whisky. This is the story of how Scottish whisky turned from an obscure bumpkin drink into a status symbol for the most powerful people in the world, a drink of the people and so much more.

How is Scotch Whisky Made?

The earliest reference to Scotch whisky goes back to 1494 with a note that said: 'To Friar John Cor, by order of the King, to make acqua vitae VIII bolls of malt.'[2] This is possibly the first reference to aqua vitae (the water of life), indicating that by the fifteenth-century, distillation techniques had made it to Scotland.

In the 1730s, the word 'whiskie' was mentioned by Bailie John Steuart of Inverness, who wanted his brother-in-law to avoid 'that poisonous drink, I mean drams of brandie and whiskie'.[3] It's thought that whisky is a corruption of the Gaelic *uisge beatha*, and Scottish distillation techniques may have been transferred over from Ireland.

Hundreds of years later, the water of life is flowing as strong as ever in bars and personal drink collections. Through the centuries, Scotch has evolved into specific categories with distinct characteristics and production styles.

There are two kinds of Scotch – malt and grain, separated into four groups based on geographical locations and distilleries:

Lowland malt whisky: The divide between Lowland and Highland distilleries was created by the 1784 Wash Act and marks an imaginary line between Dundee in the east to Greenock in the west. The Lowlands are associated with blended whisky and are generally thought to be softer and lighter than other types.

Highland malt whisky: According to the Whisky Exchange, the easiest way to divide the thirty disparate distillers that are grouped into this style is geography. In the west, there are some along the Hebridean coast, while to the south they are located near the Highland Line. In the north, it's across the eastern coastline above Inverness, and in the east, it's along the coast either side of Aberdeen with the remaining located centrally in Perthshire.[4]

Islay malt whisky: Made exclusively on the island of Islay and known for its heavy, peaty notes.

Speyside malt whisky: While this type is grouped with the Highland category, Speyside has unique weather and climate conditions. This gives the whisky area-specific flavours that include spicy and fruity notes.

Campbeltown whisky: This comes from the Campbeltown peninsula and is characterised by a complex balance of maritime, sweet and fruity flavours.

Here's how the general process for Scotch works, although each distillery will have its own approach.

Malting: High-quality barley is steeped in water and spread out onto a malting floor so it can germinate over a week and it's turned regularly so heat doesn't build up. Over that week, starch is converted into sugar through the activation of enzymes and the now green malt is placed into a kiln for drying. This stops the germination and peat may be added to give a smoky flavour.

Mashing: The dried malt is ground into a fine grist and mixed with hot water in a mash tun. Water is added in three stages, gradually getting hotter at every stage. The end product of the mashing is wort.

Fermentation: The wort is cooled at 20°C and goes into washbacks so yeast can be added for the fermentation stage. The yeast eats the sugars and produces alcohol in small batches, and compounds called congeners add to the whisky flavour. This is done for two days and the wash at the end of fermentation contains 6–8% alcohol by volume.

First distillation: The liquid, now called a wash, is put inside a pot still that is usually made of copper. The still is heated to below the boiling point of water and the alcohol and other compounds vaporise and move through the neck of the still into a condenser, or worm. The latter is a big copper coil that is placed in cold running water where the vapour is condensed into a liquid.

Second distillation: The wash is distilled twice, first in the wash still as mentioned to separate the alcohol, yeast and residue known as pot ale. The distillate from the wash still, known as low wines, is 20% alcohol by volume and goes into the second still. At the end, only the 'heart of the run' of 68% alcohol by volume is collected in the spirits receiver.

Maturation: The next stage is maturing the whisky in barrels; by law Scotch whisky must be matured in oak for a minimum of three years in Scotland. In the case of single malts, the whisky could be in the barrels for anywhere between 8–15+ years and the liquid gains a golden colour and additional complexity.[5]

Rebel Yell

Of course, Scotch whisky distillation as we know it today didn't happen overnight. It's the development of decades of trial and error and adaptation to events that have steered the course of Scottish history.

The earliest whisky produced in the Lowlands and Highlands was rough stuff, often mixed with herbs, honey and wild berries to help it go down. It was in this raw state usually out of necessity and because of the English government's refrain of wanting to control taxes on whatever was deemed a threat to law and order, or seemed like a good business opportunity.

Aqua vitae ticked both those boxes and in 1644, the first excise duty on 'strong wines and acquavite' was imposed. At the time it was only a temporary tax, but within twenty years, excisemen and businessmen had cottoned on to the opportunities that were available with this potent new spirit. One of these men was Duncan Forbes III, Scotland's first known commercial distiller who set up his operation on the Black Isle of Ferintosh.

In 1689, his distillery was burned down by angry Jacobites and Forbes demanded £54,000 in compensation from the Scottish parliament. Instead, they offered him tax-free distilling and the Forbes family took advantage of this to build three new distilleries and make profits of £2 million by 1784. At this time, Ferintosh accounted for roughly two-thirds of legal whisky in Scotland.[6]

The 1700s was perhaps the darkest century of Scotch. The more restrictions and taxes parliament imposed to control whisky, the more resistance it caused, and illegal distilleries emerged all over Scotland. A 1760 claim proposed that only a tenth of the whisky drunk in Scotland came from licensed distilleries and there were always enterprising men ready and willing to stand up in that camp.

Andrew Stein was the patriarch of one of the most famous whisky dynasties in history. Coming from a family of farmers, Stein hailed from the village of Clackmannan in the Kennetpans region of Eastern Scotland. In the twelfth century, monks had established a monastery where they panned for salt and the Stein family may have learned whisky-making techniques from this connection.

In the 1720s, Stein set up a distillery in Kennetpans; by 1733 it was the largest whisky distillery in the world. His grandson John Stein further added to the family's renown and set the table for his sons, who became distillers themselves. He also married his daughter off to another powerful whisky family, the Haigs.

Robert Haig had been building his own distilling empire in the 1600s and as his family lived within a twenty-square-mile radius of the Steins, it seems inevitable that these two influential whisky dynasties would interact and strengthen their bonds. Robert's great-great-grandson John Haig married Margaret Stein in 1751 and this union led to the grand Haig and Stein alliance that also built the Haig and Jameson whisky empires of Ireland and Scotland.[7]

As the beating heart of the Lowlands whisky, the Steins and the Haigs were naturally put out when the 1784 Wash Act meant that they would have to pay more tax and use smaller stills simply because they were south of the line from the Firth of Clyde to the Firth of Tay. The Steins adapted by getting into the gin game in the 1770s, pumping out 2,000 gallons to 184,000 gallons over five years. They went into a price war with the London gin distillers, eventually losing out, as the Londoners lobbied Westminster to drive up the duty on Scottish spirits. After the Lowland distillers were then told to give twelve months' notice of intent to export, the Stein-Haig empire fell apart under the weight of huge debts.

Eventually, they would recover with the arrival of continuous distillation in the 1800s and the advent of the Industrial Revolution where the slow, laborious processes of the pot stills bubbling away in Highland glens became a relic of the past.

The future of distilling lay in a still that would make spirits in a constant flow, and the man who'd become synonymous with the continuous still was Aeneas Coffey, with the still named after him. The continuous still was a game-changer for spirits of all categories, both blessing and curse, depending on the requirements of a distiller and the expectations of a customer.

While the continuous still allows for the mass production of neutral spirit, it can also strip away the character and complexity that gives Scotch, and many other national spirits, their identity. But have no fear. There's a brand and bottle for everyone out there who prefers the complexity of a pot-stilled single malt or a smooth blended Scotch associated with continuous column distillation.

The Whisky Kings

'Advertising is to business what imagination is to poetry.' Such was the opinion of a fast-talking, amicable Scotsman called Tommy Dewar who set off to London in 1885 at the tender age of 21 to 'wake up the south' to the magic of Scotch. But when he got to the capital, he found out two of his business contacts had died and the other one had gone bankrupt. But the irrepressible Dewar had come to London with a mission – to bring his family's whisky to the masses. He and his brother John had inherited Dewar's Whisky from their father and as the showman of the duo, Tommy understood there was no such thing as bad publicity.

In 1892, aboard the *City of Paris*, he set off to tell the world about Dewar's whisky. From the West Coast of America to the north of Canada and into Honolulu, Tommy set up deals and samples of the whisky, courting attention wherever he could.

On his trip to Honolulu, he was decried as a 'heathen grog seller' by a Scottish parson. He left samples of Dewar's with the American entrepreneur Andrew Carnegie, who then sent a 'small keg' of Scotch, likely Dewar's, to the President of the United States. This started a media storm in the press about not supporting home grown goods. 'It was the very best advertisement I ever had. And certainly the cheapest,' Tommy would say later.

In Christchurch, New Zealand, he held a raucous dinner party with toasts to the queen; naturally Tommy took along some journalists and the story was splashed across the front pages of the papers the morning after.

By the time he returned to the UK after two years of travelling, Tommy had been to twenty-six countries and appointed thirty-two agents, many of whom would remain with Dewar's for over fifty years. Dewar's White Label had become the Scotch of the world. Tommy was just warming up.

In 1895, he launched arguably the world's first narrative/serialised spirits campaign, 'the whisky of his forefathers' – a campaign that ran for nearly forty years. In that time, he set up a massive, illuminated Scotsman raising a glass of Dewar's on top of his bottling plant in London's South Bank. He got into politics, becoming a Conservative MP for Tower Hamlets and published his road trips in a jaunty book called *Ramble Round The Globe*.[8] When he and his brother John died five months apart in 1930, they each left behind estates of £270 million by today's standards.

Tommy had also left behind a treasure trove of 'Dewarisms', and some of my favourites you can quote on your next trip to the pub – lines like 'Keep advertising and advertising will keep you'; 'A philosopher is a man who can look at an empty glass with a smile'; 'We have a great regard for old age when it is bottled'; and 'We should not say how's business, but where is business'.[9]

The Dewars weren't the only brothers to see Scotch as a lucrative venture. John and James Chivas were born on a farm in the Highlands, into a big family all expected to follow tradition and embrace the rural lifestyle. Both wanted more for themselves and moved to Aberdeen in 1838. James joined a grocery store and liquor emporium, where he worked his way up, and his brother eventually joined him as co-owner of the emporium.

The Chivas brothers earned a reputation for finding and stocking bottles that couldn't be found anywhere else and when customers wanted a smooth-tasting whisky, they began blending in the emporium cellar, an act that led to what is known in some circles as the birth of the first premium blended Scotch process.

In 1843, the Chivas' luxurious products caught the attention of Queen Victoria, who supplied them with a Royal Warrant. This set the stage for the regal trappings to come. Fast forward to the early twentieth century, and US drinkers were in the market for premium whisky.

By then, the Chivas assets had been handed over to a board of trustees and this fact wasn't lost on Master Blender Charles Stewart Howard and Alex Smith, the right-hand man of one of the last remaining members of the Chivas family involved with the company. Smith and Howard bought the brand and created a blend in memory of James and John using the best malt and grain whiskies available in-house.[10] In 1909, they introduced the world to Chivas Regal, a legendary brand that is still being marketed today through the likes of partnerships with celebrities such as the UK rapper Stefflon Don.

Another whisky king might have disputed the story about the Chivas Brothers legitimising blended Scotch. His name was James Buchanan, a man who, like Tommy Dewar, had a flair for showmanship and dapper dress sense. The quintessential Victorian gentleman, Buchanan wore a top hat, sported an impeccably combed moustache and enjoyed being driven around in a red-wheeled carriage by liveried footmen. He rose to fame through his Black and White blend – but he had to work to get there.

Born in 1849 in Rockville, Ontario, Canada, to Scottish immigrants, Buchanan overcame ill health as a boy and came to Scotland at the age of 14. He began his career as a clerk and then joined his brother's grain-based business in Glasgow. By 1879, he'd dipped his toe into the whisky ocean as a London agent of Charles Mackinlay & Co – a stint that was brief and unsuccessful.

A year later he founded James Buchanan and Co. Bolstered by the creativity of Glasgow blender William Lowrie, the Buchanan Blend became a best-seller, being supplied to the Houses of Parliament and taking America by storm. Sales were helped by Buchanan's constant advertising, and his insistence that blended Scotch be well-aged and have a high malt content did a lot to make it popular and respectable. He parlayed his whisky success into retiring as a country gentleman, buying an estate near Petworth in Sussex and becoming a baronet for his philanthropy.[11]

The early groundwork of the whisky kings and barons of the late nineteenth and early twentieth centuries truly propelled Scotch onto the world stage. Many distillers and brands have followed in their rich marketing tradition, such as the Highland Park distillery found in Kirkwall on the Orkney islands. As with all good marketing stories, the exact origin of the distillery is shrouded in mystery. One claim is that it was founded by an infamous priest smuggler, Magnus Eunson, in 1798 and there is a distinctive Norse influence.[12]

The distillery has leaned into this Norse and folklore aesthetic. One such product is the 'Viking Scars' 10-year single malt, the bottle etched with Norse knots, making it a fitting tribute for Thor or Odin to consume. (For a deep dive into Norse mythology, you can read my book *Norse Fighting Heroes: Kings, Conquerors and Shield-Maidens*.)

The brand story and Magnus Eunson legend comes to life on the box:

> Centuries ago, long before Orkney became part of Scotland, it belonged to a vast VIKING KINGDOM. Does that shape the CHARACTER of our whisky? Without a shadow of a doubt. Magnus Eunson, who founded Highland Park in 1798, was a direct descendent of those first Viking pioneers who settled on our island home.... 1 IN 3 ISLANDERS BEARS VIKING DNA and we continue to craft Highland Park with a FIERCE INDEPENDENCE that's driven through our Viking bloodline.

Then there's the highly coveted Highland Park Scottish Folklore series, with the likes of the 1988 31-year-old 'Nuckelavee' bottle. Named after an Orcadian sea demon, the box features a horrific image of the creature, which looks like a giant, flayed horse with a rider sprouting out of its back with long, grasping arms.

Whisky Women

Given how many stories there are about men who turned Scotch from an obscure hooch into a sophisticated spirit prized by Mark Twain, Winston Churchill, Ernest Hemingway, Sean Connery, Raymond Chandler, Haruki Murakami and others, you'd be right in thinking that Scotch has historically been considered a boy's club. But women have had their hand in Scottish whisky for as long as it's been around.

One of the most important is Bessie Williamson, the only woman in the twentieth century to own and run a Scotch distillery. She rose to become the owner of Laphroaig and when she first started at the distillery in 1933 as a shorthand typist there was no indication that she would become a trailblazer.

What she did have was an effervescent, curious nature and it was this which brought her to the island of Islay from Glasgow for a summer job that turned into a lifelong vocation. Her gregarious spirit bypassed the grouchiness of Laphroaig owner Ian Hunter, who developed a soft spot for her and they became fast friends.

In 1938 when Hunter suffered a stroke and ended up in a wheelchair, Bessie was appointed head of distribution towards the US. After the Second World War, Bessie was put in charge of Laphroaig and took control at key turning points in the history of whisky.

By the 1960s, Bessie had become the face of what *could* be possible in Scotch, of the ingenuity that women were always capable of and which could finally start to be appreciated. The Scotch Whisky Association invited Bessie on a North American tour to promote Laphroaig's prosperity under a woman overseas. On this tour, she met her husband, the Canadian radio star Wishart Campbell whose family traced their lineage to Islay. Bessie was also the subject of a feature documentary about Islay and Scotch in the 1960s, with the narrator noting 'Whisky is no longer a drink for men only, but you would expect its production to be an entirely male preserve. Mrs Campbell proves you wrong.'[13]

Another Scottish woman who had a guiding hand in a different whisky category is still worth mentioning here because she was a bridge between worlds and a representation of a marriage between cultures. Rita Cowan captured the heart of a young Japanese man by the name of Masataka Taketsuru, who'd come a long way to learn the secrets of Scotch production.

Taketsuru and Rita were married not long after their meeting and she returned to Japan with him in 1920. Without Rita's support, Taketsuru might never have realised his potential as the father of Japanese whisky by founding Nikka. As an English teacher, Rita was responsible for teaching the wife of one of her husband's earliest investors and it was through this introduction that Taketsuru got the funding he needed to open his first distillery.

Today, women are continuing to break down barriers and bring diverse perspectives to Scotch. There's Rachel MacNeill, founder of the Islay Whisky Academy, and Karen Somerville, co-founder of the Angels' Share Glass, a whisky glass specialist, and of the Fife Whisky Festival.

There's Annabel Thompson, founder of Nc'nean whisky, a product backed by sustainable practices and a forward-thinking mindset. Annabel has described her experience in the industry as overwhelmingly positive:

> On the whole, the industry is unbelievably friendly. We have never had a bad experience inside the industry and I've had enormously positive experiences. As someone who didn't grow up, as it were, in the whisky industry, I've been blown away by how lovely and collaborative everyone is. Of course, that goes back so far into Scotch history because everyone trades with each other for blends. It's a tiny industry, so everyone knows each other, which you might perceive to be uninclusive, but it's the opposite.
>
> The problem is somewhere between the edge of the industry and consumers with this perception that women don't drink whisky, that women don't like whisky, that women shouldn't drink whisky, that women don't work for the industry etc … It goes back to the marketing in the 1980s, which is problematic but it was extremely effective and is still so pervasive today in spite of the efforts of people across the industry to change it.
>
> I don't think the industry is entirely blameless either. Because if you look at the generalised imagery, it's male-dominated. If you're a woman looking in and all you see are brands using imagery of men drinking whisky, it's a subliminal barrier that will put you off.

Like a good blended whisky, the Scotch industry performs at its best when diverse voices are allowed to flourish and bring their creativity to the table. Innovation has been the golden thread of Scotch since it came down from the Highlands and Lowlands and worked its way into every bar across the world.

The future is bright for the spirit Robert Burns defended vehemently when few outside of Scotland could see its long-term potential. Now, Scotch is bringing out the potential in people from all walks of life as they arrive at the spirit, come through the industry and are determined to leave their mark.

Chapter 3

Rum

The 1930s.

It's a sweltering day in Havana, Cuba. A bartender, Constantino Ribalaigua Vert, decides to experiment at his bar. El Floridita the place is called. It's a long dim bar with a grocery of essential cooking supplies, mixing the spartan qualities of a New York corner bodega with the refinement of the hotel bars found in Chicago, London and the big metropolises of the world caught in the transitory trap of Prohibition.

Constante, as he's known by his patrons, has worked at El Floridita since 1914. He's owned it since 1918 and has never stopped pushing forward with new drinks for his customers.

Today, he's experimenting with the daiquiri, a rum cocktail he's learned about from bartender Emilio Gonzales over at the nearby Plaza Hotel. Like everything he does, Constante has to put his own spin on it. This isn't the first time he's made a daiquiri and it won't be his last. Showmanship, precision and flavour are the name of the game.

He's imported a Flak Mark ice chipper from the US, putting chipped ice into stemmed cocktail glasses to chill them. In his cocktail shaker, he pours ingredients for several drinks, shaking them like it's a matter of life and death. In an arc of mad exactitude, the ingredients flow from one half of the shaker to the other.

Next, Constante empties the ice out of the chilled glasses, lines them up like ducks in a row and pours the drinks with a gentleman's flourish, every glass filled without a drop being spilt from the shaker. Of his current daiquiri variants, his most popular seems to be his Daiquiri Floridita, a cocktail containing five drops of a cherry-flavoured liqueur called Marasquin.

One day, Constante is doing his thing when a scruffy man wanders into El Floridita and asks to use the toilet. When he comes out, he sees the daiquiris lined up on the bar like they usually are and he's intrigued. His name is Ernest Hemingway.

Hemingway asks for a sip and replies. 'That's good, but I prefer it without sugar and double rum.'

So, Constante makes a daiquiri to the author's exact specifications and Hemingway declares that it's very good. From that day forward, history is made and the daiquiri becomes forever interwoven with the legacy of one of America's greatest authors and a bar that continues to attract people from around the world to taste that history.[1]

This iconic connection is only one in a series of countless moments of rum taking centre stage in popular culture. Of all the spirits in the world, perhaps there is none more elusive and unrestricted as rum with the number of forms and variations it's taken through the centuries.

Depending on the point of view, rum has been the spirit of America, the lifeblood of the Caribbean islands, along with other lucrative exports of slavery and sugar, the preferred drink of pirates and scallywags, the swill of the poor, the province of the rich, the artefact of a bygone colonial era, rebranded, reinvented and sanitised for modern bar patrons.

Spiced, gold, dark, light, white, overproof, navy. Styles with a reputation for being unregulated, confusing, delicious and deranged, sometimes in the breadth of a single conversation or drinking session.

The story of rum is a melting pot – of distillation, of people, of cultures – all mixed across four centuries of power shifting across Britain, the Caribbean, America and beyond. Rum is the survivalist spirit that has taken on all comers and remained in the conversation.

The Murky Origins of Rum

Everyone's got a story about the origin of rum. Some say it was first invented on the island of Barbados in the seventeenth century. Some say it was created in Cuba, or that it was the Portuguese that had first dibs. An undisputed truth is that rum is made from sugarcane and its by-products, like molasses or sugarcane syrup.

As rum has been reinterpreted across cultures and centuries, production methods have varied based on style and flavour, but gathering the raw ingredients has always remained the same. Sugarcane is harvested and crushed, and the extraction of the juice, syrup or molasses takes place for fermentation. Sugarcane juice may be used for the rhum agricole style which originated on the French Caribbean islands of Martinique and Guadeloupe.

Molasses may be used for producing a dark or spiced rum. Either pot stills or a column still will be used for distillation depending on the style and where the rum is being made in the world.[2] (Already this should give you an indication of the crazy amount of variation that looms large in the history of rum.)

In the rum multi-verse, let's stick with the story that it was developed in Barbados. Sugarcane grew in abundance on the pear-shaped island that became a sugar production mecca to feed the demands of a rabid seventeenth-century British public. Sugar had rapidly evolved from a luxury of the rich to a commodity for everyone. The wonderous white gold could get rid of the taste of rancid meat, sweeten coffee, and was key to making a new product that had arrived in England in 1657 called chocolate.

Several British moneymen were attracted to the allure of Barbados' sugar-rich shores. One of them, Richard Ligon, a businessman who'd lost his fortune in the English Civil War, set off to the island with five others in 1647.

Charmed by the succulent tastes of pineapple juice, wild pigs and the infinite sunshine, Ligon stayed on the island until 1650 and wrote a *True and Exact History of the Island of Barbadoes* while locked up in a debtor's prison in 1657. While he'd not exactly achieved his goal of reclaiming his fortune, Ligon did make observations in his text that reveal the early history of rum.

He wrote of a peculiar spirit called 'kill-devil', a rough and fiery beverage knocked back by the locals. The poor quality of the spirit was also reported on by Sir Henry Colt, who was encouraged by his Bajan companions to drink up to thirty drams daily. The French priest Jean Baptise Labat called it 'rough and disagreeable'.[3]

This wasn't surprising, as rum expert Wayne Curtis points out:

> Distillers hadn't sorted variables, and the early technology didn't allow for any sort of precision in rum making. The quality of the cane, water and fermentation would have

> played a secondary role in the quality of the output, and the taste would have been determined largely by the condition and oversight of the still.[4]

Here we see the early links between kill-devil being a rough and ready drink that morphed into the brash-sounding rum it would be known as. The origins of the word 'rum' are as varied as where the drink first came from and the most likely answer is that it derived from the British slang 'rumbullion' and 'rumbustion'. Both words meant uproar or tumult, a fitting name for the explosiveness that would come to define the spirit in the shaping of early American history.

The American Republic of Rum

In 1700, America was still several decades from becoming a nation. But the colonies that would come to define her were already embracing rum in several ways. In the northern colonies of New England, the spirit was being served from barrels across Boston, Philadelphia and Newport, shipped directly from the West Indies. It was prescribed as a cure-all for sickness, a lubricant for friendship and a trading commodity for furs. Merchants swapped rum with Native American tribes for pelts and other goods, a practice that was banned from Massachusetts to South Carolina by 1707 because of the fear of intoxicated Indians attacking settlements, while the tribes pushed for restrictions because of the destruction it wreaked upon them.

Against a backdrop of rising tension between colonists staking their claim to new lands and the First Nations people from whom those lands were taken, coupled with the growing resentment felt by the colonists towards the interference of England and France controlling their settlements, rum continued to mutate with early cocktails like flip – a drink described as 'an alcoholic porridge' made of about two-thirds beer and a sweetener of dried pumpkin, loaf sugar, molasses or anything similar that seemed available at the time. Five ounces of rum were then put into a device called a loggerhead that 'gave the flip a bitter, slightly burned taste'.[5]

Rum was the marker of independence. The symbol of a nation shaking off the yolk of Old World sensibilities, a steady burning fuse that came to represent the American spirit and finally ignited in 1764 in the aftermath of the Sugar Act.

England levied an import tax against molasses on French-colonised islands in the Caribbean. Rhode Island, Massachusetts, Connecticut, New York and Pennsylvania were all up in arms about the trading restrictions and created petitions and collateral for the Act to be repealed.[6]

The main argument from the colonies was that if New England lost trade with the lucrative islands, then it would damage the economy of Great Britain. Without the New England distilleries being able to access affordable molasses, they'd shut down. Without the money flowing in from rum, the colonies wouldn't be able to buy as many goods from England. This argument proved to be compelling for some English manufacturers and the British parliament revised the Sugar Act in 1766 to allow some wiggle room.

No blood had been spilt in this resolution, but it was a catalyst for a revolution that put America and England on a collision course in the Revolutionary War. As England swept in to introduce more taxes, such as the Stamp Act which restricted alcohol licences, legal papers and other printed materials, the colonists weren't going to be pushed around anymore.

The Boston Tea Party kicked off in 1773. A foreman at a rum distillery, Joseph Whicher, dared English soldiers to fight him in a 1775 protest on a bridge between Salem and Boston. He was cut with a bayonet. Rum merchants and distillers in Boston resisted the Crown's advances, half of which were part of the Sons of Liberty, the resistance group that was on the frontlines of the American Revolution.

In the heat of the revolution, rum turned into one of the most valuable commodities. One general writing to George Washington in 1780 claimed 'besides beef and pork, bread and flour, rum is too material an article, to be omitted. No exertions out to be spar'd to provide ample quantities of it.'[7]

In 1783, the Revolution ended and a new nation rose, finally free to chart its own course. Rum had greased the wheels of progress. And for a brief time, it stayed in the spotlight. But not for long. After the Revolutionary War, molasses got harder and more expensive to bring into the US and there was a shortage of sugar and slaves in the West Indies into the nineteenth century.

Over the next few decades, rum lost its lustre as an affluent symbol of American ingenuity. It devolved into a sign of weakness that the

American economy was faulty, a relic of the past that was being brought into the country to fill the pockets of enemies that had tried to control the United States not so long ago.

So, drinkers and distillers made the switch to a new spirit – whisky. Farmers could invest in grains like corn as a commodity. New stills improved distillation processes and by the middle of the nineteenth century, bourbon was well on its way to becoming the new spirit of Americans, a label that remains to this day. But as it had done so many times before, rum would survive and lay dormant until the world was ready to embrace it once again.

A Pirate's Life For Me

To deviate into an adjacent part of the history of rum, pirates have become another enduring motif of its story. From the iconic Captain Morgan spiced rum, aped from the life of the murderous Captain Henry Morgan of the seventeenth century, to the immortal line of 'yo, ho, ho and a bottle of rum' from Robert Louis Stevenson's *Treasure Island*, pop culture has been having a love affair with pirates for decades.

Colourful, larger-than-life characters like Edward 'Blackbeard' Teach, Anne Bonny and Jack Rackham have all made enticing symbols of grog-swilling scallywags. I'll admit I've had a hand in that too. Over the pandemic, I started a blog called The Rum Ration and wrote a running series called A Pirate's Life For Me, where I paired different rum brands with pirates and imagined the kind of bottles they would drink.

The truth is that the real-life pirates sailing the Caribbean seas of the eighteenth century weren't picky about what they drank. But when they found rum, they drank it as heartily as any other alcoholic drink that could pass the monotony of weeks at sea or take their minds off the diseases that would be rife aboard ships like scurvy and typhus.

Some pirates were more taken with rum than others, such as the infamous Boston pirate Ned Low, who captured Captain George Roberts of London. Roberts' summary of his time aboard Low's ship provides a window into the pirate's drinking habits.

The crew spent their time 'drinking and carousing merrily, both before and after dinner, which they eat in a very disorderly manner, more like a kennel of hounds than like men'. And Roberts often shared rum with Low during the nights. 'We took a dram of rum and enter'd into discourse with one another, on difficult subjects; for as a tavern or alehouse-keeper endeavours to promote his trade, by conforming to the humours of every customer.'[8]

Pirates also weren't demanding grog when they ransacked towns. Grog came after the Golden Age of Piracy, originating with the British Navy. For sailors posted in the Caribbean, it was difficult to drink water because it would become spoiled on long, tropical voyages, so it became common practice for drinking water to be cut with alcohol like beer and brandy. Then rum came along and had the benefits of remaining sweet, killing germs and more of it could be stored aboard ships because it was a higher proof than beer and wine.

After a few decades of rum being knocked back by tipsy sailors, it was starting to become a problem for the British Royal Navy and one captain wasn't going to stand for it.

His name was Admiral Edward Vernon and he proposed a radical solution to stopping the overconsumption of rum in the Navy. He wouldn't get rid of the rum ration because he knew that to do so was to invite mutinies and insubordination from sailors thirsty for their tots.

What Vernon did instead was dilute the rum in 1740, with an order of the drink to be 'mixed with the proportion of a quart of water to every half pint of rum'. This concoction of one part rum and four parts water would be served over two daily sessions between ten in the morning and noon, and the second between four and six in the afternoon. The beverage took its name from the tough, waterproof cloak Vernon liked to wear, which was made from grogram. Add to the fact that the Admiral was affectionately called 'Old Grogram' by his men, and grog became the drink of the navy.[9]

Pirate and navy-branded rum rank among the most widely distributed bottles in the category today. Pirate's Grog is a spiced rum brand in the UK that offers several fruity flavours and can be gifted inside a 'treasure chest'. Barti spiced rum based in Pembrokeshire, Wales uses seaweed as one of the ingredients and is inspired by the life of John 'Black Bart' Roberts. Red Bonny is a dark rum, blended from Guyana rum, aged for three years and named after the fiery-haired Irish lass, Anne Bonny. Mary Read Rum is a spiced rum made in the Netherlands and named after Bonny's partner in crime.

Pirates and national pride are also entwined, as is the case with the Orcadian rum brand J. Gow, which is inspired by the life of the Orcadian pirate John Gow. Founder Colin Van Schayk has plenty of passion for running one of the smallest distilleries in the world.

> We have a 2,000 litre pot still, with packed column, which we also use as a fermenter. We also have a separate 2,000L fermenter. The imported molasses comes in 1,000L IBCs, this is then pumped into the fermenters with water, yeast and nutrients and fermented for seven to fourteen days depending on which rum we're making.
>
> It's then distilled first from 8% to 30% in a stripping run, then it's returned to the still and distilled again in a final run to around 65%. It's then either turned into spiced rum with the addition of whole spices or filled into casks.
>
> We also keep some of the backset (stuff left over in the still) from stripping runs and add it to our dunder or muck pit. This is bacterially fermented and fed with dead yeast, waste molasses etc to develop heavier compounds and esters. Small portions of this are added to future fermentations to develop heavier rum flavours.
>
> We have a spiced rum that is dry with only 5 grams of sugar per litre added after distillation. It's subtly spiced. I wanted it to taste of rum complimented with spices rather than masked by them. It has citrus notes, with flavours of moist ginger cake and oatmeal with a nice warm spice finish.
>
> Our Fading Light release is fermented for fourteen days, double distilled and aged in chestnut casks for eighteen to twenty-four months. Zero added sugar or colouring. It has a slight funk on the nose, natural sweetness with estery notes of dried fruit, vanilla, honey and cream. The palate is smooth with hints of nuts on the finish.

On the other side of the battlefield is Lamb's Navy Rum, which takes its name from Londoner Alfred Lamb who blended eighteen different rums from Barbados, Jamaica and Guyana in 1849. The naval connection came much later in 1970 when the British Royal Navy stopped giving the rum ration to sailors on 31 July – 'Black Tot' Day. The brand decided to do an advertising campaign that year called 'Join the Lamb's Navy', and the connection stuck.

A rum that has a genuine naval connection, albeit squeezed through the machine of capitalism, is Pusser's rum. In 1980, the British Admiralty Board reached an agreement with an American entrepreneur called Charles Tobias to hand over the secret formula for the official Royal Navy rum blend. Tobias felt there would be a market for the rum to live on through retired sailors and the sexiness and mystique of a 325-year-old tradition.

In exchange for the recipe, Tobias paid royalties to the Sailor's Fund and Pusser's has been sold worldwide ever since.

Rum's Second, Third and Fourth Coming ...

By the time Prohibition swept America in the 1920s, rum had been hibernating for over a hundred years. It had been blasted by the temperance movement of the 1800s, replaced by bourbon as the spirit of the nation and driven even further underground by the alcohol bans brought in by the Volstead Act, which signalled the end of legal drinking. But not so far away, on a tropical island off the coast of Florida, it emerged from the long winter into golden sunshine, taking on fresh forms and styles as it always had.

In the 1920s, Cuba became a refuge from the stuffiness of the mainland, a watering hole for the rich and adventurous who flocked to Havana for the seductive nightclubs, exotic cocktails and intellectual sheen, a bonified Paris of the Caribbean.

Here visitors discovered a new, lighter style of rum lightyears apart from the rough, dark New England varieties that had once been the toast of revolutions and rebel songs. The new republic of rum was spearheaded by the Bacardi family and its patriarch Facundo Bacardi y Maso. The family had purchased a distillery in the 1860s and created 'the bat drink', a libation rural Cubans couldn't get enough of.

This name for Bacardi rum comes from a story about a colony of bats living in the rafters of the distillery or in a tree in the back garden. The bat became the brand's logo, eventually becoming one of the world's most valuable trademarks. The rum itself became iconic too. Light and infinitely mixable with water, lime juice, pineapple and orange juice, Bacardi rum found its way into cocktails like the daiquiris that enchanted Hemingway and countless other Americans seeking greener pastures.

Back on the mainland, people were thirsty for all kinds of spirits, from whisky to gin. Bootleggers and the Mafia across major cities such as New York and Chicago were meeting the supply and demand at any cost.

Meanwhile, a rum smuggling operation had developed called the Rum Row, a term which originally popped up in Florida. This came from ships that sourced rum from the Caribbean and taunted the US jurisdiction with legal loopholes that allowed the selling of alcohol on the edge of the three-mile jurisdiction limit out at sea.

One of the pioneers of the Rum Row was gentleman smuggler William 'Bill' McCoy. McCoy was born in 1877 in Syracuse, New York, and from his early days he felt called by the sea. He served as a mate and quartermaster on various ships and he set up a motorboat service and boatyard with his brother Ben. McCoy made a name for himself as a skilled yacht builder and sailor, a reputation that would serve him well in the coming years.

At the beginning of Prohibition, the McCoy brothers were struggling. Their boat and adventure businesses couldn't compete against the buses and new motorways that were being built across Florida and they needed a fix.

Salvation came in the form of a rum runner, who offered to pay them to transport booze through the Rum Row. Although McCoy declined the offer, it inspired him to become an independent rum runner and he and his brother invested in a schooner called *Henry L Marshall*. He sailed the schooner into Nassau, loaded it with 1,500 cases of Canadian whisky and returned to the US, where it sold for $15,000.

From that point on, McCoy was hooked and he expanded his operation by introducing a new schooner called *Arethusa*. What set McCoy apart from other rum runners was his thoughtful and risk-free approach. Unlike other smugglers who diluted their liquor with harmful products like turpentine, McCoy's booze was unsullied and clean. This unadulterated, high-quality spirit became known as 'The Real McCoy'. He converted *Arethusa* into a floating liquor store that operated within the three-mile marine border.

After mooring the boat just outside the three-mile limit, and so in international waters, he arranged for buyers to come through the Rum

Row and purchase rum, whisky and any other tipple they wanted. McCoy set up a strict system. Only two buyers were allowed on board at any one time and any vessels were watched by a swivel machine gun to ensure there wasn't any trouble.

This approach worked and McCoy established himself as a successful businessman. His techniques allowed him to stay ahead of the law. One example includes him renaming the *Henry L Marshall* schooner *Tomaka* and placing it under UK registry to avoid US jurisdiction.

He's also credited with creating the burlock, a package that held six bottles jacketed in straw. Three were on the bottom, then two, then one, and a hole was sewed in burlap. Not only were the burlocks compact and easy to transport, but they could also quickly be disposed of. Some were lined with salt, which helped the sacks to sink when thrown overboard. After the salt dissolved, the sacks came back to the surface.

McCoy took his smuggling empire to the next level by setting up on the island of St Pierre. A French colony, St Pierre existed outside of US law, while not having any competing factions. Under McCoy's guidance, the St Pierre economy transformed, and the island turned into a commercial merchant port.

On 23 November 1923, McCoy's luck ran out when he was captured by the US Coast Guard. In a battle with the Coast Guard's ship *Seneca*, McCoy was unable to stop *Tomaka* from being boarded. He surrendered, stating that he was fully aware of his actions. McCoy pleaded guilty to breaking the law, spending nine months in a New Jersey prison.

After his release, he returned to Florida and invested in real estate, while carrying on his seafaring passion with his brother. McCoy passed away in 1948 from a heart attack in his happy place – out at sea, aboard his private yacht *Blue Lagoon*.[10]

Men weren't the only rum runners who made the headlines. Gertrude 'Cleo' Lythgoe was a force unto herself. Lythgoe was born in Bowling Green, Ohio, and was the youngest of ten children. Orphaned from an early age, she made up her mind to strike out on her own and went to New York. She became a stenographer, graduating as a junior accounts clerk for a British booze importer.

When Prohibition arrived, Lythgoe realised that the world was changing rapidly and that she needed to change with it. She managed to convince her employer that there was money to be made by importing liquor from the Bahamas. After relocating to Nassau, Lythgoe set up a wholesale liquor export shop in the Lucerne Hotel, infamous for attracting a cavalcade of shady characters.

In her autobiography, *The Bahama Queen*, Lythgoe described the atmosphere of the hotel. 'All types and nationalities conversed on the front veranda waiting for the ringing of the dinner bell. Many newspaper reporters and feature writers sat by the hour at the bar gathering rich material to be woven into fiction.'[11]

With Nassau being a hotbed of crime and violence, it says something about Lythgoe's character that she was able to survive and thrive in such a hostile environment. More than that, she established a fierce reputation that gave her the nickname 'Queen of the Bahamas'.

One of the reasons that Lythgoe became so well known was because of her beauty. She earned the nickname 'Cleo' because she was meant to look similar to Queen Cleopatra. But despite having many suitors, she never married, running her rum empire solo. She certainly captured the attention of fellow rum smuggler Bill McCoy, who gave an account of Lythgoe to New York journalist Robert Wigley:

> She was a tall, slender girl with black hair, a brain as steady as her own dark eyes, and a history that was nobody's business. She came to Nassau as an agent for Haig and McTavish's Scotch whisky, no one knew from where. She made no secret of her background, but she told an entirely different tale to everyone who asked. She was born in California. She had been born in India. She was a gypsy. She had been raised in the Middle West. You could take your choice. Members of the rum mob who drew their own conclusions concerning her and then tried to operate accordingly, probably will recall the breath-taking fury she could show, and one or two must remember the pistol jammed into their ribs by way of making things clear.[12]

McCoy mentored Lythgoe and like her mentor, she prided herself on only smuggling the highest-quality spirits that weren't watered down. When crossed, she was ruthless. One story involved her tracking down a rival who'd been spreading rumours that she traded in counterfeit booze.

She confronted the poor sod in a barber shop, shoved a gun in his face and commanded that he leave Nassau or she'd pull the trigger.

While Lythgoe mainly operated as a middleman, she was more than happy to get her hands dirty in the field. She made several trips with McCoy to smuggle rum directly into New Jersey. It was only a matter of time before her infamy caught up with her.

In 1924, Lythgoe was arrested on Nassau and charged with smuggling 1,000 barrels of whisky and rum into New Orleans. She was transported back to The Big Easy to await trial.

While Lythgoe had arranged the delivery, she'd put her trust in a third party who'd tried to stab her in the back and sell the booze for his own gain. The man was captured by the US Coast Guard, which enabled Lythgoe to demonstrate that she was travelling elsewhere at the time of the incident. The charges were dropped and she returned to Nassau a free woman.

By April 1924, the US government had successfully petitioned to have its jurisdiction over the waters around the coastlines extended from three miles to twelve miles. This made rum running far more difficult, as smugglers would need to sell liquor further from land. Sensing the end of an era, Lythgoe decided to quit while she was ahead.

On retiring, Lythgoe moved back to America, settling first in Miami and then finally in Detroit. She spent her final years writing her memoirs, passing away in 1974 at the age of 86.

The Queen of the Bahamas left behind a hell of a legacy, best summed up by long-time admirer Robert Wigley. 'She stands alone and fearless – a woman who would grace any London drawing room … she has commanded the respect and homage of this motley and dubious throng and is known in the trade as The Queen of the Bahamas.'[13]

After Prohibition ended in 1933, America was ready to welcome back its wayward spirit, but the land was a much different place from when rum had left. Big industrial firms were pumping out alcohol with advanced systems with the same obsession for efficiency as the biggest car manufacturers of the day. 'Cuban' rum (i.e. the light stuff that Bacardi had made famous) was in big demand and so distillers shifted towards pumping out similar styles.

Into the Second World War, many distillers were contracted to make neutral spirit for the war effort, while an agreement between President Roosevelt and Winston Churchill in 1940 sent thousands of American soldiers to British-controlled islands in the Caribbean to beef up security and build new bases. Antigua, Jamaica, St Lucia, Bermuda and Trinidad's populations all spiked.

In Bermuda, rum was becoming the drink of choice for the soldiers and it was in this rowdy atmosphere that the immortal connection of rum and Coca-Cola was made. This was bolstered by big advertising campaigns by Coke, and boosted in part by a dispute over a song called *Rum and Coca-Cola*. The Trinidadian Calypso singer Rupert Westmore Grant, who performed under the name of Lord Invader, didn't care much for the American occupation. He observed the soldiers using their money to coerce local women into prostitution while drinking rum and coke.

These observations became the heart of *Rum and Coca-Cola,* a song that commented on American excess. Invader worked with fellow Calypso singer Lionel Belasco to compose the melody, which came from a song called *L'Annee Passee*. It wasn't long before *Rum and Coca-Cola* turned into a huge hit in Trinidad, becoming one of the most popular songs of 1943.

In September of that year, American entertainer Morey Amsterdam visited Trinidad as part of a USO tour. During his time on the island, he heard *Rum and Coca-Cola* and took the music back with him to the US. He created his own version of the song and later claimed that he'd never heard of the original. Amsterdam went on to record *Rum and Coca-Cola* with the Andrews Sisters in 1945. In under ten minutes, they created a record that went on to sell seven million units and topped the *Billboard* magazine chart for seven weeks.

The issue with Amsterdam's version is that it stripped *Rum and Coca-Cola* of its social commentary. Without really thinking about what he was writing, he altered the lyrics to the point where it sounded as though women were deliberately prostituting themselves.

The Andrews Sisters also failed to think about the lyrics. Patty Andrews said 'We had a recording date, and the song was brought to use the night before. We hardly really knew it, and when we went in we had extra time and we just threw it in. It was actually a faked arrangement.'

Maxene Andrews has said 'The lyric was there, it was cute. But we didn't think of what it meant; but at that time, nobody else would think of it either, because we weren't as morally open as we are today and so a lot of stuff just went over our heads.' Lord Invader and Belasco both sued Amsterdam for copyright infringement, winning the case in 1948.[14]

After the war, the next reinvention of rum spread through the tiki bar culture started by Donn Beach (born Ernest Beaumont Gantt). Donn had already been mashing up a unique blend of South Pacific décor with exotic rum cocktails in his Los Angeles bar, 'Don the Beachcomber'. During the war, he'd been drafted and spent most of his time overseeing various hotels and restaurants in Capri, Lido and the French Riviera after being wounded in an attack by a German U-boat. His ex-wife Cora 'Sunny' Sund stepped up in his absence, running the Los Angeles bar and turning it into a small but mighty chain across America.

Another titan of the tiki movement was Victor 'Trader Vic' Jules Bergeron. Vic recognised that after Prohibition ended, drinkers weren't ready to give up extravagant, over-the-top cocktails and set out on an odyssey with his wife in 1937 to locations like New Orleans, Havana and Trinidad to sip and absorb rum cocktails. He perused the tropical restaurant South Seas in San Francisco, and made a stop at the Don the Beachcomber bar in LA to soak up the magic of the place he'd heard so much about.

Research completed, he went back to Oakland to give himself and his restaurant, Hinky Dinks, a complete makeover. Just like Gantt, Bergeron needed a new name to go along with the adventurous, flamboyant attitude that he wanted to portray to his patrons. His wife mentioned he always seemed to be involved in one deal or another and so Trader Vic was born. The cult of tiki lasted until the late 1970s, when drinking tastes shifted to white spirits like vodka, a lightning-quick rise that cut whisky and rum out beneath the knees and appealed to a generation who wanted something new and edgy.

Craft Rum Revolution

Into the 1990s and 2000s, big rum brands like Bacardi, Captain Morgan and Mount Gay pushed out products at a steady rate. These drinks were mainstays in bars: comfortable and familiar, but the kind of spirit one might pick up on autopilot and mix with coke, rather than enjoying them for taste and complexity. Flavoured and infused rums offered some novel varieties, but the klaxons of rum as the spirit of America, or the lifeblood of a cocktail republic in some faraway exotic land, weren't sounding as they once did and hadn't for a long time.

Into the 2010s, rum broke out of its stasis chamber again with a surge of craft distilleries. Craft spirits, according to Wayne Curtis, are 'loosely defined as liquor produced by those making fewer than 50,000 cases per year … buoyed by a demand for local and regional products across the board, a thirst for authenticity, the Millennial desire to favour something new rather than stick with something familiar.'[15]

American rum distillers are certainly leading the charge, with the likes of the female-led Montanya rum in Colorado. Founded by Karen Hoskins in 2008, Montanya has several offerings that are worth trying.

The first is Valentia, a Spanish word that translates to courage, bravery and grit. Valentia is a pure, single-barrel, double-matured rum that's bursting with flavour. The drink is aged for four years in Laws Whisky House barrels and then finished in Rye barrels from Catoctin Creek, imparting a distinctive Scotch quality. The first sip reveals notes of chocolate and toast, while the second brings in peaty flavours and an undercurrent of coconut. Notes of caramel and honeysuckle trickle through with an awesome, fiery ambush at the back of the mouth.

Then there's Oro, which translates to gold, Montanya's award-winning product. It's made from sugarcane juice and mixed with local water. The rum is aged for a year in an American white oak barrel that used to hold Laws Colorado whisky; being fresh from whisky, the barrel imparts a full-bodied profile. What sets the Oro apart from some dark-aged rums is that there's no added sugar, molasses or caramel. It's not carbon-filtered, it maintains its natural colour, and features a dollop of honey to bring out natural flavours.

On the nose, the Oro has a warm, bready scent that invites you in and conjures images of that first slice of hot toast that pops out of the toaster for breakfast. The flavour of coffee and caramel sweeps in, providing a smooth kick that keeps on going towards the back of the mouth and crackles in the aftertaste. Subtler notes of chilli pepper, chocolate and anise sparkle in the background, like the instruments in an orchestra coming together to create a grand symphony of awesome flavours.

Maggie Campbell from Privateer Rum in Ipswich, Massachusetts, is another woman leading the charge in American rum. Her Privateer Queen's Share has rave reviews and her rum-distilling philosophy is 'what I make today is intended for years in the future, and what I am tasting now is from years in the past. The experience leaves you unstuck in time, like the movie *Arrival*'.[16]

There are other tireless supporters of the American rum resurgence, such as Will Hoekenga and John Gulla, co-founders of the Rumcast, a podcast that celebrates rum at home and abroad. In a conversation I had with both, Hoekenga and Gulla are incredibly optimistic about the future of American rum.

Hoekenga's prediction is:

> As time goes on, I think you'll start to see more distinctive regional styles develop throughout the US. Kind of like how there's not really one style of American barbecue (Memphis is the best, fight me), I don't think there will be one style of American rum. You're going to see more fresh cane juice rums in the cane-growing regions of the country. You're going to continue seeing regions that do have rum history coalescing around a style and fine-tuning its characteristics (like New England rum). That said, there are certain characteristics you can already find more often in the US. than in other places, like ageing in new American oak barrels rather than used bourbon barrels.

Gulla pointed out the growth of consumer desire to find premium rum in the same way they are looking for high-quality bourbon or Scotch.

> I think consumers are beginning to look for other, similar experiences where there are excellent and affordable products that merit our time, money, and attention. Like many others, I feel strongly that rum offers perhaps the most diverse selection of any spirit, and that many premium rums offer an incredible value based on the quality of the spirit – especially in direct comparison to those other categories and their exorbitant prices.
>
> I got out of exploring bourbon due to the insane pricing and lack of availability of the really high-end stuff. I never even started with Scotch because it felt like it was out of my price range to get the type of quality product I wanted in the first place.
>
> When you think Scotch what are the first thoughts that come into your head? For me, it conjures images of

> distinguished sipping; home bar carts with crystal decanters located in or near a home library; a large, cozy chair sat next to a warming fireplace and a classic novel sitting half-open nearby. I think that Scotch has done a great job at conveying this image, and thus creating a perceived value behind it. Likewise, I think the Scotch industry has done an excellent job at generating a high-end market that makes a large amount of product simultaneously feel unique, scarce, and interesting.
>
> Rum by contrast, as we all know has a bit of a public perception problem. Heck, even those who pay attention to rum can't seem to agree on much of it! We have pirates and beaches, Polynesian and Tiki, and now a segment that is going for a more distinguished sell, closer to the Scotch image. So, I think the very thing that holds rum back in many ways may also be what has stopped it from getting out of hand with crazy prices on the super-premium products – to the great benefit of those of us who can take advantage of a superior product without the added free-market hype.
>
> I, for one, enjoy the personality disorder that rum seems to have to a degree, but I do think it also holds the category back from being considered by the masses as a world-class spirit that should compete with whisky in terms of a quality distillate.

In the UK, there's also a craft rum revolution going on with distillers contributing to a collective British identity of regionality and local stories. In my hometown of Manchester, there's the Salford Rum Company, Rainy City golden rum from the Tameside Distillery, One-Eyed Rebel rum and Witch Kings rum liqueurs.

A standout Manchester rum is Decorrum from Lucy Wolfenden and her partner Lewis, which celebrates the art deco beauty of the 1920s. According to Wolfenden the brand is,

> heavily influenced by businesses like Belvedere and Grey Goose. The kind of brands that have bougie, sophisticated bottles and that you want to take a picture with. We felt there was a gap in the market for a rum that was on the

same level and came up with the idea for an art deco 1920s branding that appeals to both men and women.

We knew that the majority of rum in the UK came from the Caribbean so it was a case of creating several business plans, picking up the phone and seeing where we could source it from. Everyone we spoke to gave good advice and was happy to guide us in the right direction. We eventually discovered The Diamond Distillery, which is renowned for the quality of its rum. The product is imported as a white 95%+ base spirit from Guyana and then goes to a distillery in Carrington called Alcohol Solutions. They reduce the strength of the rum to 37.5%, spice it and flavour it with our recommended ingredients to give us the final bottle we know as Decorrum.

It was difficult during lockdown because we couldn't go to the distillery and try out recipes in person. We had to give them a liquid brief suggesting what colour, smell and taste profile we wanted in a Word document and then they would help us create the product. They sent us three samples in three separate batches to try and after a lot of back and forth and months of emails, calls and focus group discussions we got it right.

The bottles go on a long journey too. They are produced and imported from France, spray painted in Birmingham and sent to Alcohol Solutions to be bottled, sealed and filled with our rum.

As we're based in Manchester, we wanted to incorporate the spirit of the city into the brand. The community here is buzzing, pun not intended, so we have linked Decorrum to the worker bee, the iconic symbol of Manchester and what it represents.

On the subject of premiumisation Wolfenden said:

We understand that people are drinking less but choosing to purchase more premium, expensive drinks and spending more on a night out. There is a rising popularity for rum, it's not just a cocktail ingredient but a well-liked drink in its own right. The competition is increasing. However, the

> competition isn't simply to sell more rum, but to produce the highest quality.
>
> People are choosing quality over quantity. Acknowledging that we were determined to create a premium liquid using no artificial flavours and natural ingredients full of flavour sourcing the base liquid from the best distiller in Guyana to appeal to our target audience. With this strong competition, brands aren't just focusing on the liquid itself but also focusing on premiumising packaging. The appearance of the bottle can make a huge impact and encourages customers to choose that product over the competitors around it.

Interesting rum-blings are happening in other parts of the UK too.

Brothers Bruce and Louise Goddard-Watts are the founders of SLY DOG rum, a product in the increasingly popular spiced rum category. The brothers told me their thoughts on the category and perspective on rum:

> As rum becomes more popular, and new brands are brought to the market, they all seem to be following the same trends as the big dogs, still focusing on the traditional picture of rum as a bit of a 'pirate's drink'. While the history of rum is still important, we want to be the Sly Dogs of the pack, doing things differently, focusing on the flavour of our rum more than anything else. So, we went to the best in the flavour business, and working with the UK's leading 'Flavour Master' and rum experts, we crafted a spiced rum that would stand out and created a bottle that would stand out with it. The numbers speak for themselves in terms of the sales of spiced rum. Even before the pandemic, it was growing incredibly quickly, regaining parts of the market after the 'gin-boom'. What the closure of hospitality venues has allowed for is a chance for experimentation at home. We have had new rums delivered every week to allow us to sample what's available. This has also given rise to the popularity of more expensive choices to what is normally available behind a bar, and with that a newfound appreciation for better-tasting spirits. We hope to see SLY

> DOG at the forefront of that shift towards higher quality, flavourful spiced rums behind every bar.

Another UK rum making waves is God's Own Rum founded by Joe Dunning and Campbell Carruth in Yorkshire. Dunning and Campbell wanted to create a brand that tapped into local tradition and brought a new perspective to the category. Dunning told me:

> What we wanted to create was a fusion of old and new to provide new meaning in the rum category. It was tapping into the local Yorkshire community, that story and combining it with modern distilling techniques. Being small scale, we had the ability to play around and experiment. We have a lot more versatility than some brands who're reliant upon segments of time in the bigger distilleries. We've also trademarked our name and placed it as *the* Yorkshire rum so that's given us some leverage over competitors.
>
> We also wanted to get away from the image of pirates and palm trees. These images have been around for a long time and we wanted to create a more mature-looking rum instead of jumping on the sea creatures bandwagon. It was about tapping into the idea of premium rum.
>
> Another USP is the way we produce. You have very few British distilleries that do the distilling of the molasses from scratch. There's a lot of UK-based rum brands that just import and relabel. We distil our product at the beginning and for every twenty-five litres we put into the still, we only take twenty back out. We're getting rid of the 'meh' quality alcohol so we can start from the base product and build back up to the best quality.

Carruth also gave his thoughts on premiumisation in the category.

> The buzzword of the day is premiumisation and that is affecting the industry and different vendors from a growth perspective. The expectation is that the eCommerce side of rum will grow and people will have access to more products from different parts of the world.

> For us, we're focused on getting to the next level and scaling our operations so we can continue to promote the idea of premium rum. To me, it's class outside and class inside. What we're looking at is the full package from the consumer's point of view. Being premium is about not screwing the shit out of the distillation process and putting all the crap in. You have to factor in the cost of what you put into your product.

Rums Around the World

America and Europe aren't the only places where craft rum is taking off. There are interesting products coming out of countries you might not expect like Japan, Cambodia and Vietnam.

Nine Leaves Distillery on Honshu island in Shiga Prefecture, created by Yoshiharu Takeuchi, has been developing Japanese rum since 2013. Takeuchi-san was originally drawn to distilling whisky but opted for rum because he found there was more opportunity to be creative.

On seeking advice from the owner of Chichibu Whisky, Ichiro Akuto, Takeuchi purchased copper stills from the global distillation giant Forsyths and started to source his ingredients. He located his water source in Shiga and got his sugarcane from Okinawa. When designing the logo for his brand, Takeuchi tapped into his heritage. His family kamon (crest) features nine bamboo leaves, a symbol of the Takeuchi's family's involvement in the wood industry.

A unique product is the Nine Leaves' Angel's Half French cask. On the nose it's toasty, waxy and has hints of rye bread. In the mouth it's woody, with notes of mushroom, peanut butter, coffee and biscuit.

The Iejima brewery on Ie Island in Okinawa has a product called Santa Maria. Iejima is best known for distilling awamori, the national spirit of Okinawa that has a powerful kick. Branching out into rum distillation, the brewery decided to mix traditional Japanese techniques with a respect for the environment. The result is a 100 per cent pure Agricole rum made from local sugarcane that's been cultivated on the island since 1630. As a reflection of the company's respect for nature, the Santa Maria bottle features an elegant white feather floating above a mountain.

The Santa Maria name comes from the white Easter lily that blossoms on Ie Island during spring. In the west, the lily is a symbol of Saint Mary. It's a subtle hint to the Japanese philosophy of life being ephemeral, of the seasons changing and nature transforming the land. The rum is aged for two to three years in Nikka whisky oak barrels and has a bouquet of banana, pineapple and lychee, followed by the taste of pear, apple, cocoa, chilli pepper and caramel.

The Grace distillery, founded in 2004 by Yuko Kinjo, has also been quietly adding to the legacy of Asian rums in Okinawa. Kinjo was focused on showcasing the natural ingredients of Minamidaito, which is why the rum has been produced from local sugarcane. Interestingly, sugarcane is the main product of the island, having been grown there since 1903.

The growth of the sugarcane is a partnership between herself and the Minamidaito Island Chamber of Commerce. Production is limited to once a year to preserve the crop in an environment that is prone to typhoons and extreme weather. The distillery has two products called Cor Cor Red and Green.

The Red is bottled at 40% ABV and comes with an esoteric poem on the label that tells the story of the island and would make the legendary Japanese poet Ono No Komachi smile with approval: 'Bats, dancing in the night sky / Suspended magic, falling in drops / These are the things / That make men and women covet love / This is the magic of rum / A sugarcane love potion.' Cor Cor Red has a combination of rubber, black pepper, peach and apple on the nose, while the mouthfeel is mushroom, grapefruits and watermelon.

Going over to Cambodia, the Samai distillery in Phnom Penh produces a rum called Kampot Pepper. Samai is the Khmer word for modern and represents a new generation of rum producers that are exploring new frontiers and flavours. The distillery is the brainchild of two Venezuelans Antonio Lopez and Daniel Pacheco, who went to high school together and reconnected years later in Cambodia.

Like the creation of any great concept, the idea for Samai started in a bar, while Lopez and Pacheco were throwing around ideas about what Cambodian rum could be like if it was made. That night of drunken genius became the catalyst for something special and in 2014, Samai opened its doors.

Opening a distillery came with a certain set of hurdles. At the time, people in Cambodia didn't have much knowledge about rum and

Samai embarked on an education programme through regular tastings and workshops. Fast forward to 2024 and Samai has developed a great reputation for producing high-quality rums with diverse characteristics and the Kampot Pepper is definitely the jewel in the crown.

The production of this rum is as unique as the brand itself. Kampot pepper is like the Champagne of peppers, in the sense that it has a Protected Geographical Indication (PGI) status and can only be made in the Kampot region of Cambodia.

But the pepper isn't the only intriguing thing about the drink. The production method is unusual as well. The base of the Kampot Pepper rum is the Samai Gold rum, which is made from molasses produced from locally grown Koh Kong sugarcane. A three-month maceration process happens, with the pepper imparting a subtle red colour and unsubtle spiciness in the liquid.

Next comes a vapour infusion technique, where Samai re-distils the rum in two 60L copper alembic pot stills and uses a basket of Kampot peppers to let the alcohol vapours move through for more flavour absorption. The final stage involves taking the best cuts from the maceration and the vapour infusion and blending them to get the bottled product. Taste-wise, the rum is a spicy mixture of tomato, coriander, chilli pepper and burnt biscuit.

Vietnam is also developing into a rum destination. With its high-quality sugarcane and variable climate, it's an ideal place for harvesting ingredients, as the founder of Rhum Belami Roddy Battajon set out to do. A former chef who moved to Vietnam for a fresh start, Battajon wanted to showcase the quality of Vietnamese ingredients.

> I created Rhum Belami following my Caribbean family tradition. The first important quality is the freshness of the juice called vesou. It's sourced in Long An, to maintain a local supply chain and contributes to keeping the carbon footprint to a minimum. In order to respect local farms in partnership with Rhum Belami, we decided to implant another crop to reinvigorate the soil without using fertilisers. A lot of distilleries forget their impact on the environment and the consequences of their harvesting method, diminishing nutrients in the soil. Vietnam has perfect soil. It's well drained and the weather ensures top-quality sugarcane in the fields.

> We have several products. There's Calyx, which we distilled in 2019, but went untouched during numerous months in oak casks prefilled with Mangosteen and dried fruits. Those forgotten barrels were reserved for a different use and convey a surprisingly smooth palate for a 59.9% ABV rum.
>
> We have our Cuisse De Nymphe, a rum that after distillation, is kept in lightly toasted barrels. It has a rich, aromatic bouquet, which varies between herbaceous and floral. Powerful and perfectly balanced, it's a bartender's ideal choice for any passion martini and pina colada.
>
> Then we have Legacy. This rum is aged for thirty-six months in toasted barrels prefilled with red Phu Quoc Pepper and exotic fruits cooked in turmeric. The Legacy is our best seller and has a reddish colour, a fruity nose and a round, full-bodied taste. A woody note is persistent long time after consumption.

Thailand has a claim to fame with rum too. SangSom special rum is the country's flagship offering. The story of SangSom began in 1977 and the brand grew to take 70 per cent of the Thai spirit market share. As it gained momentum outside of Thailand, SangSom rum picked up awards in the 1980s, winning gold medals in booze competitions in Madrid in 1982 and 1983. From that point on, it seemed to fall off the map, only to come back swinging in the 2000s, picking up another medal in 2006 at a Barcelona competition.

This recognition has become a part of the bottle's identity, with the gold medals displayed proudly on the label. This led to the rum being referred to locally as SangSom Rianthong, which translates to SangSom Gold Medallion. Yet despite the awards, SangSom is virtually unheard of beyond its Thai borders, which is a shame because there's a lot of interesting things going on with this rum.

My first thought on trying SangSom was 'Bloody hell, I've never drank such a smooth-tasting rum!' Perhaps that's why it's so popular in Thailand and goes down well with tourists. It's the kind of drink you could easily shot and spend all night downing at a bar.

That's not to pass the rum off as an inferior product. Far from it. Hints of vanilla and apple arrive on the nose in a thin veil. On the palate, flavours of chocolate, strawberry and pineapple unfold in gentle waves. This is finished off with an electric tingle of heat that rises in the back of the throat. Overall SangSom is a delicate rum that doesn't shout in the mouth. It's quiet, preferring to build up after several sips.

How about a trip to Mauritius next? Rum aficionado Frederic Bestel set up Gold of Mauritius as a tribute to his homeland. Bestel's family came from the north of France and arrived in Mauritius in 1800, carving out a plot of land for themselves. Through the generations, the Bestels turned their hands to rum-making, with a young Frederic helping his dad and grandad pick local fruits and spices for moonshine rum.

Following in his father's footsteps, Frederic set out to create his own spirit and came up with a lychee-flavoured liqueur. This concoction inspired the name for his company Litchquor, which comes from the French word 'litchee' for lychee.

Gold of Mauritius is blended from a range of unaged rums from small Mauritian distillers that Bestel personally selects. He then ages them in South African port barrels which still have port residue inside them for a period of one year. But this process is dependent on the barrels, as some have less port residue than others.

After the initial ageing, Bestel chooses between ten to fourteen barrels and then blends the rum to create a consistent flavour. Caramel colouring is also added to the rum for consistency, as the port barrels can often give the finished product a red or orange shade.

The first note that strikes me about this rum is its medicinal, rubbery scent. Sipping it reveals a tangy, pear quality. Pleasant, simple and no frills. Next come flavours of stone fruit and peach. If Gold of Mauritius was a person, it'd be that reliable friend who's got your back at the bar. Easy to deal with, not overbearing and enough personality to make your night memorable.

Meanwhile, William George white rum has an African slant and is the brainchild of Andrew and Richard Nicholls. The product is a blend of six different rums, with four being sourced from Jamaica and the other two coming from Trinidad & Tobago. The Jamaican rums are pot-stilled, while the Trinidad & Tobago varieties are multi-column distilled. It's worth pointing out that one of the Trinidadian rums is aged for two to five years in ex-Bourbon barrels and carbon filtered to remove the colour. The other five rums are unaged. All the rums are blended in Amsterdam by E&A Scheer, a premier rum-blending house with its fingers in a lot of big rum brands.

While the ingredients don't come from Africa, William George certainly carries the story of a time and place. The Nicholls created their rum as an inspiration to their grandfathers, William and George. William arrived in Zambia in 1938 and then returned to England to fight in the Second World War. He then returned to Zambia to settle down for good, while George relocated from England to Zimbabwe in 1956.

Andrew and Richard wanted to provide a fitting tribute to two people who shaped them. This dedication to family is captured in the William George label. It features a compass which points towards true north at 11 degrees west. The direction was calculated from Victoria Falls at the time that William and George lived in Africa. The font for the label was taken from George's birth certificate and a message that William wrote to his wife can be read on the side. It says 'blissful happiness for decades of time'. William George has cherry, stewed fruits and banana on the nose and a tropical punch of peach, vanilla, almond and raisins on the first and last sip.

India is another place where you might not think to find good rum. The Old Monk brand is a great place to start. The story of Old Monk goes back to 1855, when the father of Colonel Reginald Edward Harry Dyer of the Jallianwala Bagh massacre, Edward Abraham Dyer, set up a brewery in Kasauli, Himachal Pradesh. Dyer set up his brewery with the intention of catering to British folks' love of cheap beer.

The brewery ended up changing hands when H.G. Meakin bought the brewery in 1855, only for a merger to occur and the brand became Dyer Meakin. Fast forward to 1949 and the brand was bought by N.N. Meakin, who eventually changed the name to Mohan Meakin in 1967.

Old Monk rum was introduced in honour of a story about a kindly British monk who enjoyed inspecting the Mohan Meakin rum barrels. During the rum production period, the monk provided good company for the master distillers and they eventually taught the monk their secrets. His good advice helped to improve the overall quality of the rum and so a legend was born.

Old Monk went on to dominate the Indian alcohol market, becoming one of the world's most popular rums. The brand has prided itself on its 'word of mouth' marketing tactics, preferring to let its reputation speak for it rather than flashy advertising.

An introductory product to try is the Old Monk 7-year-old. It has a strong hit of molasses, caramel and roasted coffee beans detected on the nose. Chocolate and liquorice notes grab the attention on the first sip, building into a sensation of sweet warmth that spreads through the mouth. There are subtle chewy hints of bubblegum and pepper and vanilla that stick around for the finish.

Another part of the world that offers interesting rum is Haiti, which is known locally as clairin. Boukman rum offers a multi-faceted drinking experience and what I really love about this rum is the rich story that's gone into making it. The name was inspired by Dutty Boukman, who led the Haitian Revolution in 1791. Boukman showed tremendous heart by casting off the chains of oppression and leading his people to a better future. This is captured by the script on the label, which reads 'Listen to the voice of freedom rising in our hearts.'

The brand was started in 2016 by Haiti native Josette Buffaret Thomas and Ireland-born Adrian Keogh. Boukman was not only started to honour the island's rich traditions, but to give rum aficionados an alternative to the more well-known Barbancourt.

Company account manager Garcelle Menos has said that Boukman's mission is to,

> showcase Haiti as the lost world of rum. There's a beauty and drinking culture there that has been left untouched and undiscovered for years. The reason why we emphasise the mission is because it's important for people to understand that Haiti doesn't need a handout and we need people to live with dignity and income.
>
> We emphasise our partners because we don't want to be the brand that just bottles Haitian rum. We are creating jobs and making sure they're not living on two or three dollars a day and are able to live sustainable lives and be secure.

Boukman is produced from Haitian sugarcane and has important terroir from two locations. The first is the canefields of Croix des Bouquets in the south and the northern cane fields of Cap Haitien, where Dutty Boukman swore an oath of liberty and started the Haitian Revolution with rum.

The sugarcane is grown without fertiliser and cut by hand. Then, the cane is crushed in a steam engine, which runs on bagasse (sugarcane by-product), providing a sustainable energy source. The fresh sugarcane juice is fermented for three days, distilled into clairin and then infused with barks, citrus peels and botanicals that are native to Haiti. The ingredients are locally foraged and include bois bandé, zou'devant, campèche, bois cochon, oak and bitter orange peel.

On the nose, Boukman has hints of cinnamon and lemongrass. In the mouth, there's orange peel, rosemary, coriander and cardamom. The herbal, grassy qualities are balanced by the sweeter notes. It's topped off with a woody, dry finish.

The breadth of these world rums is still only a fraction of the category spectrum. Like the big comic book movie franchises that dominate popular culture, there truly is a rum multi-verse out there. Every dimension is inhabited by a different origin story, a different take on a style, a different opinion that keeps the category relevant and moving forward like any consummate survivalist.

Chapter 4
Bourbon

'Good whiskey is like a good song. It requires no explanation. One taste should tell you everything you need to know. No one has to tell you how to feel about it. You simply settle in and enjoy it.'

I read this mantra across the bottle of Traveller whisky, turning it around to see every detail. Inside the bottle, illuminated by golden liquid, I see a map marked by Lexington, Kentucky, the beating heart of the bourbon industry. I open the bottle, pour myself a glass and settle into the sound of *Tennessee Whisky* by 10x Grammy award-winning country singer Chris Stapleton.

Traveller is his bourbon. A drink he created in partnership with the Buffalo Trace Distillery and Master Distiller Harlen Wheatley. It's a smooth, rambling kind of bourbon. Mild, toasty, easy to drink, exactly the kind of product that goes well with a country ballad.

In many ways, the story of bourbon mirrors the most enduring of country songs. Humble beginnings, family values, salt of the earth, small-town living, hard times, good times, rough and ready party times, commercial greed, public controversy, hope, resilience, heart-rending, catchy as hell.

Who Invented Bourbon?

As the spirit of America, bourbon has to have a great origin story. From Henry Ford and the motor car to Thomas Edison and the lightbulb, it's the American way to celebrate the inventors who changed the world and so too is it with bourbon.

A story that existed for many years is that a Virginian pastor by the name of Rev Elijah Craig created bourbon on 30 April 1789 – the day that

George Washington became president of the United States. Craig was the owner of Kentucky's first paper mills and on that day in 1789, a fire broke out behind one of the mills where barrels were being stored. The fire burned the inside of some of the barrels and workmen went to Craig to ask what they should do with them. A thrifty man, Craig told them to keep the barrels and stick corn whisky in them to see what happened. After some time, it was discovered that the barrels changed the colour and taste of the whisky.

If that story sounds too good to be true, then you're right. It's pure marketing. The story of Elijah Craig being the inventor of bourbon was invented in the 1960s when the bourbon industry was fighting to have the whisky be called a home-grown product of the US.[1] Insiders in the industry knew it was false and because there was no internet, it was a lot easier to promote the myth.

The truth is that there are several contenders for the creation of American whisky and to get to the heart of that, we must trace the ingredients back to the source. For bourbon to be considered bourbon, it has to be made with these requirements:

> Made with at least 51 per cent corn in the mash bill and produced in the United States.
>
> Distilled to a maximum of 80% ABV.
>
> Aged in charred new oak barrels and barrelled at a maximum of 62.5% ABV.
>
> No flavourings or colouring can be added.
>
> The finished product must be bottled at a minimum of 40% ABV and a maximum of 75% ABV.[2]

It's in the corn that we find bourbon's origins. When Kentucky became a state in 1792, corn wasn't the chosen grain for distillation. It was rye. But as more settlers moved west and settled in the Bluegrass State, they planted corn because of its versatility as a crop that could be eaten whole, made into flour and used as animal feed.

Between 1813 and 1818, corn started to replace rye as the main whisky-based distillate through the recommendations of influential Northeastern distillers like Harrison Hall, who wrote: 'I have ever considered the union of rye and corn in mash, as productive of more spirit and of a purer quality, than can be obtained from either grain alone; and if the proportion of one-fourth part of rye can be obtained, it is enough.'[3] In his later work, Hall also advised against rye mashing and that more experimentation had to be done, though he never advised on corn whisky being stored inside charred barrels.

Another name linked to the creation of bourbon is Wattle Boone, employer of Thomas Lincoln, the father of President Abraham Lincoln. This presidential connection adds gravitas to the Boone story. Lincoln's father worked for Boone, who resuscitated a distillery in Nelson County and he built the first Kentucky distillery in 1780, according to the Lincoln papers in the Library of Congress.

But it's believed that it was actually Boone's father Walter who set up the distillery and Wattle's moniker of the father of bourbon was fanned by newspapers that wanted to publish an attention-grabbing story. This is suggested in an 1897 *Louisville Courier-Journal* story that read 'Thomas Lincoln was engaged by Wm. Boone, a distiller … which was then in operation upon nearly the exact spot where the big Atherton distillers now are.'[4] By 1897, Abraham Lincoln and bourbon's places in popular culture were already well-established.

John Ritchie comes up in bourbon lore too. Born in Scotland in 1752, Ritchie started a distillery in Nelson County and died there in 1792. His activities were recorded in 1895 by one Dr M.F. Coones, who mentioned that Ritchie's distillery was the source of a famous red liquor in Kentucky.

The most likely candidate for the inventor of bourbon is Jacob Spears, whose family settled in Kentucky in the 1780s. The owner of the Peacock Distillery, Spears is credited with coming up with the name bourbon after Bourbon County. Several records back up this claim and bourbon expert Fred Minnick has laid all of these out in detail in his book *Bourbon: The Rise, Fall And Rebirth Of An American Whisky*.

In 1869, a New Orleans publication *The Times-Picayune* linked Spears to bourbon's early days. 'The first whiskey manufactured in Bourbon county was made by parties who emigrated from Pennsylvania about the year 1790. The first distillery was erected by Jacob Spears a short time afterwards.' Minnick also points out that in 1935, Congressman Virgil Chapman spoke of his admiration for Spears as the creator of American whisky:

> I do not know this as an accurate, historical fact in the year 1790 … a man by the name of Jacob Spears, in Bourbon County, Kentucky, where I reside now, made straight

> Bourbon whisky, and because it was made in Bourbon County … has been called Bourbon whisky ever since.[5]

A Kentucky Democrat, Chapman didn't have a reputation for hyperbole and wouldn't have anything personal to gain from mentioning Spears. He was possibly relying on anecdotes and oral history he'd learned from living in Bourbon County.

Distillation Gold Rush, Taxes and Adulteration

Into the 1800s, bourbon production got a major shot to the arm through the efforts of President Thomas Jefferson signing the Louisiana Purchase which involved America taking the Louisiana Territory of 828,000 square miles from the west of the Mississippi River to the Rocky Mountains and into the Gulf of Mexico and Canada from the Spanish and French. The crown jewel in the Louisiana Territory was New Orleans and the flow of goods into the New World.

This meant that bourbon distillers could sell their goods freely through New Orleans in barrels, turning bourbon into one of the city's most valuable commodities. Jefferson also repealed a whisky tax in 1802, increasing the growth of distillers, wholesalers and rectifiers all looking to cash in on a drink that was displacing rum as the spirit of the nation.

By the 1820s, bourbon had made an enemy of temperance movements that saw it as a demon drink alongside other alcoholic beverages. This image wasn't helped by the quality of some types of American whisky that were being adulterated by rectifiers with prune juice, tobacco spit and water after distillation. There were no regulations against this at the time and terminology was different. In these wild west days of adulterated whisky, the word straight – i.e. neat – whisky could also mean rectified. So, rectifiers could market their products as straight bourbon.

In this fight for consumer attention, distillers came out with specific brands, such as Oscar Pepper, James E. Pepper, Chicken Cock, Silver Creek and Woodcock. But the most successful brand of the time was Old Crow, named after James C. Crow, who made his bones as a distiller at the Oscar Pepper Distillery, which is now known as Woodford Reserve Distillery. Crow is credited with bringing the sour mash technique to Kentucky, which caught on at other distilleries, killing harmful bacteria in other bourbon mashes. The whisky that Crow made flew off the shelves and after his death, his name was honoured by W.A. Gaines & Co, who bought leftover stocks and created the Old Crow brand.

Meanwhile, the government that had once seemed to work in bourbon's favour would prove to be capricious. In the Civil War, new whisky taxes were imposed and by 1867, when the whisky tax was $2 per gallon, the whole industry was accused of defrauding the government. Distillers were charged with tax evasion and the strongest of these conspiracies was the plan of the US Treasury Department's supervisor, John McDonald, who presided over Chicago, St Louis and Milwaukee.

At a trial that indicted many distillers, wholesalers and collectors, deputies would point out that the Great Whisky Ring began with McDonald in 1871. He collected money from distillers and gave it to influential members of the Republican party. The secretary of President Ulysses Grant, Orville Babcock, was named as a co-conspirator. Even more telling is that some of that money was found to have funded Grant's Republican election campaign and others like it. In the end, Grant pardoned Babcock and McDonald.[6]

The trial had sensationalised the conspiracy, leaving a stain on the name of bourbon distillers who'd been fighting to keep their products authentic and free of tax reform. Hope would soon be on the horizon.

Bottled-in-bond Sagas

For a hundred years, bourbon had flowed through America. It had been protected by a passionate and scrappy group of distillers and bastardised by snake oil merchants, unscrupulous wholesalers and dodgy marketers trying to make a quick buck.

By the 1880s, the former were sick and tired of having the latter dictate the terms of engagement. But the distillers had their own share of the blame. Many weren't handling stocks properly and failed to forecast product demand. At the centre of this controversy was bonded whisky. The kind housed in government-approved warehouses and the government allowed whisky to stay in bond before tax was paid.

In 1884, there was an attempt by Congress to pass a bonded whisky act, but it didn't go through and the response from distillers was to change the bonded age limit to lower their taxation. To some, they came off as bitchy and whiny. J.M. Atherton of the Atherton Distillery said, 'whisky dealers all over the country have been making laughing stocks of Kentucky distillers because of the many changes and reforms they favour, but which generally fall through after a great deal of discussion and agitation.'[7]

But the bourbon producers wouldn't stop their filibustering. They argued that bottling spirits in bond would be a lucrative way of selling American whisky exports and that they couldn't give consumers genuine bourbon if they were at the mercy of the rectifiers and adulteration salesmen.

This came to a head in 1896 when Kentucky Congressman Walter Evans passed a bill that allowed the export of bottled goods in a large amount of proof gallons. Distillers were looking forward to greater protection against rectifiers and a step in the right direction of producing pure bourbon. The Liquors Dealer Association fought back against the Evans bill when it went to the Senate on 16 December 1896 and a hearing was granted.

The distillers argued that the wholesalers were against the bottle-in-bond act because they wanted to control the bottling themselves and continue to adulterate to their heart's content. The dealers dug their heels in, arguing that the act would only benefit the Kentucky distillers.

After a lot of wrestling from both sides, a shaky détente was agreed and on 3 March 1897, the Bottle-In-Bond Act was officially passed. The distillers now had a legally binding guarantee that bourbon had provenance and consumers could legitimately know where a product came from.[8] Reliable wholesalers also had a guarantee that they could continue to bottle whisky out of bond without the need to put government stamps on bottles and cases.

This was only a temporary armistice, as the wholesalers were determined to keep on doing what they'd always done, while the distillers wanted to break away completely and bottle their own products. Skirmishes between both sides continued to happen into the 1900s with further fuel added to the fire after the passing of the Pure Food and Drug Act in 1906.

Under this legislation, there were no clear legal definitions of bourbon whisky and this lack of definition allowed rectifiers to brand their products as bourbon, even if they were grain vodka blended with rye whisky. As more debates around the Pure Food and Drug Act cropped up, resentment in other states built towards Kentucky, especially Illinois,

Indiana and Ohio who accused the Kentucky distillers of wanting to create a monopoly for themselves on what bourbon was allowed to be. To the Kentucky distillers, they were fighting for their livelihoods.

This hundred-year-old struggle of defining American whisky had become tiring for one man – President William Taft. Not long after he took office in 1909, Taft invited everyone with a horse in the bourbon race, along with chemists and those involved in the Pure Food and Drug Act, to reach a consensus on a legal bourbon definition and blends that were deemed as imitation whisky.

The landmark 'Taft Decision' decreed:

> Some time during the Civil War it was discovered that if raw whisky as it came from the still, unrectified and without redistillation, and thus containing from one-half to one-sixth of 1 per cent of fusel oil, was kept in oak barrels, the inside of the staves of which were charred, the tannic acid of the charred oak which found its way from the wood into the distilled spirits would colour the raw white whisky to the conventional colour of American whisky, and after some years would eliminate altogether the raw taste and the bad odour given the liquor by the fusel oil and would leave a smooth, delicate aroma, making the whisky exceedingly palatable without the use of any additional flavouring or colouring. The whisky thus made by one distillation and by ageing in charred oak barrels came to be known as 'straight' whisky, and to those who were good judges came to be regarded as the best and purest whisky.[9]

In other words, the Taft Act as a whole finally etched the words 'bourbon' and 'rye' next to 'straight whisky' in the legal bedrock of the American system and called out the fraudulent rectifiers and blenders who'd been cutting corners for too long.

> The straight whisky men are relieved from all future attempts to pass off neutral spirits whisky as straight whisky. More than this, if straight whisky or any other kind of whisky is aged in the wood, the fact may be branded on the package, and this claim to public favour may be truthfully put forth.[10]

Taft did more for bourbon than any other president that had come before him, but there was still a long road to travel with many trials and tribulations before America's spirit could reach the heights that it has today.

Bourbon Barons and Bootleggers

James 'Jim' Beam had been carrying the bourbon-making legacy of his family since the age of 16 when he first learned how to make the stuff. In 1894, he officially became the head of the Beam operations, following in the footsteps of his father and grandfather, both named David, and his great-grandfather Jacob, who set down the family roots in Kentucky as a humble farmer in the 1780s.

The Beam dynasty knew how to make good bourbon and Jim was no exception. The company's Old Tub whisky had become a national bourbon brand and was popular, despite the trend of distillers having to shift to industrial alcohol production for the First World War.

In 1920, everything came to a grinding halt for Beam with the introduction of Prohibition. Forced to shut down, Beam sold all his booze holdings and moved to Florida. As is the case with many of the great bourbon barons of the twentieth century, Beam had no problem adapting – for the sake of supporting his family, and to the changing times. He took a crack at coal mining and citrus farming, though he didn't turn out to be much good at either.

Beam wasn't an outlier in turning his hand to something else or getting creative in a climate of all alcohol being banned in the States. There were always loopholes to find and whisky returned to one of its original guises as a medical product. In 1920, it was used as a treatment for the Spanish Influenza outbreak that killed millions of people worldwide.

One pharmacist, F.J. Quirin reported:

> during the influenza epidemic … whiskey was very freely prescribed by physicians for their patients and as a druggist, I have no hesitancy in saying that … it was the cause of saving many lives … Much more might be said against Prohibition of the kind proposed, but I believe the influenza epidemic alone is sufficient to convince most people of medicinal value in certain areas.[11]

Naturally, some took advantage of this medicinal clause, such as John and Mary Dowling, a couple who would fight against bourbon being an exclusively American product for the rest of their time in business. As co-owners of the Waterfill & Frazier Distillery in Kentucky, the Dowlings had plenty of equipment to lug down with them to Juarez, Mexico, where they started the D&W Distillery. While in Mexico, the Dowlings struck up a connection with the Beam family through meeting Jim Beam's cousin Joe, and Joe's son Harry. The US government allowed for small batches of medicinal whisky to be made and as it wasn't illegal to distil alcohol in Mexico, the Dowlings brought 'Mexican' bourbon to the world.

Mary was a firebrand bootlegger who never shied away from making money from whisky wherever it was to be found. Before Prohibition, she'd started unloading 22,000 barrels of whisky from the Waterfill and Frazier warehouses near Tyrone, Kentucky, and by 16 January 1920 she had 1,600 barrels left. She decided to keep the rest 'safe from the heat' by storing them at her house and selling them by the bottle with her sons John and Emmett.

In 1923, the Dowling home was raided by the police and Mary was put on trial with her children. The final ruling of the trial came in 1926, with the family being hit by fines of $10,000 and Mary's sons being sent to prison for a year. By this time, the Dowlings had already started constructing the distillation plant in Mexico.[12] The D&W Distillery had a popular following all through Prohibition, yet their Mexican bourbon was looked down on by Kentucky distillers for the lack of authenticity up until the final day of it being made in 1964, when bourbon was officially recognised and protected as a US-made product.

Back in the US, bourbon distillers didn't just face opposition from the government. They were being shaken down by criminals forming strong bootlegging rings that were producing their own supplies of illegal booze or stealing legitimate stuff. There was one instance in Lebanon, Kentucky, of four masked men taking guards hostage at the Kobert, Mueller and Wathen distilleries. The gang stole ninety-two cases of bourbon.

After two years of constant scrutiny from the government and harassment from bootleggers, the leading US whisky distillers decided to fight back by banding together and referring to themselves as the 'Custodians' of pure-bonded medicinal whisky. They protested that

Federal Prohibition Commissioner Roy A. Haynes was playing fast and loose with enforcing Prohibition standards, and their livelihoods were being taken away by criminals.

While steps were being taken to limit the influence of whisky bootleggers, the Anti-Saloon League, a temperance organisation, claimed that forwarding the medicinal alcohol movement was undermining the reason for the Volstead Act in the first place. And so raged a back-and-forth over the importance of whisky for medical purposes between dry politicians and those seeking to legitimise the sale of products perceived to help fight illness. The distillers were either passed from pillar to post in terms of who they needed to talk to, or were sometimes ignored altogether.

But a major win for the bourbon industry happened in 1930 when influential bootlegger arrest numbers increased and there was talk of repealing Prohibition from the likes of New York governor Franklin Roosevelt and President Herbert Hoover.

The voices calling for repeal started as a trickle and gradually turned into a flood as the Great Depression of the 1930s tanked the American economy. The temperance crusaders had lost their edge and their arguments no longer held weight for a nation that needed to get back on its feet and whose citizens needed work.

Alcohol taxes had also taken a massive nosedive since the start of Prohibition, so making alcohol legal meant taxes could be collected again to jumpstart the economy and buy goodwill for politicians. According to the founder of the Anti-Saloon League, Dr Howard Russell, the main reason why Prohibition was repealed was from the decision-making of 'American multi-millionaires who want liquor to pay their income taxes.' It's hard to argue against that point.

For the bourbon industry, it was fantastic news. For the first time in thirteen years, distillers like Jim Beam could start to fill barrels again and good ol' Jim himself could finally get back to doing what he did best. By 1933, Beam was 70 years old and would have been well within his rights to ride off into the sunset like a gunslinger who'd earned his reputation ten times over.

Instead, he returned to Kentucky and rebuilt the distillery in 120 days. In 1934, he incorporated the James B. Beam Distilling Company, which proudly championed bourbon for decades to come, riding out the waves of continued government taxation, the disruptions of a second world war, and the 'white spirits' terror of the decades to come.

Another bourbon dynasty would become closely tied to the Beams around the same time. Five brothers, David, Ed, Gary, George and Mose Shapira, had a string of successful general stores, including one in Louisville. Consummate businessmen, the Shapiras recognised that with Prohibition's repeal, the demand for bourbon could skyrocket and they wanted to cash in.

So the Shapiras decided to make a bet, as explained by Bernie Lubbers, brand ambassador of the Heaven Hill distillery founded by the Shapiras.

> Let's keep in mind these brothers were young. They were in their late twenties and thirties, but they had an eye for business and for spotting talent. They met the legendary Harry and Joe Beam, two brothers who had gone down to Juarez, Mexico, to distil bourbon with a woman called Mary Dowling back in the Prohibition days. Together, the Shapiras and Beams invested in the company that would become Heaven Hill. As Mark Shapira, the current owner, has told me it was between $18,000 – $20,000 and that was a lot of money back in 1935.
>
> From there, the first Heaven Hill barrel was made on the 200 acres of Bardstown land on December 13th 1935. For the Shapiras, the collaboration with the Beam family was a bet. They saw an opportunity to be at the centre of the bourbon universe in Bardstown.

Plenty of people wanted to jump on the bourbon bandwagon. In the 1930s, it was common for bourbon brands to be bought directly from distillers who wanted to get rid of unwanted stocks and put out young bourbon or blends to get in on the action. All this sounds encouraging, but new and old threats loomed for bourbon, including the spectre of the Bottle-In-Bond Act that was set to be revisited.

The Fight for Bourbon Protection

A couple of years after Prohibition, Canadian distillers and wholesalers decided it was the right time to reopen the Bottle-In-Bond wound and try to get the legislation changed. The argument was that Canada wanted blended whisky to be allowed as bottled-in-bond, while Americans pushed back to say the Act was never meant for non-American spirits. Congress wouldn't budge and introduced a law that foreign distillers who didn't comply with this jurisdiction would be embargoed. The Canadian government wasn't pleased with this decision and warned that it could hurt trade between both countries.

Yet trade agreements dropped tariffs on Canadian whisky from $5 to $2.50, encouraging Canadian distillers to advertise 'Canadian bourbon'. For example, Seagram proudly displayed on a product 'every penny of tariff saving is passed on to you … Seagram's V.O. 6-years-old Bottled-in-Bond under Canadian Gov't Supervision, $2.09 a pint.'[13]

This must have been insulting to American whisky makers whose forefathers had campaigned so hard to get the Bottled-In-Bond Act approved. The simple sentence 'stored in bonded warehouses under US government supervision for no less than 4 years' had become a trusted sigil among American consumers and a brand awareness piece. Bourbon distillers had nothing to protect them against foreign bourbon labelling in 1937.

Salvation came the year after when Canadian distillers were encouraged financially to make blended whisky instead of bottled-in-bond. This led to the realisation from Canadian distillers that it wasn't worth the hassle of continuing to push the bottled-in-bond point and they gradually moved to exclusively promoting blends.

As was the case with the First World War, industrial alcohol became the focus of distillers during the Second. In a storm of strict whisky price enforcement and antitrust allegations towards liquor companies, the 'Big Four' bourbon makers emerged: Schenley Distilleries, National Distillers, Hiram Walker and Seagram.[14] All four megacorps were touted as controlling half of the whisky production in the US, gobbling up smaller bourbon makers and brands through aggressive acquisitions and being regularly indicted and investigated for illegal practices and monopolisation.

Two other distillers, Continental Distillers and Brown-Forman, were also grouped into this bourbon illuminati, butting heads with the Department of Justice and the Senate over advertising, pricing and political contributions towards the Democrat and Republican parties. Those same political contributions aided the Big Four in allegedly getting the DOJ to drop certain cases and any attempt to break them up by the government was unsuccessful.

Into the 1950s, flashy and creative advertising was the name of the game for bourbon brands looking to stake their claim to American drinkers. Interestingly, this was a time when bourbon ads were geared only towards men because distillers didn't see women as a feasible market. They had no issue with using women in their ads to entice more men to drink, as evident from Jim Beam, Old Crow, Early Times, Yellowstone and others buying ad space in *Playboy* magazine.

Ancient Age ran a campaign with model and actress Sophia Loren so her likeness could appear in stores as a cardboard cutout in 1967. The brand also featured women heavily in their print ads. One version is a pretty woman holding a bottle of Ancient Age while pointing suggestively towards the male consumer who'd probably be looking at it. The copy for the ad reads: 'If you can find a better bourbon … buy it! Ancient Age Bourbon is full 6 years old. It's distilled in one place to assure you of exceptional quality in every bottle … every drink! That's why Ancient Age is America's Largest Selling 6-Year-Old Kentucky Bourbon!'

Ironically, a woman would be instrumental in creating arguably the most successful new bourbon of the 1950s – Maker's Mark. Margie Samuels and her husband Bill Samuels Snr started the brand in 1953 after purchasing the Burks Distillery, which had started in 1805 as a gristmill. Margie was the type of forward-thinking woman who could see the distillery being a travel destination and historical landmark, as she spent time collecting as much history about the place from neighbours as possible and maintaining the original equipment and feel of the distillery.

She also came up with the Maker's Mark name, a disruptive choice that went against the Southern heritage and imagery that had become standard fare with bourbon. Capped off by the iconic red dripping wax seal, Maker's Mark launched in 1958 at $6 per bottle, the most expensive bourbon on the market at the time, compared to the general $2 price tag for other products.

The brand leaned into this expensive imagery, putting out some of the most creative adverts to ever be seen in the bourbon industry, as seen from a 1966 campaign:

> It tastes expensive … and is. Maker's Mark is made expensively; by hand; in small amounts and flavoured with

> homegrown wheat to make it softer. It's the softest spoken of the bourbons; you can stay with its easy taste ... Unless you really care how your whisky tastes, don't pay the price for bourbon as good as Maker's Mark.[15]

The '60s became the decade of bourbon. The Bourbon Institute had been formed in New York to champion and develop universal standards and an ambitious marketing campaign was launched to make bourbon as glorious as white picket fences, apple pie and baseball in the American consciousness. This was the time when the myth of Elijah Craig creating bourbon was invented. It was a press release picked up by various press outlets and the more the story circulated, the more patriotic and red-blooded American bourbon became.

The Bourbon Institute lobbied for bourbon to be officially named and protected as a US product, a decision that was finally achieved in 1964. This was after several years of back and forth between Congressmen, especially the stubborn holding out of one New York Congressman by the name of John V. Lindsay. He had ties to a Mexican bourbon distillery but no amount of stonewalling could stop the inevitable. The two hundred years of struggle for recognition by bourbon distillers had finally paid off.

But just as there seemed to be sunny skies ahead, a storm of white spirits blocked out the light.

Riding Out the White Spirits Wave

Into the late '60s and 1970s, vodka captured the imagination of the American consumer. The reasons for this will be explored in Chapter 5. What's interesting about the rise of vodka in relation to bourbon is how distillers responded and tried to adapt.

For example, Ancient Age took a cue from vodka as a mixer with soft drinks by positioning its products with orange juice. There was also the rise of 'light whisky', a movement motivated by the colourless appearance of vodka.

Perhaps the most infamous case of a bourbon distiller making light whisky is Brown-Forman. This involved filtering out the colour of an 8-year-old bourbon made in Pennsylvania and bottling it at 80 proof.

This 'Frost 8/80' was meant to be Brown-Forman's answer to vodka, a spirit that could be blended into cocktails like martinis and daiquiris. The only problem was that the product had a taste and smell that was unsuitable for vodka cocktails and it ended up being an epic failure. Brown-Forman had sunk $4 million into advertising and now had to buy back every unsold bottle they could find. Once they'd collected everything, the company destroyed the stocks and from that day the word Frost became a curse, never to be uttered again in the halls of Brown-Forman.[16]

The single most damaging year in the history of bourbon might well be 1972. This was when the light whisky madness was in full gear and vodka was close to becoming the top-selling American spirit. The Bourbon Institute was on its last legs in terms of being the leading bourbon education hub in the world. A year later it would fold into the Distilled Spirits Industry Council with other national spirit lobbies. But as a last hurrah, it published an ad about the ten-year reign of bourbon being the number one best-selling whisky in the world, even if the bourbon industry looked like a sinking ship at the time.

But bourbon was still selling and some of the old guard dug their heels in. Chief among them was Jim Beam, who backed away from the light whisky trend and championed American heritage. Meanwhile, Tennessee whisky brand Jack Daniel's branched out from its humble country roots and flooded into pop culture on the back of the punk movement in New York and the hair- and glam-metal bands on the Sunset Strip in California in the 1980s.

Maker's Mark also seized its opportunity as arguably the sexiest bourbon in the 1980s, going head-to-head with Jack Daniel's in advertising warfare. The rivalry between the two brands was built on potshots and one-upmanship, and Maker's Mark had some creative bullets with which to load up its gun.

Bill Samuels Jr, a savvy marketer who'd picked up his skills from his father, signed an editorial letter that claimed he'd received a phone call from the wife of Jack Daniel, and that her husband's favourite whisky to drink was Maker's Mark. 'She told me that for years, and for obvious reasons, the only whisky her husband, Jack Daniel would drink was the one with his name … Now, according to Mrs Daniel, Maker's Mark is the only whisky Jack Daniel drinks.'[17] Brown-Forman owned the

Jack Daniel's brand and it's tempting to think that with such a brazen shot, the conglomerate would retaliate by suing the jumped-up 'mom-and-pop' outfit that had the audacity to oppose it.

Apparently, Samuels Jr invited members of the Brown family to a private party. Owsley Brown, the former Vice President of the company, was said to be there and it's rumoured he told one executive to make a brand that could compete with Maker's Mark. This would be Woodford Reserve, and stories have varied on whether this was true or not.

The Maker's Mark brand, although positioned as a scrappy underdog, wasn't the mom-and-pop operation it appeared to be on the surface. For one thing, the brand was growing at a lightning pace after the Burks distillery was awarded National Historical Landmark status by the US Department of the Interior and Bill Samuels Snr leveraged that fact to stir up a media sensation. Sales shot through the roof and the Samuels had to put out a memo to say they couldn't meet the current demand. It was only a matter of time before Maker's Mark became a victim of its own success and the Samuels decided to sell to Canadian company Hiram Walker.

Bill Jr tried to buy the brand from his father but couldn't match the $15 million offer from the Canadian powerhouse, or its distribution networks and manpower. He settled instead for being a member of the Hiram Walker board.

A positive outcome of the bourbon brand rivalry is that it elevated the industry, demanding that its stewards and champions fight to preserve it, as had always been the case when outside influences threatened to derail momentum.

This carried through in the 1990s, with a renewed interest in bourbon coming from outside of Kentucky in other states and from the rest of the world. In 1999, the Kentucky Distillers' Association created a brochure for what would become the iconic Kentucky Bourbon Trail. A 'holy trail' of distilleries was presented for bourbon pilgrims to slake their thirst and drink from the well of local history. The year after, a press release was sent out along with a passport that could be stamped and this marketing campaign created a whole new subcategory of bourbon tourism.

The success of the Kentucky Bourbon Trail pointed towards a return to glory for the category, though it wouldn't be until the mid-2000s that it would achieve heights to match those of the 1960s.

The Modern Bourbon Boom

At the turn of the new millennium, a host of bourbon fan clubs and magazines were cropping up in every corner of the internet. Specialist bars like the Bourbons Bistro opened in 2005 in Louisville, enticing consumers from across the globe to fly in and try bottles they'd never heard of.

Seeing the growing appetite for Kentuckian culture, the Louisville Convention Visitors Bureau flew reporters in to review the Kentucky Derby and knock back drams in Bourbons Bistro, Brown Hotel Bar, Galt House and dozens of other local bars that were keen to take advantage of the renewed interest in America's spirit.

These flames were fanned even more by the online bourbon community that had grown across social media and bloggers who sang the category's praises from the UK to Alaska. A generation of whisky writers rolled up their sleeves, got their boots on the ground and told readers everything they needed to know. Chief among them was Chuck Cowdery, an author who produced a popular book called *Bourbon, Straight.*

According to him,

> the biggest change in thirty years is that people are actually writing about whisky now. Thirty years ago, there were a couple in the UK but no one here. When I got into the business, whisky was dead. I worked on many distilled products but few whiskies because whiskies were barely ever promoted back then. Even when I started American whisky writing about twenty years ago, I was a lone voice crying in the wilderness.[18]

Writers like Cowdery were flying out to meet and visit master distillers who'd attained godlike status among bourbon enthusiasts for the way they conducted themselves and pushed the industry forward.

The purest representation of this was Booker Noe. Jim Beam distiller, promoter and raconteur extraordinaire, Noe had a magnetic presence built on down-to-earth Kentucky charm and impish wonder that kept him young and energised. The innovator of the small-batch bourbon technique, Noe popularised mixing the contents of a select group of single-barrel bourbons together to create a product with a unique blend of flavours.[19] He produced his own iconic bottle called Booker's and promoted the illustrious legacy of his family until his eventual passing in 2004.

However, the modern bourbon boom hasn't been a total love affair. When controversial practices have happened, fans have been quick to call it out and demand answers. For example, between 2008 and 2016 bourbon brands were lowering proofs and dropping age statements so they could keep up with demand. Age was an obsession for distillers and they chose to free themselves of worrying about it so they could bottle more of a specific brand.

A bonus was that it also made stock forecasting easier, but the passionate bourbon fans who'd started this modern movement sometimes felt betrayed when brands changed age statements. In some cases, it's led to mass boycotting, as was the case with Heaven Hill and its twelve-year-old Elijah Craig.

At first, Heaven Hill moved the age towards the back label of the product and stated openly that it would keep the 12-year label. Bourbon aficionados weren't convinced. Commercially, Heaven Hill was thinking that it couldn't price a 12-year-old bourbon at $30 while other brands were priced at $50. While fans were pissed off at first, they eventually got over it, which highlights the passionate nature of bourbon fanbases and tribes.

Bernie Lubbers acknowledges the goodwill that Heaven Hill has built up over the decades and revealed what's on the horizon at the distillery when I interviewed him.

> We've recently relaunched our flagship Heaven Hill Brand, and now that shines alongside our Evan Williams Brand #2 selling Bourbon and Elijah Craig and others. Mostly, Heaven Hill has stayed within Kentucky and a couple of other states and Evan Williams has been the value brand for the company in the past. We've spent the last ten to twelve years trying to revamp the name because it's the name of the facility that we started at.
>
> So, we discontinued the value bourbon brand and then relaunched with a 27-year-old Heaven Hill Select too. Other recent releases are a 20-year-old corn and an

> everyday 7-year-old bottle in bond. We've got a grain-to-glass release, which is grains that have been grown at the distillery in Bardstown. The corn wasn't grown there, but the wheat is Kentuckian. There are three different recipes of that and it's a 6-year-old product. Heaven Hill isn't the first to do it. But the whole Shapira family are excited to bring it out, especially Max, who even at 80 is spry as ever and in the office six times a week.

Lubbers is one of the most passionate educators in the bourbon industry whose journey has been evolving since day one.

> I came into the bourbon industry in 2005 and believe it or not there were only ten distilleries in Kentucky at the time, making up 95 per cent of the world's bourbon. The only ambassadors that were representing the distilleries were the distillers themselves. They were production- and technical-based people who didn't have the skills to stand in front of a group of strangers and deliver a talk.
>
> Coming from the comedy world, that gave me an advantage. My first role in the whisky industry was working at Jim Beam and I'd already been putting those skills to use by running events and promotions at corner bars to have people taste their products.
>
> Instead of using a pre-approved slide deck, I decided to write my own bourbon presentation for a representation of Knob Creek's 9-year-old product. Since I wasn't a distiller or a member of the Beam family, I decided I was going to talk about the words on the label and no one was doing that back in 2005. That put me on the map and I was hired as one of the first official ambassadors for Knob Creek. Without my comedy background, I'd probably have been scared shitless to put myself out there like that and do something that no one else was doing.
>
> It wasn't until I got into the industry and started talking about the words on a label that I saw how trends develop and come back around. Early on, I researched how Pappy Van Winkle and his company, Stitzel Weller, had taken out

> advertisements on how to read a bottle. So, that confirmed to me I was on the right track. Everything comes back around every twenty to thirty years.
>
> The deeper I went into my research, the more I learned about the rich histories behind the people who created bourbon. Whenever I'd pick up a bottle in training or tastings, I'd tell my audience that the person on the label has a story. The story was what got people interested.
>
> As a storyteller and comedian, I've focused on my strengths. I'm not a distiller or in production. I'm the face of the brand in the marketplace. Because when I first started bourbon training, distillers were telling me about fermentation and temperature settings and I was like 'Why are you telling me all this technical stuff that I'll never be able to present?'
>
> So, I told them to give me something I can digest. Give me something I can get excited about that'll make me want to drink the products, so I can get customers excited about doing the same thing.

Lubbers also told me it's new blood that'll make a huge difference in bourbon's future growth, highlighting Heaven Hill's current master distiller Conor O'Driscoll as an example.

> Conor is amazing at what he does and I can say that from having worked at the two biggest bourbon companies in the world. He's the only guy I know who's had experience running small, medium and large distilleries. He's worked pot stills at Woodford and column stills and done everything in between.
>
> One of his biggest strengths is that he's come in with a younger set of eyes and is moving Heaven Hill forward for new generations and that does make a difference. Because sometimes you just do what your daddy said, right?
>
> That's certainly true with Parker Beam, who was the master distiller emeritus when I first started. He should be on the Mount Rushmore of distillers but he was always focused on distilling exactly like his dad Earl Beam. He was the master distiller after the Second World War before Parker

> took over in 1960. If Earl told Parker to do it a certain way, it'd be done a certain way.
>
> I remember Parker always using his body to try and figure out what the state of the bourbon would be like. He'd make assumptions based on how the temperature rose and how it made him feel. Now, doing things the traditional way can be good but it also hinders you. Conor is willing to experiment and make the best possible spirit he can make.
>
> One more thing about Conor I've noticed is he'll put his foot down and take a stand against the usual way of doing things when a company might be building a new distillery and they pay consultants a bunch of money to tell them what to do. But he's ballsy enough to say we're going to do things our own way and stand by the name that's on our bottles.

Indeed, the future of bourbon is bright, with new products, trends and personalities propelling the industry forward. For example, bourbon investment has grown in recent years, with consumers investing in bourbon casks in a similar way that Scotch lovers invest in casks. Jeremy Kasler, the founder of CaskX, is at the centre of this bourbon investment boom.

In an interview with Forbes, he said:

> we think bourbon barrels will continue to rise in value. A couple of things are going to drive that. The first thing that will affect prices is the cost of raw materials to make bourbon. Barrel prices have almost doubled in the last three years; corn is more expensive, and shipping is more expensive. The entire infrastructure surrounding whisky is more expensive, so that's driving the price higher.[20]

The second thing Kasler pointed out was that the increasing demand for the liquid will also force prices upwards, alongside big spirits conglomerates buying distillers and creating scarcity in the market.

Kasler also believes,

> bourbon represents a good investment because it is a tangible commodity. When you buy whisky in barrels, you own

> something, and your money isn't tied up with something that only exists on trading desks. It's something you can lay your hands on, especially if you visit the distilleries with us on one of our VIP trips. This is becoming increasingly rare from an investment perspective.[21]

Elsewhere, distilleries are becoming increasingly focused on sustainability. Angel's Envy started a campaign in 2014 called Toast the Trees, which focuses on championing the planting and conservation of white oak, which has powerful biodiversity qualities. Angel's Envy works with the Arbor Day Foundation to run this reforestation programme and in 2021, there was enough white oak planted to sequester roughly 55,000 metric tons of carbon.[22]

Others, such as writer Michael Veach, see the bourbon craze levelling off, but he envisions new artisan distillers providing a 360-degree experience of bourbon tourism, small warehouses for storage and high-quality products. Veach argues that artisan distillers,

> need to make their top priority making good whisky. The distilleries being built with the main goal of making a lot of money by selling out their brand and distillers to the big companies are in trouble … The big companies have plenty of brands already and don't need to increase their portfolio or production. Next, the artisan distilleries need to make bourbon tourism an important part of their business plan. Tours are an excellent way to get your product in front of consumers.[23]

And so, we've reached the end of our song. The ballad of bourbon has been an epic ride of highs and lows, triumphs and heartbreaks, rebirths and falls. Every year, new lyrics are added to its story and drinkers will continue to listen along and dance to the music.

Long may that song keep playing.

Chapter 5
Vodka

1864, Russia.

A man named Piotr Smirnov had an idea. A businessman who'd risen far from his humble origins as a serf in the tiny Russian village of Kayurovo, Smirnov was always thinking about the next thing that could push him up to the next rung of society.

His latest idea was vodka.

Within twenty years, Smirnov vodka was one of the most famous vodka producers in Russia and Piotr had become one of the wealthiest men in the country. In 1886, he'd even received a special designation from the Tsar as a Purveyor of the Imperial Court, meaning the Smirnovs were the official vodka makers to the royal family, and the people.

It was all going so well until the early 1900s, when the Tsar nationalised the Russian vodka industry. By this time, Piotr had died and his son Vladimir had taken over. With this nationalisation, Vladimir was forced to sell his factory and it only got worse during the Russian Revolution of 1917. As the Bolsheviks seized power and the line of Tsars was broken, Smirnov and his family fled the country.

In the 1920s, Vladimir created a factory in Constantinople (Istanbul) and eventually settled in France, where he changed the family name from Smirnov to Smirnoff. This name sounded less Russian and less likely to have his family oppressed, so Vladimir revived the vodka brand under the Smirnoff name.

By the 1930s, the Smirnoffs had sold the rights to their vodka to an American tycoon called John G. Martin, the co-founder of the Heublein alcohol distribution company.[1] His board thought he was mad. For decades, Americans had been staunch whisky drinkers. Vodka was alien and strange. How was it possibly going to sell?

Martin rolled the dice and his gamble paid off. Smirnoff vodka exploded onto the scene, leading a revolution as loud and as wild as any dreamed up by the Russian people. In 1939, the year that Martin bought the rights to Smirnoff, vodka represented a poxy 35,370 gallons of what was consumed in the US.

In 1961, it jumped by 50 per cent between 18–44-year-old men[2] and this was a sign of things to come. Vodka didn't just come after whisky. It looked to topple rum, gin and other categories as the world's most consumed spirit. For a time, it looked like that was going to happen.

First, let's go back to the origins of this upstart spirit and how the stage was set for its American invasion.

The Origins of Vodka

Vodka, a spirit made from fermented cereal grains and potatoes, has a history that may date back to as early as the eighth century in Poland or the ninth century in Russia. Both nations have a claim to fame on it, but there is little if any documented evidence to suggest this was the case,[3] as suggested by Scott Simpson in his paper *History and Mythology of Polish Vodka.* Instead, it would be more fitting to say that vodka developed through a natural exchange between the Slavic tribes that would settle the land of Poland and all the other cultures that formed countries like Ukraine and Russia.

The early drink of these cultures was beer and fermented wine and the first record that is meant to exist of a vodka distillery comes from 1174 in Russia from the *Vyatka Chronicle*.[4] This may or may not be true. We can assume, like the path of other spirits, distillation techniques came to Russia and Poland around the thirteenth century and distillation was used for alchemy and medical purposes.

One of these early physicians, Nicholas of Poland, likely carried these techniques back home with him after studying at the Medical School of Salerno. A couple of centuries later, another Polish physician Stefan Falimirz, published a book called *Of Herbs and Their Powers*, which detailed the medical uses of a wide variety of plants and other ingredients. In it, he also refers to the preparation of 'wódki', by way of distillation. Here we see the substance that would become vodka referenced for the first time in the Polish language. According to Simpson,

'Falimirz' wódki differed subtly from what we call 'vodka' today. For Falimirz, wódki included all 'medicinal distillates, both distilled ethanol and steam-distilled essential oils'.[5]

Wódki became interchangeable with another Polish word 'gorzatka', a beverage that steadily grew in popularity for the Polish working class throughout the fifteenth and sixteenth centuries. Alongside it, 'vini cremati' (burnt wine) was also a popular choice.

Gorzatka still had a long way to go before it became universally accepted, especially as the literary scene evolved in Poland. A popular literary image of the gorzatka-drinker of Polish Renaissance poetry was a petty nobleman getting sauced and suffering from brutal hangovers. The moral decay and chaos caused by distilled alcohol were also blamed on outsiders, as the poet Klonowic mentioned that the stuff must have been created by Satan himself in 1584.

Into the seventeenth century, opinions began to change about gorzatka. The Krakow writer Jurek Potański wrote a tract in 1614 about vodka being a local tradition and acknowledging that neighbouring nations had their own version of it as well. From that point on, vodka was established as the drink of Polish culture.

This was observed by Ulryk Werdum, a noble German who visited in 1671 and said gorzatka was the 'favourite drink' of 'the most aristocratic Poles'. They 'carry it with them ... and must drink it almost every hour'.[6]

With vodka now firmly entrenched in Polish culture, there was room for experimentation with ingredients. By the 1760s, grain vodka was the most popular type that was being made, but there was also a tradition of fruit vodkas that has lived on into the modern day.

The most prominent of the period was 'sliwowica', also called plum brandy. In 1777, botanist Jan Kluk said 'wodka from all of the fruits can be excellent, but among them the best is from plums'.[7] Recent Polish legislation has attempted to banish sliwowica from the vodka canon and place it in a new category called 'okowita' (an old Polish word that comes from the Latin aqua vitae), but fruit vodka and vodka remain generally intertwined in the mind of modern consumers. Sliwowica has certainly been more enduring than other types of vodka, such as rye when it was dethroned by an invader in the eighteenth century.

The Rise of Potato Vodka

The most well-known story about how potatoes made it to Poland was that King Jan Sobieski III brought them over from Vienna in 1683. In the next century, potatoes were officially recorded as a food item for sale when they were listed as an expensive import in the Krakow market in 1739.

At the time, it was difficult to conceive of turning potatoes into vodka because of the number of technical issues to deal with. For one thing, grains were able to produce their own enzymes and convert starch into sugar, and then yeast could convert it into alcohol. Potatoes needed an additional step to make sure that the right amount of sugars could be produced for vodka.

By 1760, these issues seemed to have been worked out, as a distillery in the Kingdom of Prussia was the first to make potato vodka at scale and then improvements and potato distillation techniques spread throughout Europe towards the end of the eighteenth century. But the humble potato still wasn't the main ingredient of choice for vodka. That came in the nineteenth century, when the potato became the main source of carbs at the Polish dinner table, replacing millet. This was because they were cheap, easy to farm and grew out of even the poorest plots of land.

Adding to the attractiveness of potato vodka was the incentives given in the 1860s for running agricultural distilleries on Polish lands. These distilleries were owned by individual landowners who farmed potatoes in the growing season on big plantations and distilled alcohol from the crop in small factories connected to the land in the off-season. Plus, the advancement of distillation stills throughout the nineteenth century further increased the renown of potato vodka, speeding up processes and enabling distillers to turn a bigger profit.

At the height of the potato vodka craze in the nineteenth century, it eclipsed beer as the drink of choice among Polish peasants, as the price of vodka had been brought down dramatically by this wonderous carb.

This wouldn't remain the case forever; into the twentieth century, grain vodka started to come back into fashion. There are a multitude of reasons for this, with one of the biggest being that the old manor systems and agricultural collectives were broken down by new political changes sweeping across Europe, with much of these changes happening in

Russia and rippling outwards across Eastern Europe like a stone being dropped into a pond.

Certainly by the 1900s, wodka had replaced gorzatka as the dominant phrase for vodka in Poland. Here was another ripple effect from Russia, as wodka had become the word of choice there too and likely carried over.

From Russia With Love

Like Poland, vodka has a storied history in Russia and possibly the first ever spirit to be tasted in the country was called 'zhiznennoy vody' (living water), which is the equivalent of aqua vitae. From there, the process of distilling vodka may have stemmed from Genoese merchants distilling for the Grand Duke of Lithuania in the 1400s. Russian clerics also visited Italian monasteries to see distilling techniques first-hand and brought it back with them.

In the fifteenth century, the growth of vodka started to increase in Russia because of new distilling technology and we see an early example of how the perspective of vodka becomes tied up with the man in charge.

Tsar Ivan IV, better known as Ivan the Terrible, saw the commercial power of vodka. While previous rulers like Grand Prince Ivan III had forbidden the making of strong spirits, the Tsar went on to build the first 'kabak' (tavern) for his palace guard in Moscow and sanctioned state-owned distillers so he could control and profit from them.

This didn't mean Ivan the Terrible enjoyed knocking back vodka. He even restricted drinking in kabaks and took a hard line against public drunkenness. This set off a pendulum swing of rulers either banning alcohol production, or pushing it for their own agenda. The next Tsar, Fyodor, tried to tear down kabaks. Then his successor Boris Godunov saw the money to be made in the vodka trade and aimed to grow kabaks across Russia, while also permitting it to be bought and taken off the premises. The first of the Romanov Tsars, Mikhail, took the opposite stance and tried to limit vodka growth with limited prohibition in the mid-1600s, only for his son Alexis to reverse the decision when he took power.

Tsar Alexis' most enduring contribution to the history of vodka is the codifying of the state's monopoly on alcohol production and sale. In 1649, he introduced the Law Code, which spelt out that any private production of alcohol would be met by brutal punishment and any money earned from vodka sales would go into the royal coffers.[8]

This was bad news for peasant distillers, who nevertheless went on making 'samogon', homemade vodka. It was good news for aristocratic distillers who could earn favour among the Russian elite with their fashionable beverages and vodka varieties mixed with herbs, fruits and berries. A popular gimmick of seventeenth century Russian noble feasts was to include a selection of vodka with flavours that started with each letter of the Russian alphabet.[9]

Into the nineteenth century, vodka had become a pillar of the Russian national identity and so businesses and brands wanted to shout about it and bring any kind of legitimacy they could as part of Russian pride. It was out of this desire that the connection between vodka and one of Russia's most famous scientific minds would be forever intertwined.

Dmitri Mendeleev, chemist and creator of the periodic table, has been caught up in more than one romantic legend over the years. For example, there's one popular story about how Mendeleev supposedly created the periodic table in his sleep. On a February night, after a long day of work, Mendeleev fell asleep and dreamed the chemical elements could be arranged into groups with similar characteristics if grouped by atomic weight. There's no documented evidence to support this myth.

Another myth claims that Mendeleev invented vodka. Or if not that, he created the perfect mixture of 40 per cent ethanol and 60 per cent water. It became the literal Russian Standard, as a Russian vodka brand of the same name proudly states. 'In 1894, Dimitri Mendeleev, the greatest scientist in all of Russia, received the decree to set the Imperial quality standard for Russian vodka and the "Russian Standard" was born.'[10]

While Mendeleev wrote a dissertation called *A discourse on the compounds of alcohol and water*, and did experiments to test the precise measurements of ethanol and water mixtures at various ratios, he didn't state anywhere in his writing that vodka at 40% ABV is the best quality. His area of study wasn't about the best way to mix vodka. He was commissioned by the Russian government to find more efficient ways to bring in excise tax on alcohol. His research helped to do exactly that. Nor was Mendeleev a vodka drinker himself. He didn't want to become an alcoholic like one of his older brothers. So, he sipped red wine instead.[11]

At the turn of the twentieth century, Russia again went through massive political upheaval with the ousting of the Romanov line, the Bolsheviks taking power and the rise of Communism. Party leader Vladimir Lenin was a staunch opposer of alcohol, using his anti-vodka rhetoric to strengthen his position. He claimed that in vodka, Tsarist Russia had supplied society with the means to abuse itself, lulling the common man into torpor and rendering him too drunk to challenge the status quo.

The Bolshevik ban was essentially the Russian equivalent of American Prohibition and went down about as well as it did in the States. In the 1920s, it's estimated that about a third of rural households in Russia were once again making samogon, and so by 1925 the government had given in. Private homebrewing was legal, so long as the alcohol wasn't going to be sold.

In the lead-up to the Second World War, the pattern of leaders switching from demonising vodka to promoting it continued when Stalin took over as the head of the Russian government. He used the revenue from spirit sales to fund national defence programmes and increase his political strength. At the end of the '30s, the ABV of vodka spiked from 20% to its 'natural' level of 40% ABV, as Mendeleev had 'recommended' years ago.

Vodka was the fuel that kept the Russian military going throughout the Second World War. It was served to the troops as part of their rations. To some high-ranking officials in the Russian command centre, such as Sergei Witte who created the State Vodka monopoly as finance minister, vodka could single-handedly fund wars, such as the conflict with Japan back in the early 1900s. He wrote in his memoirs about his successor:

> When the war with Japan began, the then finance minister Vladimir Nikolaevich Kokovtsev began to use the liquor monopoly primarily as a means of increasing revenue, by raising liquor prices and increasing the number of liquor stores. And the work of excise officials was judged by increase in revenue rather than by decrease in alcoholism.[12]

Like many of his policies, Stalin was ruthless in how he executed them and wouldn't let anyone get in his way of achieving his vision of a powerful Soviet Union.

For example, prior to him being in office, so-called 'social hygienists' had placed a lot of emphasis on alcoholism being a social-based disease. They advised the Soviet people to be weaned off this alcohol dependence to make sure the nation could be strong. This view was echoed by psychiatrists, who believed only they had the ability to solve the social ills of alcohol abuse and cure suffering patients. According to author Patricia Herlihy, 'touting the results of their empirical studies of the patients in psychiatric institutions, the psychiatrists maintained that they alone had the knowledge to treat this type of alcoholic effectively'.[13]

There was no room for this kind of intense scrutiny in the new world Stalin was building and these social hygienists and psychiatrists either quietly moved into new lines of work or disappeared in more permanent ways.

Herlihy also writes:

> With the question of alcoholism thus 'solved', in 1930 Stalin ordered the production of vodka to be increased and placed directly under central government control. New factories were built, and by 1940 there were more shops selling drink than meat, fruit and vegetables put together; the output of alcohol rose sharply as a result.[14]

Of course, the Russian government would once again return to dimming vodka's commercial star once the Second World War ended. But over in the West, vodka was about to shoot straight for the moon and seize the spotlight in America.

Shaken, Not Stirred

1958 became a watershed year for white goods like vodka. It was the year Ian Fleming's James Bond uttered the immortal line 'shaken, not stirred' when ordering a martini in the novel *Dr No.* In 1964's *Goldfinger*, Sean Connery made the line even more famous when he said it for the first time on screen as Bond. Not that America's infatuation with vodka rested solely on the shoulder of Fleming's iconic spy, but it certainly helped with its image as the spirit of a new generation.

Vodka appreciation had been steadily growing in the States since the end of the Second World War. In 1950, only 40,000 cases were sold. Five years later, that number had jumped to 4 million. It's interesting that at the time of the Cold War, when Americans feared Communism on their doorsteps and the invasion of Red armies, it was a colourless liquid that popped up everywhere and radicalised the American youth who were fed up with their parents' and grandparents' fuddy-duddy taste in brown spirits like Scotch and bourbon.

Further bolstering vodka's appeal was the fact that it was colourless, odourless and could be mixed with anything. Smirnoff took advantage of this with its 'Leave You Breathless' campaign. This slogan, along with 'It Takes Your Breath Away', tapped into the idea that people who drank vodka wouldn't be caught over the limit on breathalyser tests.

Then there was the variety of cocktails that could be made with Smirnoff. A 1967 advert read:

> You can't decide which one you like the best. Smirnoff Screwdrivers with the zestful taste of orange juice. Bloody Marys with tomato juice. The Smirnoff Mule with refreshing 7-Up. The dryest Martinis. The smoothest drink on-the-rocks. Filtered through 14,000 pounds of activated charcoal, only Smirnoff makes so many drinks so well.[15]

Chief among these cocktails was the Moscow Mule, an invention from Smirnoff that boosted sales even more. This zingy mixture of Smirnoff vodka, ginger beer and lime first appeared in 1940 in a Los Angeles restaurant called Cock'n'Bull. The owner, Jack Morgan, needed to move a lot of homemade ginger beer, while his girlfriend Ozeline Schmidt, was the heiress of a copper factory that struggled to sell its products. Smirnoff CEO John Martin and his advertising manager met with Morgan and Schmidt to create a cocktail that combined the bar's ginger ale and was served in a copper mug.

It wasn't until 1946 that the Moscow Mule started rolling out to bars across the country because Smirnoff wasn't being produced during the Second World War. Martin launched an aggressive marketing campaign to get it onto menus, though it kept getting refused by every bartender he put it in front of. Common responses included 'what, drink that stuff? Russian dynamite? No sir!'[16]

Traveller bourbon is a collaboration between country singer Chris Stapleton and the Buffalo Trace Distillery. (Author's own photo)

Highland Park's 10-Year-Old Viking Scars Scotch whisky. (Author's own photo)

Woodford Reserve bourbon. (Author's own photo)

William Hogarth's *Gin Lane* painting. (Public domain, Wikimedia Commons)

Above: Cor Cor Red is an example of a growing number of Japanese rums on the market. (Author's own photo)

Right: Boukman rum from Haiti. (Author's own photo)

Old Monk Indian rum. (Author's own photo)

Udisan awamori is a great entry-level awamori to try. (Author's own photo)

Witch's Kiss shochu is good for drinking in the autumn and winter. (Author's own photo)

Beniotome red maiden shochu is made from sesame seeds. (Author's own photo)

Tatsugo gold shochu is a brown sugar shochu from the Amami Islands. (Author's own photo)

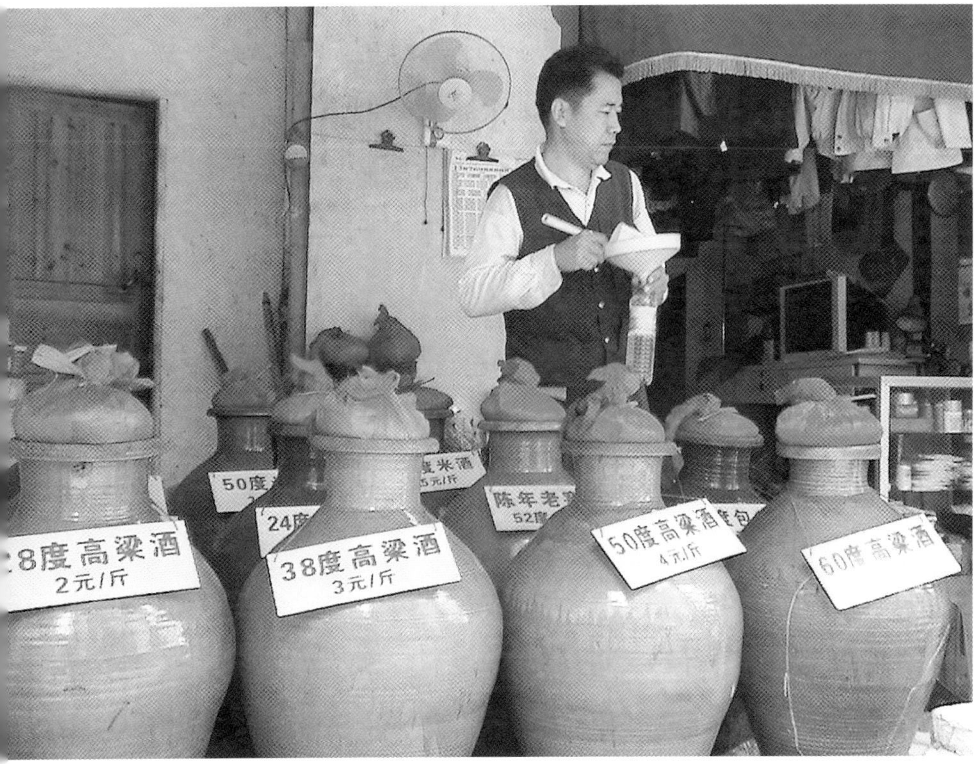

Baijiu. (Public domain, Wikimedia Commons)

A bottle of soju. (Public domain, Wikimedia Commons)

Yokka koji awamori is made with a four-day koji fermentation instead of the traditional two-day koji fermentation in Japan. (Author's own photo)

Absolut vodka collection. (Public domain, Wikimedia Commons)

Gusano worms are associated with mezcal. (Public domain, Wikimedia Commons)

Ada Coleman was one of the most famous female bartenders in history. (Public domain, Wikimedia Commons)

'Cocktail' Bill Boothby was known for his flamboyant serving style and larger-than-life persona. (Public domain, Wikimedia Commons)

To get around this, Martin came up with a stunt that involved Polaroid cameras. If he could get a bartender to try the cocktail, he'd snap a picture of them drinking it out of a copper cup. He'd take two photos. One was for the bartender's wife, the second was to take it to the next bar across the street and so on and so on until the Moscow Mule was 'firmly entrenched' in the American zeitgeist by 1954 according to the *New York Times.*

Another vodka was able to capture the imagination of the American public through the same kind of bold marketing campaigns and risk-taking attitude. Absolut vodka.

The story of this iconic brand goes back to nineteenth century Sweden when a man known as Lars Olsson Smith set out to make an absolutely pure vodka and challenge the city of Stockholm's booze marketing monopoly by selling his product outside of the city at a cheaper price. Smith's decision to thumb his nose at the Swedish government's control of liquor marketing was successful and his Rent Brännvin (pure vodka) was a big hit.

Smith ended up controlling half of all vodka sales in Sweden, brashly offering free ferry services to his customers to the island of Reimersholme where he made his vodka. As you might expect, Smith's antics earned him his fair share of enemies. He survived two assassination attempts, eventually becoming ill with appendicitis.

Believing he wouldn't survive for much longer but holding out hope for a lifesaving operation in London, Smith left his money to his family in case he didn't make it.

He did.

And when he returned home, his wife, sons and daughters refused to give him back his wealth and he died destitute in 1913. It was an ignoble end for the vodka king of Sweden, even more so when his products were taken over by the Swedish state liquor monopoly in 1917 and run into the ground.[17]

By the 1970s, the Swedes had lost their thirst for strong spirits, due to various government campaigns to try to change local drinking habits. Wine was being presented as the better alternative, while other initiatives were encouraging Swedes to stop drinking altogether.

Lars Lindmark, CEO of Vin & Sprit, saw an opportunity to relaunch the once-illustrious brand a hundred years after it was first developed by Smith. He rightfully saw that vodka was considered a premium product in America, but for his vision to catch on, he understood that the product would need to have an incredible design and memorable marketing in a highly competitive market.

To do this, he worked with Gunnar Broman of the Carlsson & Broman agency on the key task of exporting Swedish vodka with a sexy and sleek product. Broman went to work and found a pharmacy bottle in an antique shop in Stockholm's Old Town. This was the first part of the puzzle, as vodka had been sold to pharmacies as medicine in the sixteenth and seventeenth centuries in Sweden.

Next, Broman sat down with the creative team of the Ayer advertising agency in New York, presenting five different concepts. At the time, it was fashionable to create premium bottles that were decked out in gold and silver – anything with flash. Broman went against commercial tastes by wanting a design that was understated and transparent.

So the bottle used for Absolut would be see-through, which drew a viewer's eye through it. Put a lot of Absolut bottles together and they'd look like a vacuum.

Another design choice was to make the label on the bottle look like an old-fashioned ad, i.e. with the brand name appearing as a headline above text that went into history and traditions. Like a phoenix rising from the ashes, Smith was resurrected on the label, his name etched into the saga of Swedish vodka.

The final piece of the puzzle came with the name. First, Absolute Pure Vodka was suggested but was quickly shot down because of trademark issues in the US and 'pure' couldn't be used either because of legal restrictions. So, the name was shortened to Absolut in honour of the Swedish spelling.

At last, Absolut was ready to go to the American market and Vin & Sprit found the right partnerships to make sure the product was ready to launch for the spring of 1979 at a trade fair in New Orleans, and then across the East Coast soon after.

Before long, Absolut was stirring up a craze on the Manhattan cocktail scene. New Yorkers were curious about trying an Absolut on the rocks and any time a bartender said they hadn't heard of the new superstar Swedish vodka on the block, the intrigue and excitement got bigger. Much of Absolut's success came from the innovative bottle design, which earned first prize from the Art Directors Club in New York in 1980.

It even caught the eye of artists from all strata of society, with the most famous being Andy Warhol. The story goes that Warhol saw Absolut in Studio 54, the club he liked to hang out in with his friend Michel Roux, the CEO of Carillon. Something about the bottle spoke to the artist and in 1985, Warhol painted it. Absolut Warhol hit the public eye in 1986, a luscious pink, purple and red homage to the legacy of Lars Olsson Smith.[18]

Vodka's Refinement and Reinvention

By the 1990s, vodka was in danger of becoming permanently stuck with its image as an unrefined odourless, colourless spirit that didn't have much else going for it. In the mid-'90s, another shift happened, with vodka becoming more complex and flavoursome, a move towards refinement and a celebration of natural ingredients.

Arguably, the brand that started this trend was Grey Goose in 1997. American entrepreneur Sidney Frank teamed up with French cellar master Francois Thibault to develop a French vodka that could take the category in a bold new direction. Frank had come from a rural background and established himself as a savvy businessman, though he didn't have any spirit-making experience. Thibault had earned his stripes in the wine and cognac trade and the two men's skills complemented each other.

Both agreed that to make a stand-out vodka, full control of the ingredients was necessary. Instead of buying existing spirit and re-distilling it, Frank and Thibault sourced wheat from Picardie and spring water from Gensac-la-Pallue, making and distilling the vodka from scratch. These ingredients celebrated the terroir of French grains and landscape, pointing towards a premium spirit that stood out above other products on the market. This came across in how the vodka was positioned, being called single-origin because of the provenance of the two main ingredients of wheat and water.

But first, before the ingredients and the brand story could be created, there had to be a memorable name. A few stories have been given for where the Grey Goose name originated. One romantic tale involves the famous geese that are meant to gather and drink from the fountain in front of Hotel de Ville in Cognac, France.

I suspect that to be a wild goose chase. The most likely origin comes directly from Frank, who said he got the name from a German white wine he sold back in the '70s and was defunct in the '90s. It couldn't have hurt that he owned the worldwide rights to the name.[19]

Armed with a memorable name, a luxurious-looking logo and bottle, and a fine-tasting liquid, Grey Goose took the world by storm, going head-to-head with fellow luxury vodka Absolut and carving out its own corner of the market. With its success came the freedom for new brands to enter the premium vodka space, adding their own flourishes and flavours to the mix, like Belvedere, which tapped into its heritage to reintroduce to the world what Polish vodka is capable of in a luxury setting.

But with this premiumisation has come a certain kind of association, according to Ross Haddow, the chief marketing officer of Dutch Barn Orchard vodka, which is co-owned by comedian Ricky Gervais.

> For a long time, vodka entered this space of overt status projection with rappers, bling, sparklers and big bottles, particularly successful when those on-trade party venues were flying. This world will always resonate with a certain consumer, but there are a growing number of them looking for something and until now vodka has failed to evolve with this. There is a reappraisal of how good vodka can be.[20]

Dutch Barn certainly contains an echo of the old, rural roots of vodka, a down-to-earth, rustic process that involves apples from North Yorkshire being blended with potato spirit.

Another emerging field in the modern vodka revolution is the ready-to-drink category, packaged alcoholic drinks with spirit bases. Vodka is one of the most popular bases according to Adam Rogers, the North American research director of the alcohol data intelligence platform IWSR:

> Many of today's younger legal-drinking-age consumers are opting for RTDs as their entry into beverage alcohol, with many of the RTDs being vodka-based. Since RTDs act as a bridge product to the full-length strength version, vodka will eventually experience an increase in consumer attention once they cross that bridge.[21]

An example of this is Sprinter, a line of 100-calorie vodka sodas from reality star Kylie Jenner. Sprinter comes in flavours of black cherry, grapefruit and lime. Established vodka brands like Absolut are getting in on the trend as well. The company launched its 5% ABV Absolut Vodka Sprite, indicating that RTDs are moving away from the sugar-filled alcopop explosions of the early days.

Premiumisation continues to be the driving force behind vodka, as it does with many other spirits. But few perhaps have the chameleon-like ability that vodka does in its ability to work across cocktails, mixers, RTDs and beyond.

The once-upstart spirit that came down from the frozen climbs and rustic settings of Eastern Europe has found itself a place in the Western imagination, as told by many celebrities, artists, leaders, movers and shakers.

Here are some of my favourite lines:

> 'I no longer know if I wish to drown myself in love, vodka or the sea.' – Franz Kafka
>
> 'There are no absolutes in life – only vodka.' – Mick Jagger
>
> 'I have a punishing workout regimen. Every day I do 3 minutes on a treadmill, then I lie down, drink a glass of vodka and smoke a cigarette.' – Anthony Hopkins
>
> 'Money, like vodka, turns a person into an eccentric.' – Anton Chekhov
>
> 'I began to think vodka was my drink at last. It didn't taste like anything, but it went straight down into my stomach like a sword swallower's sword and made me feel powerful and godlike.' – Sylvia Plath

Chapter 6

Mezcal and Tequila

Once upon a time, an enchanting young Aztec goddess named Mayahuel brought light and warmth to the world. She was the goddess of fertility, who danced in the darkness of the sky until she was kidnapped by her wicked grandmother Tzitzimitl.

A monstrous conqueror, Tzitzimitl was on a mission to slay all the lightness of the universe and bring eternal darkness. Like others of her kind, she feasted upon human flesh and hearts and demanded sacrifices in her name. She guarded her granddaughter savagely and jealously.

Meanwhile, Mayahuel longed for love and companionship. She longed to dance and feel the same joys she once did when she was free. Every night, the goddess sat on the edge of a cloud and sang, until one day she was heard by the honourable feathered serpent god Ehecatl. He rose into the sky, searching for the owner of the voice that bewitched him and as soon as he laid eyes on Mayahuel he fell deeply and madly in love.

The lovers caressed and frolicked with each other every night, though it wasn't long before Tzitzimitl found out. Enraged, she plotted to kill them. Aware of the demonic crone's plan, Ehecatl swept Mayahuel out of the heavens and down to Earth where they could hide. Wrapping themselves around each other, the serpent god and the fertility goddess turned into a massive, majestic plant called a Maguey with many spikes to keep the wrath of Tzitzimitl away.

Yet Tzitzimitl was as crafty as she was vindictive. She found and recognised the plant, and in her rage she split the plant in half with her machete, butchering and quartering her granddaughter. These dismembered pieces of flesh were thrown into a broth that the demon cooked and fed to her legion of hungry servants.

But there was one piece of the Maguey that had been missed, a glittering green spire that had been left to wither in the desert. Ehecatl, overcome by grief, swept the single piece of his lover into rich volcanic soil, his tears watering the ground as he rose back into the heavens to battle and kill Tzitzimitl.

While this battle raged across the sky, the tears that had been shed brought life back to Mayahuel and she was reborn in Maguey form.

Another legend tells of how Mayahuel was married to and impregnated by the god of healing, Patecatl. He provided relief to his followers through magic mushrooms, peyote and other hallucinogens. From their union came the 400 rabbits, known as the gods of drunkenness. This legion of merry deities was known for drinking the nectar of the maguey/agave plant and representing the characteristics of an intoxicated person.

In both stories, the agave plant is the root that connects everything else together, reflecting its importance within Mexican culture.

A plant with near-limitless symbology and properties in the wider history of Mexico, the agave is the source of mezcal and tequila. It's also where pulque comes from, a beverage sacred to the ancient Aztecs that still has a vital role in the modern day. Indeed, the entire journey of mezcal is a fascinating one, through the mythology that connects people to the land and sky.

Mezcal Making

Before diving into the history of mezcal, it's worth finding out how it's produced to appreciate its beauty and complexity. And it starts with this simple understanding – all tequila is mezcal, but not all mezcal is tequila. Mezcal is a spirit made from the agave plant, while tequila is a specific kind of mezcal made from an agave varietal called blue Weber and produced in five Mexican states: Jalisco, Michoacan, Nayarit, Guanajuato and Tamaulipas.

As there are over 300 different species of agave, each with its own unique qualities, you can imagine the level of complexity that comes with different mezcals depending on where they are produced in Mexico, the choices made by the mezcaleros who make them, and the conditions of the palenques where the spirit is made.

The following is a general overview of mezcal production:

Growing: Every agave plant has its own growth cycle, so it's best to think in terms of terroir, i.e. the conditions in which the plant grows. This involves the soil, weather patterns and maturation rate, which can be anywhere between seven and thirty-five years.

Harvesting: Once an agave is matured, the leaves are chopped away to reveal the piña (heart) of the plant. It can weigh up to 80 kilos and is extracted using an agricultural tool called a coa, an instrument that looks like a mix between a hoe and a shovel.

Cooking: The piñas are chopped and placed inside an earthen pit at a palenque. The pit contains volcanic stones that have been set on fire and retain heat. The fire usually starts early in the morning and will burn for hours, after which the agaves are arranged in layers and covered with earth. The cooking time ranges between two to five days and the natural sugars in the piñas are caramelised to create a smoky flavour.

Milling: After the piñas have been roasted, they're crushed and milled to extract juice for fermentation. This is a laborious process but it's done to preserve the quality of the sugar and stop fibres from breaking.

Fermentation: In this stage, the wort is fermented with naturally occurring yeasts in a container that can be made from various materials like stone, wood or clay. Fermentation time is between ten and twelve days.

Distillation: Once the fermentation is done, the mezcal is distilled in either copper stills or in a more traditional fire-heated clay or wooden still. Both mezcal and tequila are double distilled and the final product comes in at 40–50% ABV.

Resting: Sometimes, mezcal is left to rest for several months to a year in oak barrels so the flavour can develop. Other times, mezcal is bottled without ageing.

This process can create several types of mezcal:

Espadin	The most common agave type which creates a mezcal with an earthy, smoky flavour.
Tobala	Agave that produces a floral tasting mezcal.
Madrecuixe	This type of agave creates mezcal with herbal, medicinal flavours.
Arroqueno	An agave varietal that produces spicy mezcal.
Tepeztate	This agave produces a powerful smoky kind of mezcal.
Pechuga	A special kind of mezcal mixed with fruits, nuts and spices during distillation. The flavours are complex.
Raicilla	Technically, this a different category to mezcal but is sometimes grouped with it as a fellow agave spirit. Raicilla is made from agave in Jalisco and has a signature bouquet of herbal, floral and earthy notes.

Mesoamerican Origins

All mezcal cultures of Mexico can trace their origins back to the ancient past of the first inhabitants of the country migrating across the Bering Straits between Russia and Alaska, through mainland North America and into what is now Mexico, thousands of years ago. They inherited agave from the land they cultivated, using it as a source of food, drink, augury and communication with their gods, as far back as ad 200.[1]

In the great city of Teotihuacan, the Birthplace of the Gods, found in the Valley of Mexico, northeast of Mexico City, pulque (fermented raw agave sap), powered the city and the rituals of its people communicating with Mayahuel and the rest of their gods.

When the Spanish Conquistadors swept through the Americas conquering Mexico and subjugating the indigenous communities in the 1500s, they brought distillation techniques with them that some people believe led to the development of mezcal as we know it today. Others believe the indigenous people were already fermenting and distilling spirit before the Spanish showed up. But a third origin has been given – Filipino sailors who brought distillation technology with them in the 1570s.

As mezcal expert Tom Bullock writes:

> upon arrival in Mexico, Filipinos established coconut plantations along the west coast. Here, using techniques mastered back home, they made a spirit called lambanog by distilling fermented coconut mash. Studies point to the origins of mezcal production taking firm hold along the coast beneath the Colima volcanos, right where the coconut palms grew.[2]

It's possible that the rise of modern mezcal was a combination of all three factors and the Spanish may have destroyed earlier records of mezcal because they had reason to want it outlawed. Depending on sources, the first written record of mezcal is dated either in 1608, 1609 or 1619, as a prohibition against the spirit from the Castellan crown. There was fear of mezcal outcompeting Spanish wines and brandies, so restrictions were introduced to try and stop its production. As has always been the case when the government suppressed alcohol production and consumption, the mezcal industry was driven underground.

Into the seventeenth century, mezcal remained popular among Mexican communities all over the country and a cat-and-mouse game between rebellious mezcaleros and Spanish authorities sprang up for the next hundred years. An enterprising mezcal bootlegger of the seventeenth century had several advantages on their side. The first was that mezcal was mobile, as the only kit needed to transport the spirit was copper pans. All the other utensils – a trunk for the stills, wood for the fire, the water needed to cool the alcohol, were readily available in the wild. Plus, any pits and ovens could be hidden if a constable came riding by on horseback to scan the landscape, checking for smoke. The nimble mezcalero could pack up shop, disappear into the next valley and set up anew. In fact, this constant bait and switching is responsible for mezcal distilleries being called palenques, meaning 'clearing', as in clearings in the wild, where mezcal could be produced as nature intended.[3]

By the end of the seventeenth century, the Spanish government relaxed mezcal restrictions, recognising the futility and wasted effort of trying to repress a spirit as old as the land they'd conquered. This provided new opportunities for mezcal distillers to come back into the light and push the industry forward in ways that had never been seen before.

The Great Break-Up

The 1600s were a turning point in the history of mezcal. A Spanish aristocrat, Don Pedro Sanchez de Tagle, had seen a business opportunity that very few others had. In 1595, King Philip II of Spain banned the planting of new vineyards in Mexico to maintain the market for Spanish products. Sanchez realised the potential of making mezcal from blue agaves, building the world's first tequila factory around 1600.

This is how the popular legend goes anyway. In truth, Sanchez didn't come to Mexico until 1695, so he couldn't have cottoned onto tequila being a genuine commodity because it was still in its infancy as another variety of mezcal.

The myth was likely started in the 1800s at a time when tequila was truly on the rise by wealthy land owners and distillers, who wanted to reinforce their own social status as successors of a manufactured narrative that positioned tequila as a premium spirit and mezcal as a poor man's libation.

Due to its popularity, a local tequila industry boomed in the state of Jalisco and was taxed by its governor, and the town of Tequila became the most advanced region of mezcal production. For example, the Cuervo family were given the first official licence to commercially produce tequila by King Carlos IV of Spain in the mid-eighteenth century, protecting their interests in times of further mezcal prohibition.[4] Meanwhile, other tequileros separated themselves from the archaic landlord hacienda systems that had sanctioned mezcal production, turning into private enterprises.

The cracks between mezcal and tequila became even bigger in the War of Independence, which kicked off in 1810 and eventually brought an end to Spain's 300-year rule of Mexico. Soldiers on all sides of the conflict were drinking a lot of tequila and after the new nation of Mexico was established, its new leaders were quickly enamoured by European engineering, especially the Industrial Revolution going on in Britain, and the surge in distillation technology.

Within a couple of decades, the town of Tequila was thrumming with continuous copper stills, while agaves cooked and simmered in big stone masonry ovens that had replaced the ancient earth pits. Tequila the drink was being made on a mass scale and by the time of the Mexican Revolution in 1910 it had been kicked up another notch.

For soldiers amid battle, tequila became alcoholic morphine, a shot of courage to be taken from a bamboo shoot called a canute, worn around the neck. According to Bullock:

> the lines of tequila production needed to be increased, essentially industrialised. Tequila took to the task, set their new innovations to maximum and jumped production to unprecedented levels. This is the fork in the road … Mezcal, as we still know it, and tequila, as it was fast becoming, in the midst of the chaos and confusion of war, part ways. It would be another hundred years until they'd begin to see eye-to-eye again.[5]

After the Mexican Revolution, mezcal was left to flounder, while tequila carried a sexy, rebellious image to it. Inside Mexico, it was the drink of the badass renegades who'd fought to create a constitutional republic. Outside of the country, tequila flooded into America on an alcohol tide that wouldn't be pushed out by Prohibition.

Mexico became a getaway for Americans looking to escape from the stuffiness of the Volstead Act, giving rise to the original Sin City: Tijuana. For many Californians, Tijuana was practically a stone's throw away from San Diego and they hopped over the border into a sleepy town of about 1,000 people that ballooned into a mecca of excess, gambling, prostitution and crime.

A lavish casino called the Agua Caliente attracted high rollers and big-name celebrities like Clark Gable, Bing Crosby and Charlie Chaplin. Even Al Capone paid a visit when he wasn't ruling the roost in Chicago.[6] Bars prospered in every corner of the city and there wasn't a speakeasy in sight. Here tequila flowed in abundance, even becoming a catalyst for one of the most iconic cocktails in history – the margarita.

The origin of a cocktail is always a murky affair. Most sources agree the margarita was invented after Prohibition ended, with a faithful encounter happening in 1936.

In the summer of that year James Graham, owner and editor of *The Moville Mail* newspaper in Moville, Iowa, took his wife to California for a holiday. Like many tourists, the Grahams got sidetracked on a visit to Tijuana and found the debauched jewel to be a shadow of its former self. Of the 150 bars that had once shone brightly, garishly and proudly in the Mexican evening only four years ago, there were now only ten left standing.

The Grahams wouldn't be deterred.

On the recommendation of a taxi driver, they stopped at a bar owned by an Irishman called Madden. He was known for his incredible drink-making skills and an alluring concoction called the Tequila Daisy.

As Graham would later write:

> As a newspaperman seeking information, I entered the joint and told Mr Madden my curiosity was aroused regarding The Daisy. Mr Madden was not the most talkative of men, but eventually, he was persuaded to admit that the drink's creation was a mistake. 'In mixing a drink, I grabbed the wrong bottle and the customer was so delighted that he called for another and spread the good news far and wide.'[7]

Graham never said what was in the Daisy or hinted if he'd even tried it, but we do get a hint of how the cocktail got its name. (Daisy in Spanish is Margarita).

Other stories claim the margarita was invented just south of Tijuana in Ensenada at Bar Andaluz in 1948. Or maybe it was invented in 1941 by Don Carlos Orozco up the street at Hussong's. Whatever the case, the margarita has been adopted as the Mexican cocktail celebrated all over the world.

Throughout the 1930s and '40s, tequila continued to grow in popularity. For example, during the Second World War, production increased because European spirits dropped in inventory, as white and brown spirit makers were tasked with making industrial alcohol for the war effort. Between 1940 and 1950, agave fields in Mexico grew by 110 per cent, bolstered by agricultural reforms introduced by President Lopez Mateos granting 30 million acres of land to farmers, many of which ran agave farms.[8] It was in this decade the Mexican government also started campaigning to officially label tequila as a Mexican product by stating it could only be produced by distilling agave in Jalisco. These standards, made between 1944 and 1947, were constantly updated.

The 1960s were another successful decade for tequila, especially when the Olympic Games were hosted by Mexico City in 1968. This truly brought tequila onto the world stage and set the wheels in motion for it to be gradually associated as a 'party' drink, a label that has persisted into the modern era.

But even that paled in comparison to 9 December 1974, when tequila officially received a Denomination of Origin (DOC) protection, classifying it as a product that could only be made in Mexico. But this wasn't without controversy. Borders between Mexican states expanded to accommodate political ambitions, damaging tequila's reputation and shifting it into a soulless corporate product in the eyes of some. This is ironic, considering DOCs are put into place to protect the craftsmanship and originality of spirits.

According to Bullock, 'in the decades to come, blights from over-farming and further industrial/political manoeuvring – coupled with the introduction of mechanical equipment that could dramatically further the kind of productivity needed to meet market demand – powerfully drained tequila of its original character.'[9]

Don't get me wrong. There are plenty of interesting tequila brands out there today that are focused on championing the craft nature of tequila makers in their local communities.

For example, El Rayo Tequila, founded by UK-born Jack Vereker and Tom Bishop in 2019, is a modern take on tequila, celebrating Mexican culture. They spent a long time working with tequila maestros like Oscar Garcia to get the recipe right.

This is what Vereker had to tell me about this journey of El Rayo:

> One of the fundamental reasons for launching the brand was that we wanted to push the idea of tequila and tonic as the next gin and tonic. We wanted our tequila to be delicious on its own and stand out when paired with a mixer.
>
> Oscar was instrumental in helping us find the right partner in creating this unique mix. Without him, we wouldn't have had meetings with distilleries. The tequila industry is close-knit in Mexico and essentially we were two gringos from London knocking on their doors.
>
> We wouldn't have got much out of the distilleries and Oscar helped to navigate those conversations. He was also involved with our production team at every step of the process. It was a nine-month process and we went through over fifty samples until we got to the spirit we wanted. It was a labour of love.
>
> The name was probably one of the hardest things to come up with. We knew we wanted it to be in Spanish and

> we came across the story of the origins of tequila and agave spirits.
>
> What people tell their children in Mexico is that an agave farmer saw a lightning bolt strike his agave plant. He went out to the plant, saw it was cooked and charred and there was nectar coming out of it. So, cooking agave meant you could get tequila and that was an awesome story for us.
>
> We thought it was perfect because it's a historical story and ultimately tequila is a heritage-based product. We didn't want to get rid of the tradition. We wanted to link to the heritage but display it in a modern way. The label of our bottle is telling the lightning story and it means we're trying to add electricity and vibrancy to the category.
>
> We want to be the brand that showcases all this creativity to the world and so every year we partner with new artists who create custom art for El Rayo. We are a tequila brand but we're also a lifestyle brand. We want people wearing our clothes, buying our artwork and steeping themselves in the modern Mexican culture.

It's also become fashionable for celebrities to cash in on the popularity of tequila and while there are some who may launch brands as a money-making exercise, others have done it for a genuine passion for the spirit and culture.

Dwayne 'The Rock' Johnson is an example of this with his Teremana tequila. As he revealed in an interview with *The Spirits Business*, agave spirits have been an enjoyable part of his journey. He's enjoyed it 'in the good times, the not so-good times and everything in between'. He's been with the production of the liquid 'since day one. I insisted on such participation because it's the only way to truly learn the process from beginning to end. I needed to educate myself.'[10]

Founded in 2020, the brand is inspired by the Polynesian word 'mana' for spirit, which is a celebration of The Rock's Samoan heritage. There is also a reference to his three daughters Tiana, Jasmine and Simone on the bottle's packaging, embossed in the word 'Tijasi'. To create the three varietals, The Rock and his team went through 113 distilleries to find the right recipe and worked with the Lopez family, who've been making tequila in Jalisco for decades.

Production involves 'only one process' on the purpose-built Teremana distillery on the grounds of the Lopezes larger facility:

> Everything involved in the production process is made there, including brick ovens, copper pot stills, open fermentation tanks … we harvest only fully mature agave, slow roast in old brick ovens, and distil in small [3,800-litre] handmade copper stills to bring out rich, flavourful tequila that reflects the earth it comes from.[11]

Arguably, this shift towards artisanal, hand-crafted tequila wouldn't have been possible without the modern mezcal revival.

The Mezcal Revival

While tequila had been building a reputation as Mexico's premier spirit, the rest of the mezcal category had been kept well away from the spotlight. Outside the big urban areas, in the rural and mountain communities of the country, mezcal was being made and drank as it had been for centuries. Organically grown, crushed by hand, fermented with local and airborne yeasts, heated over an open fire, every measurement and decision made by master mezcaleros relying on touch, taste and smell, passing knowledge down through generations.

But given the runaway success of tequila, it was inevitable that there would be an attempt to commercialise mezcal. This came with mixed results, depending on who you speak to. In the rush to capitalise on the tequila boom, industrial-grade mezcal had a rushed process and created some potentially damaging associations.

For example, a common phrase to hear about people who've never drank mezcal is 'you mean that drink with the worm?' The worm being referred to is the gusano, the mezcal worm larvae that live and feed off agave.

Gusano worms can be dropped into mezcal bottles to mask the flavour of bad products or provide some additional complexity with a fungal taste. Or they can be eaten whole and are known to be a delicacy. Depending on how you look at it, the gusano's association with mezcal can be either good or bad, but either way, a myth has been created that all mezcals must come with bizarre-looking worms that have to be consumed.

The reason this myth has got out of control is through two mezcal brands called Gusano Rojo and Monte Alban. The first was started in the mid-twentieth century with a different name and became what it is today through the experimentation of a former art student and employee called Jacobo Lozano Paez.

It's said that Paez was experimenting with different mezcals and noticed that each tasted the same because of the gusanos that infested the agave leaves. This gave him the idea to drop the worms into mezcal and sell the bottles as a marketing stunt that caught on so well that the brand changed its name to Gusano Rojo.[12]

However, this story has been disputed in other corners of the internet, as the trademark for Gusano Rojo was filed in 1948. This was two years before Paez supposedly had his flash of larval inspiration. It was a false narrative invented by 'The Straight Dope' drinks columnist Cecil Adams in 1999.[13]

Due to the popularity of Gusano Rojo, Monte Alban followed in their footsteps and launched influential marketing campaigns throughout the 1970s and '80s to implant the idea in the mind of a male Western audience that mezcal and gusanos go hand in hand.

An ad from 1985 entitled 'The Monte Alban Never-A-Dull-Moment Party' features a festive-looking worm wearing a sombrero chilling beside a bottle of Monte Alban.

The introductory copy reads:

> Next party invite the Worm. The authentic agave worm in every bottle of Monte Alban Mezcal. By tradition, the person who gets the last drink in the bottle gets to eat the Worm. Which means your next party will be anything but dull. And you'll be looking for an excuse – any excuse – to have another party.

Further down the ad, there's a 'worm party guide' that lists everything that should be done to have a proper Monte Alban party, while a paragraph by the bottle features copy such as: 'The worm. The proof of our mezcal. The life of your party. There really is a real agave worm in every bottle.'[14]

In the 1990s, everything began to change, with a push towards artisanal mezcals that arguably kicked off when mezcal received a Denomination of Origin (DO) in 1994 and a governing body called Consejo Regulador de Mezcal (CRM) was set up in 1997 to oversee it. This was an interesting move when you consider a DO is assigned to a region in the making of a specific product e.g. champagne in the Champagne region of France. Mezcal is a category, not a specific place like Tequila. It covers the entirety of Mexico, making the CRM's job to protect mezcal and enforce regulations a difficult task.

Again, there have been mixed reactions to this labelling of mezcal. Some producers have found it difficult to register their products, simply because their palenque was built in the wrong municipality. Other distillers have seen the regulations as a step in the right direction for showcasing the authenticity of craft agave spirits.

Any revolution or revival needs an opening salvo, some daring shot across the bow that announces to the world that a flag is being planted in the ground. This shot was fired by a Los Angeles artist who decided to cruise on down to Ensenada, a tiny surf town south of the border with his arty crew one day in the 1960s. His name was Ron Cooper and he and his buddies rocked up to Hussong's one night, one of the fabled bars in which the margarita is meant to have been invented.

Cooper sidled up to the bar and tried mezcal for the first time. It blew his head off and gave him a crippling hangover the next morning – and he immediately got a taste for it. He recalled:

> this was my first experience with an agave spirit, a bottle of mezcal that tasted like diesel fuel. I hadn't even tried tequila. The next night I crawled back to Hussong's for a cerveza to recuperate. As I sat there sipping my beer, I thought, 'Man, I am going to try that mezcal again.'[15]

After the trip to Ensenada, Cooper returned to LA and eight years would go by before he tried mezcal again. Into the '70s, Cooper had become known for his paintings and acquired a fortune that allowed him to idle some of his time away on more road trips. He jumped into a VW bus with two friends and on a trip to Panama, they stopped off in Oaxaca.

The Oaxaca of the 1970s was filled with traditional Mexican weavers and artists that caught Cooper's attention and it was through them he learned the ritual of mezcal, how it was venerated at weddings and sipped at funerals in remembrance. Cooper steeped himself in these rituals, staying in Oaxaca for much longer than he had expected. He arrived in Panama four months later.

Twenty years later, Cooper returned to Oaxaca to celebrate the creation of two bronze statues that would take pride of place in LA and Santa Monica. On this second visit, he was truly on a mission to make the most of mezcal. Cooper scoured the landscape, searching for stone grinding wheels that marked farms that had mezcal stills. When he found these hallowed places, Cooper bought directly from the founder, gathering twenty-eight distillates by the time he returned to the US.

Getting this elixir back into the States wasn't easy. At one point, Cooper brought a five-gallon jug of wedding mezcal over the border in a big wooden basket strapped to an already cluttered truck that raised the eyebrows of border patrol. They told Cooper in no uncertain terms to get rid of it, forcing Cooper to pour away his finest mezcal at the time.

> I couldn't believe it. I slowly lifted the jug, and there were about two gallons left. I was half expecting to be shot in the back as I walked to my truck, put the bottle back in the basket, and opened the squeaky door. I hit the ignition and split. The three gallons I drained was a sacrifice. They didn't tear my truck apart and find those other twenty-eight mezcals. That's how Del Maguey began.[16]

Del Maguey became the mezcal that kicked off the revolution. With its bright green bottles and labels inspired by the traditional Mexican art that Cooper fell in love with so many years ago, it proliferated on back bars across the US and beyond. The three products Vida, Chichicapa and Iberico all celebrate the artisanal values of what makes mezcal mezcal.

By 2010, Cooper had ignited a new mezcal boom in the US, fuelling competition and driving him to scale up. He'd spent seventeen years as his own importer and worked with Sazerac, fending off offers from several big companies. In 2016, Cooper finally met his business partner in Paris, Alexandre Ricard, CEO of Pernod Ricard.

Over a private dinner at the Peninsula Hotel, Ricard told Cooper how his grandfather, an artist, started the company – the same way that Cooper had used his artistic creativity to will Del Maguey into existence. This struck a chord with Cooper and he knew he'd found a home for Del Maguey. The rest is history.

The spark Ron Cooper lit has become a torch carried by many passionate mezcal advocates, all eager to leave their own mark on an industry that is becoming more and more popular every year.

In 2004 John Rexer, owner of bar Café No Se in Antigua, Guatemala, started bringing mezcal back from Oaxaca to Antigua to supply the bar. Rexer has described his 'candlelit dive bar on a cobblestone street … the walls with faded photos, smoke-stained artwork and dents from thrown bottles – carry the memories of the many deliriously beautiful nights of music and mezcal.'[17]

A New Yorker who'd moved to Guatemala, Rexer had developed a taste for mezcal and smuggling cases across the border, including hooch made from the now-legendary fourth-generation mezcaleros Armando and Alvaro Hernandez, who'd illegally crossed the border into the States when they were young. Rexer's own cross-border shenanigans are the stuff of noir and crime thrillers. One story involved him having to dress up as a priest to get his bootleg mezcal past the checkpoint.

Everything converged into Rexer setting up his mezcal brand, Illegal, in 2006 and at the time of writing this book in the 2020s, Rexer sees plenty of potential ahead for Illegal and mezcal as a whole:

> The biggest opportunity, but also biggest challenge, is to apply as many best practices as possible and to learn from the mistakes of others. Tequila has had boom/bust cycles which over time has created economic instability and has led to hyper industrialisation of many brands. Mezcal, as an international business, is still young enough to build a more sustainable model that benefits everyone throughout the chain, one that evens out the highs and lows, and protects environmental diversity.[18]

Foreigners aren't the only people who've built successful mezcal brands. Brothers Julio and Eduardo Mestre set up Los Siete Misterios in 2010, after visiting the municipality of Sola de Vega in the Sierra Sur region of Mexico, known for being the home of tobala agave and clay-pot distilled mezcal. The brothers wanted to bring this traditional mezcal production method into the mainstream and so worked on building trust among the local growers.

Los Siete Misterios translates as The Seven Mysteries, named after the seven plants chosen from the Sola de Vega hills for the production of their products. The brothers have an ethos of working with the Sola de Vega mezcaleros in a collective effort:

> It's an alliance between the mezcaleros and us, in which we pursue to learn the best practices from each mezcalero invited, and then share it with all the other mezcaleros we work with, not only the ones that produce in Rancho Concordia, but all we work with in five villages, seeking to elevate the production process through community sharing and learning.[19]

It would also be a mistake to assume that men are the only ones doing amazing things with mezcal. Women have long been flying the flag, breaking boundaries and pushing the category forward. Yola Jimenez is one of many examples.

As a child, Jimenez spent summers at her grandfather's mezcal farm in Oaxaca, breaking into his office along with her cousins to steal sips from the bottle. When she grew older, she moved to London and New York to pursue her studies. But when her grandfather died, Jimenez felt the pull of home and returned to Mexico to carry on his dream.

Taking over the family business, Jimenez opened a mezcal bar in Mexico City and eventually the mezcal she made from her grandfather's secret recipe caught the attention of singer Lykke Li and stylist Gina Correlli Aglietti. The three women went into business together and founded Yola Mezcal, dedicating their time to supporting the economic freedom of women by employing them and providing growth opportunities.

According to Jimenez:

> I studied in university economic proposals that said that when women get a paycheck, 80 per cent of that goes back to the family – clothes, food, and education – especially in third world countries. When men do, it's only 50 to 60 per cent. You can really see that clearly in the towns in Oaxaca. I wanted to have a way to do things differently. I think one of the things that is problematic with Mexico too is that people treat poor people, or indigenous people, like they deserve charity … I think that the more you provide payment for work, real payment for work, that's what gives people dignity.[20]

Dona Vega Mezcal is another women-owned brand that's worth looking at. Founder Sonya Vega grew up sipping mezcal with her family and had a knack for identifying trends through her PR agency The Wetherly Group. This intuition led her back to rediscovering the wonder of mezcal and inspired her to create a modern mezcal that's not as smoky as other varieties.

> I found that many versions are a little too rugged … too smoky. I wanted to create a modern take on mezcal, with a flavour that is complex and playful, while honouring the authentic core and tradition. Travelling through the mountains of Oaxaca, I visited countless farms, agave fields and distilleries … After years of research, I teamed up with an amazing female-led production team.[21]

It's also refreshing to see an increase in the number of women mezcal and tequila educators. In the UK, Jenn Aspell and her husband run a bar called 400 Rabbits in Nottingham, and an online shop called Casa Agave, that specialise in agave spirits. Aspell's journey into the category has been a long and infinitely fascinating one:

> When I first moved to the UK in my early twenties my experience of tequila was very much the same as most people at the time and in the shape of late-night cheap shots.
>
> After trying some sipping tequila that was recommended to me, I immediately fell in love with the incredible diversity of agave spirits and started a journey of discovery, opening up a whole world of history and traditions and began working at 400 Rabbits in Nottingham.
>
> My passion for the spirit allowed me to progress in the business to the extent that running the bar was not enough anymore. I needed to show everyone why agave spirits are so amazing and why we should all be enjoying them and so I launched Casa Agave.
>
> Another hugely important thing for me is the fact that it is such an honest and humble spirit. There is nothing quite like tasting something which was created through generations of ancestral knowledge. The humble background of the families and their distilleries is admirable and I want to do whatever I can to support them.

> Agave spirits are much like wine as the terroir has such an impact on flavour, this to me is a huge reason it stands out so much in comparison to other spirits. Each expression can be different, even if it is produced by the same master distiller, using the same techniques and the same agave species. With each passing year, even slight changes to the environment will have an impact on the complexity of the spirit to a far greater extent than with other spirits.
>
> However, it goes so much further than just the remarkable flavours. There are so many aspects to mezcal which are sometimes forgotten about, starting with how the spirit is produced.
>
> The back-breaking work that goes into producing an artisan or ancestral agave spirit is unlike that of others around the world. Not only does the physical work stand out to me in how this spirit is different but also the care that goes into producing each bottle.
>
> To me one of the most fascinating comments made by a mezcalero we work with about the care he gives his wild agaves, was how he would regularly use a damp cloth to clean each one by hand.
>
> Plants taking a minimum of eight years to reach maturity, with wild agaves from other sub-species taking more than twenty years. It's mind-boggling that a mezcalero has so much dedication to looking after these agaves. When you start to look at the time it takes and the amount of work that goes into producing a single bottle then you begin to appreciate the value in a new way.

In terms of recommendations, Aspell has lots of great bottles for first time tequila and mezcal drinkers to try:

> Most of the time people already know tequila (or think they do) and have not had the best experience if it has always come in the form of shots. What I like to do is start someone off with an aged tequila (Anejos for whisky drinkers and reposados for rum drinkers) as these categories of tequila

> share those familiar flavours that people enjoy, such as dry fruit, raisins, oak, char, vanilla, butterscotch, caramel etc.
>
> When they have enjoyed sipping on a glass of aged tequila I'll introduce a blanco to the mix. Usually in tasting the order is the opposite way around Blanco-Anejo. For this, I highly recommend Mexican-owned 30-30 tequila. The distillery itself is very eco-conscious and runs off the waste material produced by making their tequila, which is entirely without additives and 100 per cent agave. There are loads of other great tequilas available in the UK ranging from entry level to top shelf. Some of my current favourites are Don Fulano, ArteNOM, Tapatio and Cascahuin.
>
> To get into mezcal I highly recommend starting with an espadin, as this is the most commonly used agave species and will ease you into tasting more variety. The flavours can still be exciting and different from one expression to the next but probably won't throw you in the deep end of funky flavours as much as other varietals.
>
> My favourite to introduce to people is La Medida Espadin, as their single variety range offers the best stepping stones into exploring the different flavours each agave varietal has to give. They are also great value and can lead you on to trying some spectacular ancestral Mezcal Real Minero or other top mezcal such as Derrumbes and Neta. Dangerous Don is also great because they triple distil with some lush flavours, so fabulous for getting into mezcal.

And it's not just consumers Aspell has recommendations for. She also shared her recommendations on how bartenders can promote agave spirits:

> The best way in my opinion is through cocktails and talking to people. What I've seen over the years is that customers immediately skip a cocktail that lists tequila on the ingredients of a drink if they haven't been converted yet. The trick is to find out their preferred flavours/classic cocktails and suggest one that uses tequila as a base. Tequila is perhaps the most versatile spirit out there, other than

> vodka, as its flavours are very delicate and so it lends itself perfectly to cocktail experimentation.
>
> I would even go so far as saying you could switch out any base spirit in a classic cocktail and play around with agave spirits as a replacement. May that be an Old Fashioned using an aged tequila, a Martini, Mai Tai, Mojito or a Negroni using a blanco or even a mezcal.

As great as the industry is, Aspell also acknowledges that there's a lot that needs to change:

> The rise of celebrity owned brands and those who are looking to hop on the tequila/mezcal bandwagon to make a quick buck, fuels the drive for a cheaper, more accessible product for the consumer. This, in turn, takes its toll on those who produce the spirits, the agaves themselves and the land where they grow, their wildlife and pollinators. Overharvesting of espadin agaves has actually meant that the species is producing less and less healthy seeds naturally.
>
> It's so important that we as consumers can respect the work gone into the spirits, or anything which we purchase and try to focus on the brands that are more sustainable, eco-conscious, or owned by Mexican families to directly support them. It's a fine balancing act to both be a promoter of these wonderful spirits and do it in a way that is sustainable.
>
> The growth of the agave spirits category is not a trend and it is here to stay and will keep growing. I hope that as it grows more people will become more passionate about supporting brands and producers who are sustainable in growing their agaves and in their production methods. With each passing year I notice more people asking about where something is from or how it's made, and with that they will pass on that knowledge and continue a steady, natural and healthy growth of great products.

With the cornucopia of new mezcal brands appearing in Mexico and beyond, the future of the category looks like it's going to keep going from strength to strength. These stats offer a window into just how much growth potential is on the horizon:

- The global mezcal industry is expected to reach $1,536 million by 2034.[22]
- Between 2024 and 2034, the value-based compound annual growth rate of mezcal is predicted to increase by 14.2 per cent.[23]
- The rising interest in Mexican culture and cuisine is a main driver in the surge of mezcal interest.[24]
- Artisanal and premium sipping mezcals that can also be mixed with cocktails are going to appeal to an increasing number of young consumers who are open to trying novel products and new experiences.[25]

There's a big, bold and bright mezcal universe for you to discover at your own pace. Try the introductory tequila as a shot. Then look past the party image. Dig deeper by trying an interesting-sounding mezcal brand. Take a sip, then another sip. Move onto the next bottle, improve your education, hang out in a mezcal bar. Start small, go big, do whatever you want to do. So long as you try a glass of Mexico's beautiful agave spirits and make your own decision about what you like and don't like.

Chapter 7
Baijiu

A cup of wine, under the flowering trees;
I drink alone, for no friend is near.
Raising my cup I beckon the bright moon,
For he, with my shadow, will make three men.
The moon, alas, is no drinker of wine;
Listless, my shadow creeps about at my side.
Yet with the moon as friend and the shadow as slave
I must make merry before the Spring is spent.
To the songs I sing the moon flickers her beams;
In the dance I weave my shadow tangles and breaks.
While we were sober, three shared the fun;
Now we are drunk, each goes his way.
May we long share our odd, inanimate feast,
And meet at last on the Cloudy River of the sky.[1]

This poem, *Drinking Alone Beneath The Moon*, is written by the legendary Chinese poet Li Dan and is an exceptional window into the drinking culture of China that has been the same for thousands of years. Li Dan's poem is a celebration of alcohol being a source of creative inspiration for the poet himself and for how all great art is made.

He compares wine to a divine elixir poured from heaven down to earth, an elixir that binds people together in bonds of friendship. This wine, huangjiu, would be toasted in the cups of Chinese royalty and lead to the development of China's premier spirit, baijiu (pronounced bai-joe) in the years to come.

Like huangjiu, baijiu is at the heart of Chinese drinking customs and is felt across all aspects of society, from business meetings to family meals. Quite possibly the world's oldest spirit, baijiu is history, tradition and prestige in a bottle, a spirit consumed across the world, yet has very little recognition outside of China.

This is its story.

What is Baijiu?

Translating to 'white alcohol', baijiu is a collective name for Chinese spirits that can be as different from each other as different rum categories are. There are various types and production methods which baijiu expert Derek Sandhaus describes as going beyond the 'faintly industrial bouquet, phenolic sweetness and oesophageal afterburn' associated with how the spirit tastes to Westerners. Instead, there is,

> [a] combination of unique ingredients and techniques [that] creates the flavours and aromas instantly recognisable in Chinese spirits. Subtle distinctions in material and process can produce great variation under the baijiu banner, and a number of sub-categories emerge. So radical are the differences between baijiu and its Western counterparts, however, that Chinese spirits may rightly be said to represent an entirely distinct school of production.[2]

The main ingredients in baijiu are:

Water: Perhaps the most essential ingredient. It washes and steams the grains, triggers fermentation and dilutes the alcohol once it's been distilled.

Qu: Pronounced 'chew', this is a special kind of Chinese yeast block that is used in making Chinese wines and spirits. It's made from moistened grains that have been clumped together along with yeasts, bacteria and other microorganisms.

Grains: There are several types of grains used for baijiu to impart different flavours. This includes sorghum, rice, wheat, corn, millet etc.

Grain husks: The outer shells of the grains have a multi-purpose use. For example, they can act as a filler for the mash as an extra source of starch to stop clumping. Or they may be used to adjust the acid, moisture and starch levels in the mash during fermentation.

To produce baijiu, there are several steps involved:

Qu preparation

Either big qu or small qu is used at the beginning of baijiu making. Big qu is made primarily from wheat or wheat bran and ingredients are soaked together in warm water and then ground into a powder. From there, more water and ingredients are added to the grains and pressed into bricks.

The bricks are stacked in an incubation chamber on straw mats, and microorganisms flourish in the small gaps, while the straw helps to insulate the bricks to trap moisture. More water is added regularly and the bricks are flipped if the temperature becomes dry or warm. The big qu bricks sit in storage for several weeks, steadily gaining in flavour and in the final stage it's mashed into pulp so it's ready to be used.

Small qu is made from rice or glutinous rice flour, which is drenched in water for hours. It's then turned into a paste and shaped into balls, coated in old qu powder to encourage bacterial growth and put on a bamboo sieve. Then, it's moved to a controlled environment for five days, eventually being mashed into powder.

Grain preparation

Depending on the type of grain used, preparation methods differ. As a general overview, the kernels are ground into powder and added to warm water to jack up moisture levels. Positive signs include the grain being gelatinised, cooked through and soft.

Once steaming is completed, the grain is air dried at a temperature that promotes more bacterial growth, but not so high that it kills the yeast and bacteria that's already grown on the qu.

Fermentation and saccharification

Like other grain spirits, baijiu needs fermentation and saccharification. Bacteria break down yeast starch into sugar, while the yeast converts sugars into carbon dioxide and drinking alcohol in the mix of water and qu. What makes Chinese spirits stand out here is that the grain is always fermented in a solid or semi-solid quantity.

Distillation

Most varieties of baijiu are distilled using traditional Chinese pot stills. This contraption is built with two cylindrical barrels, a steamer and a condenser joined by a tube. The steamer has a sealable pot that holds the grains, attached to a container of boiling water separated by a grate so steam can rise into the grains.

Grain is put into the pot after the water has boiled and as the mash temperature rises, vapours rise into the tube and travel into the condenser filled with cold water. The alcohol vapours pass into the tube, are cooled by the water back into alcohol and carry on into a spigot at the base and into a receptacle.

The grain steaming done before fermentation is also done in the steamer. Sometimes, new grains are added to the mash and steamed in tandem with distillation before more qu is added in baijiu which needs multiple fermentation and distillation cycles.

Ageing

After distillation, the liquid that has been distilled is considered yuanjiu (original spirit). In other words, an incomplete spirit that has to be aged for it to be complete. The ageing process helps remove raw and rough flavours and most baijiu is aged for at least six months, while the premium stuff may be aged between three to five years.

The process of ageing Chinese spirits is unique because clay vessels are used. The vessels are stored in subterranean cellars and the properties of the clay interact with the liquid, further tamping down undesirable flavours.

Blending

As different baijiu types incorporate multiple fermentation and distillation cycles, the liquid produced at each step is often stored and aged separately. So, blending helps with creating a finished product of aged distillates that are balanced and put into the bottle.

Generally, a blend with be a combination of the lighter flavours of the heart distillate and the intense burn found at the end of the tail. This combination adds complexity that's topped off with water to bring down the alcohol level that most often sits at between 36% and 65% ABV.

Different Styles of Baijiu

There are several distinctive types of baijiu associated with different regions and production techniques, which I've categorised as 'main' and 'others'. This classification of baijiu is a modern invention and is intended as a general introduction:

Main Styles

Strong aroma: The most popular and widely produced style, strong aroma baijiu is associated with Sichuan in the south of China and the eastern provinces of Jiangsu, Shandong and Anhui. It has a fiery, fruity sweet taste and is distilled from one or more grains.

Light aroma: The second biggest category, light aroma is split into two subcategories called Erguotou which is associated with Beijing, and Fenjiu is associated with Fenyang in Shaanxi Province. Light aroma can be distilled from sorghum and rice husks and fermented with big qu made from barley or peas. It has a mild, floral taste.

Sauce aroma: This type has ties to Sichuan and northwestern Guizhou and involves repeated fermentation in subterranean pits set with stone bricks. As the name suggests, sauce aroma is so-called for its soy sauce-like fragrance and flavour that features notes of herbs and fermented beans.

Rice aroma: Rice baijiu is made across southern China and is mostly linked to Guangxi and Guangdong Provinces. It's made from long-grain or glutinous rice or can be a combination of the two and may have tastes that are similar to Japanese sake.

Other styles

Phoenix aroma: While not quite named after a bird that rises from its own ashes, Phoenix aroma baijiu does have something of a legendary reputation. It's named after Xifengjiu, 'West Phoenix Spirit' from Fengxiang County in Shaanxi.

It's a mixture of strong and light aroma baijiu, distilled from sorghum and fermented in earthen pits with a barley, wheat and pea-based qu.

After distillation, Phoenix is aged in the 'seas of alcohol' – big rattan baskets stuffed with cloth sacks and hardened with beeswax, vegetable oil and pig's blood.

Sesame aroma: A cousin of sauce aroma, this baijiu is fermented at a higher temperature for less time and comes with a nutty, burnt taste. It's produced mainly from sorghum with wheat qu.

Chi aroma: Not to be confused with the inner energy that is spoken of in Taoist philosophy, this baijiu gets its name from douchi, a salty Chinese condiment made from fermented beans. It was invented by the Shiwan Distillery from Guangdong Province in 1895 and is unique in the fact that it's aged with an infusion of pork fat, giving the spirit an oily, bacony flavour.

Mixed aroma: This is a combination of other categories. Mixed aroma baijiu is produced using different distillation, fermentation and blending techniques from two different categories.

Medicine aroma: This style was invented by the Dongjiu Distillery in Guizhou. Created using a sorghum base, the spirit is fermented in two pits, with the bigger one performing the fermentation with big qu, and the smaller pit using rice filled with Chinese herbs. The result is a spirit with sweet and savoury notes.

Extra-strong aroma: The name of this category was coined by master blender Madame Wu Xiaoping and is a combination of at least three different baijiu, making it different from mixed aroma, which mixes two baijiu. It's aged for at least three years and comes with an earthy, spicy and sweet taste.

While baijiu is prevalent today, it took hundreds of years for it to develop and be recognised by the Chinese people. And to understand how it came to be, we must now go back to the dawn of alcohol development to appreciate the rich traditions baijiu hails from.

The Cradle of Alcohol Invention and Consumption

Many sources across alcohol scholarship seem to agree that if China is not *the* cradle of alcohol invention and consumption, it is certainly one of the oldest regions of the world for both. First, alcohol development in China predates its recorded history, as archaeologists have unearthed pottery artefacts in China's Henan Province that date back to the Jiahu period (7000–5700 bc). Analysis of the pots confirmed traces of alcohol made from a mix of grapes, hawthorn fruit, honey and rice.[3]

Early on, alcohol had a revered place in the shaping of China's political and religious landscape. It was drunk as a gateway to spirits and gods, exchanged between warlords as gifts of tribute and became a symbol of wealth and power. Unlike in the West, where alcohol was viewed as medicine in places like Europe and the Mediterranean, China viewed it as a luxury to be enjoyed.

The first advancement in Chinese alcohol arrived during the Han Dynasty (206 bc – ad 220) with the invention of qu, which enabled the development of hangjiu. Thus, Chinese wine became a favourite drink of aristocrats, developing at the centres of civilisation across Shaanxi and Shandong down the Yellow River and out into the Yangtze River down south.

Distillation came to China centuries later, perhaps from trade in the Middle East through the Song Dynasty (960–1279) or the Mongolian Yuan Dynasty (1271–1368). From these techniques, baijiu was born.

Spirit of the People

A divergence between baijiu and other types of Chinese alcohol developed in the early days. While hangjiu remained a drink of the elite, baijiu became the spirit of the people, sipped by farmers and labourers. As hangjiu was more refined, it's little wonder that baijiu took the role of its humbler, simpler cousin and quality standards for the spirit were poor in the beginning. Yet as hangjiu was more expensive, it couldn't be accessed by the average Chinese peasant. Baijiu, by comparison, was stronger and cheaper.

One famous peasant will forever be linked to the origins of baijiu. His name was Du Kang and according to legend he created baijiu through serendipity. In the fourteenth century, Du Kang, an exile, aimed to ferment wine by burying ingredients underground but feared what a bad winter could do to his sorghum grains. So, Du Kang hid the sorghum in the hole of a tree and when he came back to the spot a few weeks later with his uncle, they were drawn in by a fragrant aroma. The sorghum had mixed with rainwater, fermenting into baijiu.

An even earlier legend places the origins of baijiu in the Xia Dynasty (2070–1600 bc). A consort to the mythical ruler Yu the Great tasked an imperial subject, Yi Di, to make a new type of liquor. Yi Di put his thinking cap on and came up with baijiu, which the consort then offered to Yu the Great. The king enjoyed it so much that he ordered that future generations should drink it for all of eternity.[4]

What these myths reveal is the powerful folk tradition and history at the heart of baijiu production. Every village and city developed their own recipes and techniques as the spirit of the people flowed across the provinces. In the southwest, it turned into lighter rice spirits, while sorghum spirits dominated the rest of the country. Baijiu trucked along at a steady pace for hundreds of years and it's only in the last hundred that it's stepped into the world stage.

Spirit of the Republic

Since antiquity, China had been ruled by an imperial system, with an emperor serving as the ultimate ruler at the top of an empire of royal prerogatives and nobility. That all changed in 1911 when the Qing Dynasty fell and the People's Republic of China was formed. Many factors brought on this brutal regime change, carried out in the centuries and decades leading up to the collapse.

The problems of the Qing Dynasty go back as far as the 1700s and involve trade with Europe. There was growing dissatisfaction among British merchants that the Qing government declined the trading of wares for the tea and silk they wanted. As there was nothing the government wanted, they insisted the British and the rest of Europe pay with silver. Determined to get out from under the Chinese yoke, some British merchants began to sell opium. They brought it from India, and in time it became a commodity that China accepted as a trade resource.

As opium addiction rose in China, destroying communities and lives, the Qing banned the sale and trade of it. That didn't stop the British from smuggling it into the country and all this growing tension reached boiling point when the Qing confiscated and burned 20,000 tonnes of opium in 1839. The British government retaliated, kicking off the First Opium War that lasted between 1839–42.

England emerged victorious and the Qing were forced to sign the Treaty of Nanking, which meant they had to give Britain the island of Hong Kong, open more ports for foreign trade and make the English exempt from Qing law. This was the first of the Unequal Treaties that further weakened the Qing, forcing them to pay money, surrender land and allow foreigners to do as they pleased on Chinese soil. As the name suggests, every one of these treaties were unequal because they never benefited the Qing.

Further pressure built up with multiple civil wars that exploded across China through the 1800s. One of the most devasting was the Taiping Rebellion, a religious movement led by a man named Hong Xiuquan. Rising up over southern China like an angry tidal wave, Hong created a state called Taiping Tianguo (The Heavenly Kingdom of Great Peace) and rallied the poor to his call against the aristocratic Qing.

Ultimately, the Qing won, but the rebellion devastated Southern China and sowed more discontent against the royal family. By the late 1800s, the Qing held on to power by a thread. The Civil War period of 1850–78 had crippled China, and the country faced the threat of being eclipsed by Japan, who won a decisive victory in the Sino-Japanese War of 1895 by adopting Western technology. Meanwhile, European leaders were debating among themselves how they would divide China among their empires.

Something had to change.

In 1901, reformers in the Qing government introduced Western policies to modernise military, infrastructure and communication networks across China in the hopes that it would make a difference. Yet it seemed the writing was already on the wall, as no amount of reforms could stem the tide of resentment that had built up in the Chinese people.[5]

In 1911 came the Xinhai Revolution, led by the Revolutionary Alliance under the direction of Sun Yat-sen. At the time, Sun was in the US on a fundraising tour and was oblivious to the fact that many provinces rose in support of the Alliance. He hurried back to China, arriving after the rebels had taken over Nanjing. Sun was elected as the provisional president of the new Republic of China.

Further bloodshed didn't follow. Sun telegrammed the Premier of China, Yuan Shikai, to say that if he agreed to the formation of a republic he could have the presidency. Shikai was happy to oblige and with provisions made for the continuance of the royal court for ceremonial purposes, the Qing emperor and family abdicated the throne.[6] The 1911 revolution laid the groundwork for the revolution of 1949, as the government of the newly formed republic couldn't unify China under its control. Power vacuums sprang up through different provinces and warlords stepped in to make their own mark.

It was these sweeping political changes that transformed the course of baijiu and created the conditions for it to be showcased to the world. In 1915, a landmark visit was made by Chinese alcohol producers sent by the government to the Panama-Pacific International Exposition in San Francisco.

The exhibition was the opportunity for the Chinese Republic, hardly three years old to prove to the West that it should be taken seriously as a superpower of commerce. It was an opportunity to introduce products steeped in Chinese tradition and gain new insights into Western methods that could also be used to improve China's standing.

According to Chinese media, the San Francisco World Fair was a shining moment of glory for baijiu producers. Famous brands like Moutai and Luzhou Laojiao cleaned up with a slew of awards. The *Beijing Review* claims 'China won 1211 awards … becoming the focus of the event.'[7]

However, dig deep enough into this story and you'll find several falsehoods. Derek Sandhaus carried out extensive research into Moutai and Luzhou Laojiao's gold medal-winning claims and found them to be false (which is ironic, considering Sandhaus is now a brand ambassador for Luzhou Laojiao and a founder of Ming River, a baijiu made by the distillery).

In the case of Moutai, Sandhaus found that the second-place gold medal that it bragged about winning was actually a fourth-place medal. In his words:

> [the judging] committee awarded a total of over 25,000 medals, meaning that there must have been a category for just about everything. In this light, winning one of five medals in a 'best baijiu' category feels equivalent to receiving a participation trophy on field day.[8]

On investigating Luzhou Laojiao, Sandhaus found they were passing off the lowest-ranked fifth-place bronze medal as a 'best-in-show' award.

Other sources seem to back up that baijiu didn't receive the hero's welcome in 1915 that is so often touted. According to Moutai factory director Qiao Hong, the presentation of the brand was a disaster:

> The bottles were black without clear and distinctive labels. Visitors at the expo walked past the exhibition without noticing the product and even the judges were reluctant to take a taste from the suspicious-looking bottles … One of the Moutai representatives got so frustrated with the poorly organised trip to the exposition that he smashed one of the unattractive bottles on the floor.

But because of this fit of pique, Moutai's dim prospects were suddenly reversed:

> The bottle shattered into small pieces and the extraordinary odour of the drink spread into the exposition area. People gathered around, attracted by the smell, and ultimately the drink received several mentions … International recognition served to lift the spirit of the Chinese and Maotai was accorded the title of national drink in 1915.[9]

This is another inaccurate claim. Moutai became the national drink of China in the 1950s because it was used to entertain dignitaries by former president Zhou Enlai. Despite these truths that have been conveniently buried beneath a mountain of marketing spiel, Moutai remains China's most popular baijiu brand, regularly going for hundreds of thousands of pounds and dollars at auction.

The reasons for its popularity are as much government-based as they are location-based. Maotai, a remote village in Guizhou Province, has historically been a poor, ethnically diverse region that has failed to produce the kind of high-quality spirits compared to Sichuan, where the bulk of baijiu making gets done.

During the Qing Dynasty, a state-wide salt monopoly was introduced and Maotai became a distribution hub. Northern merchants sequestered in the village decided to import top distillers from their home provinces and blend the most advanced distillation techniques with local tradition.

This created alcohol called 'huisha' (native soil) that gave off potent smells and tastes when aged.

In the early twentieth century, Moutai became the ideal patriotic alcohol for Chinese businessmen, politicians and warlords. It was a favourite of Mao Zedong's Red Army and they passed Maotai's Red Water River four times during Mao's Long March, using the local baijiu to boost morale and clean wounds.

After the success of the 1949 Revolution, the Moutai brand had secured its place as the go-to alcohol of the people in charge, even becoming the preferred official banquet alcohol for the Chinese Communist Party.

Yet the iconic spirit made by the Kweichow Moutai Distillery could be on the decline in the coming years. In 2022, the market capitalisation of Moutai was $500 billion, whereas at the time of writing this book in 2024, that number has been cut in half.

Several reasons have been given for this slump in sales. Firstly, Moutai is no stranger to being accused of benefiting from bribes, and a 2020 accusation from State TV knocked $25 billion off the market capitalisation, according to *The Economist*.[10]

There are a few more colourful theories about the decline. One of the most popular is that the quintessential Moutai customer, the Chinese property tycoon, has decided to go through a dry spell.

Another theory has to do with a Chinese card game called guandan (literally, egg or bomb tossing). This game involves two players attempting to empty their hands by playing a high combination of cards, and is a fixture at Chinese banquets and a favoured pastime for even the most senior of officials. It requires a lot of concentration and is an indispensable business networking activity. With this in mind, there's speculation that Chinese businessmen and politicians are replacing competitive baijiu drinking with guandan games and staying sober.

What has remained constant since the Chinese Communist Party seized control in 1949 is the increase in baijiu investment, and unification of alcohol production practices. Many small distilleries have been consolidated into state-backed megacorps like Moutai and Luzhou Laojiao.

Further expansion was made in the 1970s under Chairman Deng Xiaoping's 'Reform and Opening Up' policies. The previous regime of Chairman Mao had rationed baijiu, whereas these new policies promoted private enterprise and stimulated the growth of new brands.

This expansion reached a peak in the 1990s with an estimated 18,000 to 36,000 baijiu distillers putting products into the market, ranging from premium bottles priced at outrageous prices to new styles that show the distinctive techniques of specific provinces.

Into the twenty-first century, baijiu has experienced rises and falls the same as many other spirit categories. But whereas categories such as Scotch and rum have produced a large range of established brands with devoted followings across the world, there is only a handful of baijiu brands that are recognised outside of China.

When I interviewed Derek Sandhaus he went into detail about why it's much harder to find interesting entry-level baijiu bottles outside of China:

> There's a real problem outside of China in terms of acquiring good entry-level baijiu. One of the reasons for that is most of the products that are exported to the Western market i.e. Europe and the United States, aren't aimed at entry-level customers. They are aimed at Chinese businesspeople overseas and the Chinese diaspora who already have brand loyalty.
>
> To take the UK for example, there isn't anything cheaper than £70 and reaching upwards of £300. That's a huge barrier to entry and it's asking a lot for a casual drinker who doesn't know anything about the category.
>
> It's different in China. There are tens of thousands of baijiu for every price point, from one dollar to thousands of dollars. Twenty to fifty dollars is the sweet spot usually. At that price point, you've weeded out anything low-end and crap. At that point, you're going to be drinking products that are traditionally made baijiu and not blended with neutral spirits.
>
> For specific brands in the UK that I think are affordable, you have Moutai Prince, which isn't like Moutai's high-end £400. Prince retails at £70. There's Laobai Fenjiu, a ten-year aged export version that retails at £90.

Even so, connoisseurs at home and abroad have been willing to pay massive premiums for bottles, in part for their collectability, prestige and rarity and perhaps because of the gift-giving culture that's prevalent in China. As part of gift-giving etiquette, supplying a bottle of good baijiu is an expected societal norm. (If you ever find yourself in this position, it's always better to go with a mid-range well-known baijiu brand if you can't afford an ultra-premium bottle. Better to avoid a low-end baijiu at all costs if you don't want to risk offending the receiver of your gift.)

Since 2012, baijiu distillers have also had to contend with the withdrawal of government patronage since Chairman Xi Jinping made the announcement. This was an unexpected blow to an industry that for decades relied on huge government orders for ceremonial drinking at banquets and official functions. This has resulted in brands lowering prices to compete in a crowded market, while also pushing innovation and experimentation.

Accessible Baijiu

I've chosen the bottles in this section based on being interested in the backstory of the distillery and their accessibility for first-time baijiu drinkers.

The first bottle that comes to mind is Ming River from Luzhou Laojiao, which Derek Sandhaus explained more about in our interview:

> Ming River falls into the strong aroma baijiu style, which is the most popular style of baijiu in China. Luzhou Laojiao is credited with inventing that style and has been making it longer than anyone. The liquid you find in a Ming River bottle is made the same way as everything else the distillery does.
>
> The difference between Ming River and their other products at similar price points is the blend. In order to land on the blend we did we had a couple of considerations. The first is that we wanted it to be used in a more traditional banquet style to accompany food and we wanted it to be something that we could use in cocktails.
>
> Our distillery usually does two different strengths. One is 52% ABV and the other is 38% ABV. There's not really one that's considered real baijiu over the other. It's a matter of personal preference. I'd say 52% is the standard but when

we're out with people at our distillery, they're drinking the 38% because you have to drink of lot of spirit every day.

So, we split the difference and went with 45% for Ming River. It's strong enough to add a little something to your cocktail and not so weak that if you're drinking it neat with food, you'll still get the taste. It isn't overwhelmingly strong either for non-Chinese drinkers.

As we wanted it to work in cocktails, we did taste tests with bartenders in Berlin and New York and asked the master blender to give us four different blends that she thought would highlight different aspects of the strong aroma baijiu flavour profile. We tested them with the bartenders and did round after round until we homed in on the right blend.

Red Star, or Hongxing, is the everyman baijiu brand in China, contrasting with the elitist Moutai. The distillery goes back to the Zhao brothers, who invented the Erguotou style in 1680. You wouldn't be wrong in thinking that the name of the brand has Communist ties. It received the first business licence from the People's Republic of China in April 1949 to make booze for China's national celebration in October of that year.

The higher ticket product styled 'Redstar' is a 43% light aroma baijiu that comes in a white hip flask bottle design. If you're in the mood for a cheaper, supermarket-style of baijiu you can pick up Hongxing Erguotou, which comes in a green bottle similar to Jinro soju discussed in Chapter 9.

Quentin Sterling, author of *Baijiu by Definition*, suggests Jing Xiao Bai:

I'd definitely recommend Jiang Xiao Bai because of it being light aroma style. It's a lower ABV baijiu at 40% and tends not to have some of the stronger, pungent flavours compared to strong aroma baijiu.

Jiang Xiao Bai is targeting a younger crowd. It wants to rejuvenate baijiu as a drink for a younger demographic. Founder Tao Shiquan is a standout personality in the industry because he wears hoodies, Jordans and camo pants. He doesn't fit the traditional image of a Chinese businessman. He's incorporated traditional Chinese music, hip hop and graffiti art into the narrative of the brand.

Byejoe is another Western-tailored brand. The brainchild of Houston-born Matt Trusch, Byejoe combines the best of East and West in the branding and tasting profiles. Trusch first became enthralled by Chinese culture in 1988 as a language student, travelling across the country over the next two decades.

In 2006, he launched Byejoe, relying on the guiding hand of managing director Silvio Leal, an alcohol product veteran who's handled launches for Seagram and Moet Hennessey. According to the team, the challenges that baijiu has to overcome in the West are down to the four Ps: proof, pungency, purity and price tag. Put another way, strength, smell, safety and savings. That's why the products are geared towards addressing the four Ps. Byejoe Red is a lower ABV light-aroma style at 40% ,with a base distilled from Maotai Town and blended in the US. Dragonfire comes in at 35% and is the first infused international baijiu with ingredients of sorghum, dragon fruit, lychee and hot peppers.

Looking for some timeless Chinese wisdom? You might want to get your hands on a bottle of Confucius Wisdom. Marketed as a 'wise man's spirit', this philosophy-inspired baijiu was created by Beijing native David W. Zhou in 2012. Zhou founded his business Everest Spirits after he couldn't find one bottle of baijiu in Washington, DC outside of the local Chinatown.

Even baijiu isn't immune to the influence of the big Western corporations; Diageo wanted to get in on the action with Shui Jing Fang. The British spirits titan entered into a joint venture with the Shing Jui Fang distillery of Chengdu, Sichuan, in 2003.

A distillery that recalls some of the old glory of Chengdu winemaking, Shui Jing Fang developed out of the 600-old ruins of another distillery on Chengdu's Shi Jing (Water Well). Unique yeast cultures were discovered in the ruins and were used in the fermentation pits of the distillery's high-end products in 2000.

Thanks to the partnership with Diageo, Shui Jing Fang has tapped into a global bar network and placed its products Wellbay and Forest Green on top shelves. The former is a strong aroma baijiu made from sorghum, rice, glutinous rice, wheat and corn and bottled at 52% ABV. The latter is in the same style and ABV class but is filtered with bamboo and charcoal to mellow out some of the harsher flavours of the Wellbay.

For more adventurous drinkers, there's Guomi, the world's only medicine-aroma baijiu from the Dongjiu distillery. The name of the distillery comes from the Donggongsi Temple in northern Zunyi, a suburban area famed for its winemaking in the seventeenth century. There was a unique alcohol-making technique in Zunyi that was distinct from the nearby Maotai production method.

This technique was lost to history until it was revived in 1957. It involves sorghum being fermented in big pits with big qu and small qu fermented in small pits. The pits are covered and coated with white mud, star fruit stems and lime and are sealed with coal. Everything is then combined before distillation. Guomi, meaning 'state secret' is an extension of the mystique that the distillery has cloaked itself in.

There's even baijiu inspired by Li Bai, the booze-loving poet that kicked off this chapter. The Baiyunbian distillery from Hubei Province is a leader in the mixed aroma baijiu style and was founded in 1952. The name of the distillery comes from a famous Li Bai poem where the poet stares out at Hubei Lake and pictures himself drifting in a boat up into the night sky, drinking 'beside the white clouds' or baiyunbian. An entry-level product to enjoy from Baiyunbian is Wuxing, a 42% ABV mixed aroma baijiu that has been described as having a minty, floral taste and aroma.

In terms of what the future has in store for baijiu, there's a lot of positivity to be found and education will be the driving force according to the specialists. Sandhaus told me;

> This might sound like a weird thing to say but Ming River needs more competition in the West. We need a lot more brands that are promoting baijiu as mainstream products that bars want to work with.
>
> One of the difficulties I have as a brand owner and spirits educator is that sometimes there's a perceived conflict of interest in terms of cooperating with other baijiu brands and distilleries. My distillery might not like to see me doing events where another baijiu brand is promoting it because it can be perceived that I'm promoting that brand instead. Then there's the other side where other brands see me as being Luzhou Laojiao's ambassador.
>
> So, over the next ten years, I'd like to see more educators in the US and beyond. But I think that is happening slowly and we'll also see a lot of new baijiu brands in the coming

> years. This can't come soon enough and I'd also like to see some kind of impartial third-party organisation that acts as a baijiu promotion vehicle outside of China. Japan has done an excellent job of this was sake and shochu organisations.

Quentin Sterling also weighed in by saying that specifics are key for getting baijiu into the right hands:

> When a new Chinese business trend is released, everyone will go after it and mostly it tends to be successful with a younger demographic e.g. millennials across all industries. My criticism is that isn't enough. Millennials are a big, general target and I think you have to be specific.
>
> What I've seen in Chinese citizens living abroad is that they're not necessarily interested in drinking baijiu. They are more enthusiastic about spirits like gin, tequila or bourbon. So, there's going to need to be a lot of ingenuity to make baijiu more accessible to not only these Chinese people living overseas, but also Westerners.
>
> I always love to look at tequila as a comparative journey for baijiu. Tequila has had a fifty-year journey to make it into the mainstream and even now it's still working to get a dominant market share. But tequila is a similar spirit to baijiu in its cultural relevance and could go on a similar journey.

From the first time you sip baijiu to the last sip you take, remember that you're imbibing thousands of years of tradition and beauty and now we return to where we began with a final Li Bai poem to send you off along your drinking sojourn:

> Life in the world is but a big dream;
> I will not spoil it by any labour or care.
> So saying, I was drunk all the day,
> Lying helpless at the porch in front of my door.
> When I awoke, I blinked at the garden-lawn;
> a lonely bird was singing amid the flowers I asked myself,

had the day been wet or fine?
I asked myself, had the day been wet or fine?
The Spring wind was telling the mango-bird.
Moved by its song I soon began to sigh,
and, as wine was there, I filled my own cup.
Wildly singing I waited for the moon to rise;
when my song was over, all my senses had gone.
Facing my wine, I did not see the dusk,
Falling blossoms have filled the folds of my clothes.
Drunk, I rise and approach the moon in the stream,
Birds are far off, people too are few.[11]

Chapter 8
Shochu and Awamori

Of all the alcohol categories I'm intrigued by, the one I feel the most connected to is Japanese drinks. That's probably because I'm a Japanese culture enthusiast, and when given any opportunity to get on my soapbox about this particular interest, I'm going to take it.

Having written regularly through my Japanese culture publication *Yamato Magazine* for several years and published a book called *Japanese Fighting Heroes, Warriors, Samurai and Ronins*, I enjoy spreading awareness about Japanese history, culture, food and drink and it was through this creative project that I fell in love with Japanese alcohol like sake and its spirit cousins shochu and awamori.

In recent years, the popularity of Japanese drinks has shown a steady increase across the globe. The Japan Sake and Shochu Makers Association (JSS) routinely conducts initiatives that promote Japanese booze on a worldwide scale, statistics show sake premiumisation and exports are on an upward trajectory,[1] shochu brands like Iichiko are breaking into the mainstream in the US,[2] and Japanese restaurants and bars are having their moment in the sun with ramen joints, sake bars and fusion-style chains growing year on year, especially in the UK.[3]

Perhaps this surge in culinary and beverage interest is being fanned by the popularity of Japanese pop culture too, with big shows like FX's *Shogun,* Netflix's *Blue Eye Samurai* and *Age of Samurai: Battle For Japan* all telling incredible stories while showcasing the diversity of Japanese food and drink across the centuries.

In short, it's a fantastic time to be interested in Japanese culture and if you have no idea what shochu or awamori is, then this chapter is an introduction to the Land of the Rising Sun's indigenous spirits.

What are Shochu and Awamori?

The first thing to understand about shochu (pronounced show-chew) is that it's not nihonshu, which is called sake outside of Japan. Nihonshu is its own category, a fermented alcoholic drink brewed anywhere between an average 13–17% ABV to a legal maximum of 21% ABV. As a distilled spirit, shochu is much stronger, coming in between 25%–37% ABV.

There are two kinds of shochu to be aware of called honkaku (genuine/authentic) and korui (multi-distilled) shochu. Depending on your mood and wallet, both kinds are worth exploring, though I do confess to having a honkaku bias because I feel it's the purest representation of what makes shochu such a fantastic spirit.

For example, one of honkaku shochu's biggest selling points is the fact that it can be made from a huge range of ingredients, each producing different flavours and drinking experiences. The five most common core bases for shochu are satsuma imo (sweet potato), mugi (barley), kome (rice), kokuto (brown/black sugar) and soba (buckwheat). This is only a small fraction of the universe of ingredients. Other varietals include carrot, kelp, radish, tomato, cactus, perilla, chestnut, milk, sesame, aloe and pumpkin.

At home in Japan, honkaku shochu and its older cousin awamori have held an esteemed position among drinkers. In the words of shochu expert Christopher Pellegrini:

> Over the past decade and a half, awamori and shochu have quietly overtaken nihonshu in terms of domestic consumption. According to the Japanese tax office, sales of awamori and shochu eclipsed those of nihonshu in 2003, and the gap has mostly increased ever since.
>
> In 2015, for instance, distilleries shipped 245,000 more kilolitres (64.7 million US gallons) of product than the nihonshu industry. That put it second in the country behind beer in terms of domestically produced alcoholic beverages.[4]

There is also shochu's lesser-known cousin awamori, which comes from the island of Okinawa, a place with its unique culture built on a mix of Malayan, Ainu, Chinese, Korean and Japanese influences. Generally, awamori is stronger than shochu and ranges between 30–43% ABV. It's also a distilled beverage that can only be made from long-grain indica rice, water, black koji mould and yeast.

How is Shochu Made?

The process for making and distilling honkaku shochu requires several steps:

Step 1: Koji preparation

Koji is a special kind of Japanese mould that's used in the making of sake, shochu and awamori. Its superpower is the fact that it can trigger a process called multi-parallel fermentation, where koji tag teams with yeast to convert starches to sugar and then sugar into alcohol.

Different types of koji are selected depending on the type of drink being made and there are three to choose from. For example, yellow koji kin (the mould spores sprinkled onto a starch base like rice) is the most used for making sake and can be used for some types of shochu and contributes to a lighter and fruitier kind of drink. White koji-kin is more likely to be used in shochu production and it's valued for the citric acid it creates in the moromi (mash), which protects the moromi from unwanted bacteria.

The final type of koji that can be used is black koji kin, which also has citric acid that adds a more complex flavour to the shochu. Black koji kin is also used for making awamori and is one of the regulated ingredients for making the Okinawan spirit.

Once the koji type has been chosen, spores are sprinkled onto rice or another starch base like potato or barley and are left to propagate in a carefully heated room for forty-eight hours. The spores break down the rice into glucose and get it ready for the yeast to be added in the next step.

Step 2: First moromi fermentation

After the koji kin has spread through the rice the koji is ready. It's mixed with water and yeast to create the mash. This starter fermentation may take place in clay pots or stainless steel vats.

In the five to eight days of the first fermentation, distillery workers might be busy preparing the sweet potatoes that have been delivered. They are washed and carved to remove any blemishes. This is generally one of the most labour-intensive parts of shochu making because washing and peeling potatoes isn't easily automated.

When the potatoes have been prepared, they are put into a steam drum and transported to a shredder and cut into smaller pieces to make life easier for the koji kin and yeast in the second fermentation.

Step 3: Second moromi fermentation

When the mould spores and yeast have been given plenty of time to multiply, more crushed sweet potato and water are added and the second fermentation could go on for a week to ten days.

Depending on the size of the distillery, this mixture might be left to bubble in a large vat or separated among several pots before the introduction of additional water and potatoes. However, there isn't a set formula for all types of shochu. Brown sugar shochu might have a third fermentation stage and in the case of awamori, there is only one fermentation step of koji, water and yeast.

Step 4: Distillation

It's worth pointing out at this stage that shochu distilleries don't make the shochu. They specialise in koji making. It's the stills that do all the heavy lifting for the liquid and will be at the discretion of the distillery.

If the intention is for honkaku to be slapped on the bottle label, then a pot still will be used to boil the completed moromi in batches. With this method of distillation, many characteristics of the esters in the mash add complexity to the distillate. This ester-rich liquid is called hanatare that comes in at 70% ABV, which tapers off as the run carries on. The final part of the run is known as suedare and the ABV has dropped to 10%, which Christopher Pellegrini describes in his *Shochu Handbook* as exuding:

> an organic acid-based aroma that adds depth and complexity to the distillate … the rice koji, sweet potato, yeast and water all spend a considerable amount of time together before distillation, so it's only natural that you will notice the complex interplay between them when taking a sip.

> Honkaku shochu prizes these aromas and flavours and distilleries across Japan have laboured for generations to perfect the conditions and techniques necessary to create the ideal moromi for distillation.[5]

In the case of korui shochu, a patent still is more likely to be used to create a distillate with as much alcohol in it as possible that is neutral.

For both types of shochu, the unprocessed/undiluted alcohol is called genshu.

Step 5: Ageing

The next step in honkaku shochu production is to decide on the method of ageing. One method is to age the genshu in wooden barrels in a similar vein to whisky. A more common option for large distilleries is to use large stainless steel containers that make it easy to age massive quantities of the spirit at once.

A third option is to age shochu and awamori in earthenware pots, which create softer and rounder notes in the finished product. This ageing method has a particular resonance with awamori, as many Okinawan families engage in an activity called kusu. This refers to awamori that's been aged for a minimum of three years in clay pots, and the act of ageing.

Families may choose their own pots to mark the birth of a new child and then open the pot years later to celebrate certain milestones like birthdays or going to university. This has created an intriguing drinking culture in Okinawa that foreigners are welcome to be a part of, as Maurice Dudley, awamori educator and founder of Blue Habu, pointed out to me:

> I enjoy the togetherness that comes with sharing a bottle of awamori with family and friends. If you cannot finish a bottle in one sitting, no worries, bar staff will write your name on it and 'keep' it for you for up to two months.
>
> Because Ryukyu awamori can only be produced using black koji, rice and water, many distilleries are experimenting with unique ageing methods such as cask ageing or creating awamori-based liqueurs such as awamori-coffee or shiquasa (Okinawa lime) liqueurs and much more.

Japanese spirits educator Stephen Lyman also provides interesting details on the kusu maturing method in his book *The Complete Guide to Japanese Drinks*. 'When spirit from the oldest jar is drunk, awamori from the next oldest pot is added to replace it. What is taken from the pot is in turn replaced by the next oldest jar and so on down to the youngest container, which is filled with newly distilled spirits. This has the benefit of allowing the kusu to be exposed to air and to interact with other spirits, promoting changes in the alcohol.[6]

Step 6: Dilution

After ageing, shochu is blended from different vessels and water is added to bring the ABV down. This could be anywhere between 20%–30% ABV.

Step 7: Filtration

Filtration is another step that can be used to ensure consistency in the flavour of your shochu. Organic compounds in the shochu provide flavour but it may be filtered to remove anything that is not liquid. These methods range from porous cloth bags to sophisticated charcoal filtering systems.

Interestingly, white birch charcoal filtration is prohibited by law in the making of honkaku shochu. But other types of charcoal are accepted and the only time you'll see any mention of filtration on a label is with the word 'muroka'. Yet, muroka means the liquid hasn't been filtered. The reason the word is mentioned at all is because a brand wants to signal to a consumer that there is further complexity to enjoy in the shochu.

Step 8: Bottling

The final stage is done through an automated machine that seals the liquid in 720 ml – 1,800 ml bottles. At least at the bigger distillers. Small producers rely on hand-bottling methods, which may sometimes contribute to a bigger price tag in line with the craft elements.

Tangled Origins

The origins of shochu and awamori can be traced back to the fifteenth century, by way of distillation technology coming from either China,

Korea or Thailand. For example, an official record kept by the Joseon Dynasty in Korea states that Okinawans were making distilled alcohol in 1477 because of constant trading with Thailand.

Another theory is that distillation originated in China, crossed over to the Korean Peninsula and then made a journey to Japan's Kyushu Island, which would go on to become the heartland of shochu production. A third origin story claims that distillation techniques were transported from Shanghai and went directly to Kyushu, while a final theory posits that spirit-making came from southern China straight to Okinawa.

Regardless of which theory is correct, it's safe to assume distillation knowledge travelled across all water routes throughout Asia at some point or another. Most likely, the first Japanese spirits were made and tasted in Okinawa in the Ryukyu Kingdom.

At the height of its power, the Ryukyu Kingdom ruled over all the Ryukyu Islands, a chain of Japanese islands stretching from Kyushu to Taiwan, with Okinawa as the centre of the crown. The early history of this kingdom was founded in the fracturing of Okinawa into three polities after an inept king called Tamagusuku who was unable to maintain control in the twelfth century.

The three polities included Nanzan in the south, Hokuzan in the north and Chuzan in the centre. Each region consolidated their power over the next hundred years through the building of many fortresses and setting up trade agreements with China, Korea and Japan.

It was in Chuzan that the history of the island would be defined. By the fifteenth century, an enterprising lord called Sho Hashi came to power and overthrew the previous king of the region. Then he went to war with the other two polities and unified Okinawa under the Sho Dynasty.

The new king wasted no time in securing his legacy by changing the capital of the island from Urasoe to Shurijo Castle and setting his new trading mecca in the lively port of Naha. In this way, Hashi built the foundations of the Ryukyu Kingdom and made Okinawa a thriving trading destination with Japan, China and Southeast Asia.

Among the Ryukyuan aristocracy, alcohol was a luxury item, especially awamori. The famed Ryukyu courtier Sai On believed distilled alcohol should only be allowed for the elite, and common folk weren't allowed to drink it. This attitude is confirmed by Maurice Dudley:

> During the era of the Ryukyu Kingdom, awamori was considered a valuable trade commodity. The Ryukyuans carried jars of kusu/aged awamori and offered them as tributes to the Chinese Emperor during tributary missions. Kusu was also shared with foreign visitors who travelled to the Ryukyus for trade and other diplomatic missions. As a result of such high regard, awamori was reserved for royalty. According to the royal decree, laymen were not able to produce or consume the cherished beverage.

There's a famous story about the Chinese imperial envoy Tung-yen Li visiting Okinawa in 1800 for the crowing of king Sho On. Two big pots of awamori were gifted every morning and the locals were expected them to drink it at a superhuman rate. Eventually, Li wrote to the royal family to politely ask if the king could send less of the stuff, even though it tasted amazing.

When awamori wasn't being used for wooing royalty, it was being consumed for creative inspiration. An event known as otori developed in Ryuku and on the southern island of Miyakojima and is still alive today. Otori involves a storyteller called an oya, who downs a shot of awamori, refills it and then sends the glass to the next person. Each member of the circle tells a story, gives a speech or recites a poem and the celebration continues.

Indeed, it was out of this cauldron of Okinawan creativity and love of life that the techniques needed to make shochu carried over to mainland Japan.

The Early Days of Shochu

The first known documented reference to shochu comes from an essay written by a Portuguese merchant named Jorge Alvarez who spent time at Yamagawa Port near Kagoshima Bay. According to him, 'people were drinking [a spirit] made from rice in the Yamagawa area'[7] which he likened to arak. This spirit was made with rice and was probably the precursor to rice shochu.

In 1559, the first Japanese reference to shochu popped up on the wall of a shrine in Northern Kagoshima. This graffiti was written by a frustrated carpenter who was annoyed that the head priest of the shrine and his employer had been stingy with his booze and essentially translates to 'the head priest is a cheapskate. He didn't give us shochu at all! What an a##€0§¢!'(The actual translation is a lot politer than this. But there's bound to be more than one disgruntled drinker out there in Japan who's had some strong words to say about a lack of alcohol sharing.)

Into the Edo period (1600–1868), shochu became increasingly popular and Okinawa and the southern Kyushu regions found it difficult to keep up with demand. Because of this, Japanese officials began ordering sake breweries to produce shochu from sake lees, the leftover solids separated from the liquid after pressing the fermented mash. This type of shochu became known as kasu-tori, producing a drink with a specific sweet, dried grass-like aroma and taste. Kasu-tori also took on sacred connotations because of its role in the local agricultural cycle and was often served in Shinto rituals across northern Kyushu.[8]

Another key alcohol milestone of the Edo period was that the term awamori appeared for the first time in official documents to draw a line between the locally produced shochu and the highly prized Okinawan booze. Truly, there was a lot of upheaval between Japan and Okinawa.

In 1609, Japan launched a full-scale invasion of Ryukyu after years of the Okinawan royal family continually ignoring or resisting demands from the Japanese leadership. This dissension may have started when Toyotomi Hideyoshi, the second great unifier of Japan, was determined to invade Korea and sent word for the Ryukyu Kingdom to submit troops and resources to him through agents of the Shimazu clan. The Okinawans only sent half of the supplies they were expected to send.

When Hideyoshi died in 1598, he was replaced by Tokugawa Ieyasu. The third great unifier of Japan expected the Ryukyu king Sho Nei to acknowledge the Tokugawa shogunate. In addition to ignoring this demand, the king also refused to be an intermediary for the Tokugawa to reestablish a relationship with the Ming Dynasty of China. Further slights from the Okinawan government followed and the Shimazu clan used the narrative of a failure to pay proper respects to the Japanese and were able to get permission from Ieyasu to invade.

After several battles on smaller islands, samurai forces took control of Shuri Castle and the Sho family was brought before the Tokugawa. They were forced to agree to several demands, the most binding of which annexed Okinawa into Japan and established it as Okinawa Prefecture.

A century later, a resilient vegetable made it to Japanese shores via Okinawa. In 1705, a 22-year-old farmer and fisherman Riemon Maeda visited Okinawa and noticed the people were eating the weird-looking bulbous roots of a vegetable called sweet potato.

When Maeda questioned them, the people said the sweet potato had come to Okinawa from China and he tried it for himself. Enjoying the flavour, it inspired Maeda to want to grow this exotic food for himself and so he brought seeds back with him to southern Kyushu Island and planted them in his garden. Once the sweet potatoes grew, he shared a few with his neighbours.

Unfortunately, Maeda died at sea in a typhoon just two years later. But his neighbours wouldn't forget him. They set up a gravestone for him, engraved with the words kara imo don (Lord Sweet Potato). A few years later, the grave of Lord Sweet Potato was turned into a shrine called Sweet Potato Shrine, with Maeda officially being deified as a Shinto god.

Maeda had certainly started a revolution with his curiosity. Sweet potato cultivation spread throughout Satsuma (the former name of Kagoshima Prefecture), reaching all the way to the Izu islands south of Tokyo by 1734. Such was the power of the sweet potato that it caught the attention of the shogun Tokugawa Yoshimune, who was told that even with famines destroying Japan, few people in the southern province of Satsuma died. Intrigued, the shogun tasked one of his masters of Western culture Aoki Konyo to cultivate the Satsuma sweet potato as a defence food against future famines.[9]

Maeda's efforts also led to the development of sweet potato shochu, with Kagoshima Prefecture being the reigning king of this type. According to Pellegrini, the prefecture produces 'over 40 per cent of the domestic supply on a yearly basis. The citizens of Kagoshima also set the national standard in honkaku versus korui consumption – the former makes up over 97 per cent of all the shochu that Kagoshimans enjoy annually.'[10]

Satsuma shochu is one of four World Trade Organisation (WTO) protected regional appellations that honour the traditions of honkaku shochu. For a distiller to include the teapot-like logo of this designation on a product, the shochu must be made with ingredients sourced from Kagoshima. This includes potatoes and water, and only rice or sweet potato koji may be used during fermentation. Plus, the entire distillation process has to be carried out in Kagoshima.

The other three appellations are just as rich in history. There is Iki shochu from Iki Island in Nagasaki Prefecture. This is a barley variety that is one part rice and two parts barley. Iki Island itself is thought to be the origin of barley shochu because of the trading connection is has with the Korean peninsula. The third designation is Kuma shochu from the Kuma region of Kumamoto Prefecture. This is a rice shochu distilled in the Hitoyoshi Basin from a 100 per cent rice mash and water from the Kuma River. Recognised as one of the three fastest-flowing rivers in Japan, water from the Kuma River supports twenty-eight distilleries all collecting water from a subterranean stream to make official Kuma shochu. The final designation is Ryukyu awamori as a way to honour where the shochu industry came from.

The First Shochu Boom

With the proliferation and success of sweet potato, base ingredients for shochu making increased into the nineteenth century and there was another interesting ingredient waiting in the wings: kokuto. Translating to brown/black sugar, this ingredient had been flourishing since the seventeenth century in the Amami Islands, a southern gathering of islands in Kagoshima.

It's thought that sugarcane first arrived in the Amami Islands from China in 1610 and with the islands going through various regime changes, shochu production was bound to develop and evolve.

From 1609, the Amami Islands were put under the direction of the Satsuma Domain and there are records of the domain levying shochu taxes. According to an exiled Satsuma samurai called Nagoya Sagenta, Amami islanders were making shochu out of chestnuts, chinquapins and Japanese sago plants, using the juices from crushed sugarcane.

Of all these varied ingredients, brown sugar seemed to be the most highly prized, as the Satsuma Domain owned the monopoly on it and commoners couldn't handle it without permission.[11]

After the Tokugawa Shogunate was overthrown in the Meiji Restoration of 1868, Japan began its ascent to becoming a world superpower and while the new government started unifying alcohol production, there still wasn't any commercial brown sugar shochu production in the islands. The people of Amami continued to make shochu at home, a trend that followed all shochu to an extent, with Japan's indigenous spirit hardly making it outside of Kagoshima.

This all changed after the Second World War after the Amami Islands and Okinawa were taken over by the US military. During this transition of power, there was the crucial rediscovery of black koji used to make awamori, which had itself been discovered in 1910.

In 1944, an air raid on Shuri Castle destroyed ancient stocks of aged awamori, along with a large amount of black koji. A desperate search led to a straw mat being found at a distillery with traces of the koji intact and after several attempts, the black koji was restored, even in the wake of the occupying Americans banning the production of awamori and limiting commercial transactions to and from Japan. Because of the US's heavy-handedness, there were rice shortages. On the other hand, there was a surplus of brown sugar products that could be used to make kokuto shochu.

By 1953, after the US had handed control of the Amami Islands back to Japan, the Liquor Tax Law classified brown sugar booze as a spirit and put high tax rates on production, which limited the sales appeal. Enterprising islanders fought back by lobbying the National Tax Agency to make sure that only authorised distilleries in the Amami Islands could produce kokuto shochu and it finally joined the honkaku club.

As a spirit made from sugarcane, it's tempting to think that brown sugar is the category's answer to rum. But there are key differences between kokuto shochu and rum. First, kokuto shochu must be made with rice koji. Second, it's not nearly as sweet as you might expect because the koji tamps the sweetness down. Third, brown sugar shochu generally is lower in ABV than most rums at 25–30%.

With this innovation and increased accessibility to ingredients, the first shochu boom kicked off in Japan in the 1970s and the spirit spread far and wide across the country. Further experimentation took place in this decade with the development of the first buckwheat shochu from Unkai Shuzo in Miyazaki Prefecture.

This was a difficult process, as buckwheat isn't easy to ferment. The husks are hard and have to be removed before the kernels are roughly crushed and steeped. Also, as buckwheat retains a lot of moisture it makes koji preparation difficult too. To get around these issues, Unkai used barley koji to create a smooth-tasting shochu that has become extremely popular today. In 2004, Takara Shuzo, also based in

Miyazaki, solved the buckwheat conundrum and was able to make the first 100 per cent buckwheat shochu, called Towari.

Shochu's Expansion Across the World

Into the 2000s, shochu continued to grow in recognition and popularity across Japan with the plethora of ingredients and ways to taste it, which we'll come back to later in this chapter. However, with a shrinking population, a new generation of drinkers and lower levels of alcohol consumption, shochu has seen a decline in domestic sales by 25 per cent sales volume compared to a 2007 sales peak.

The Japanese government and JSS are doing plenty to introduce shochu to new markets abroad. For example, the government listed honkaku shochu as a key category in its export expansion category in 2020, with a planning value increase of shochu experts to $27.6 million in 2025.[12]

The JSS has also promoted shochu through cocktails as a gateway to entry for many foreign bartenders who have been invited to Kagoshima to learn and take this knowledge back with them. An example of this was a trip that Hong-Kong based bartender Devender Sehgal took in 2019, along with other bartenders. Sehgal recalls:

> one thing most of us had in common was that we didn't know much about shochu. We visited around nine distilleries in different prefectures like Kumamoto, Kagoshima and Oita, which was eye-opening – but still, my understanding was very limited until I returned and began to explore [the role of shochu] more in the world of cocktails.[13]

Sehgal has since gone on to head up The Aubrey, a specialist shochu bar in the Mandarin Oriental Hong Kong and has spawned a branch in London's Mandarin Oriental Hyde Park.

Another shochu convert is Elliot Faber, co-owner of the alcohol distributor Sunday's Spirits and sake shop/bistro combo Sake Central in Hong Kong. With the help of partners, he created a mixology-inspired coffee shochu with La Colombe coffee beans and then Stumptown coffee beans. Faber said:

> Shochu is a bartender's secret. The varying levels of ingredients, alcohol strengths and ageing methods make for a myriad of textures and flavours to dominate or add subtlety to any original or classic cocktail. I've been saying for a long time: the bartender who masters the art of the shochu cocktail will have the world's attention.[14]

Chandrakant Mohanty, founder of the Japanese spirits distributor Mizunara: The Shop, feels shochu could follow a similar path to mezcal, in that a relatively obscure spirit could one day soon be a staple bottle on the back of bars across the world:

> Today, we are still at a very nascent stage of discovery of this hidden gem from Japan. In my opinion, shochu will continue to find favour across the globe quite rapidly in the immediate term – not only from the cocktail world, but also from sommeliers and chefs alike who will probably find the range of flavours in different ranges of ABV [suitable for] different serving styles with which to accompany food.[15]

Maya Aley, the first non-Japanese to be a certified Shochu Meister, has also weighed in on shochu's growing popularity abroad:

> There's long been an interest in Japanese culture, and with sake and 'washoku' [Japanese cuisine] having become available nearly worldwide, I think people have continued to look for the next new Japanese product.
>
> As more and more shochu is exported from Japan and reaches new consumers around the world, there will soon be more shochu produced at distilleries in countries outside of Japan as well. I think the localisation of shochu production will lead to new variations and exciting flavours that may be different from what honkaku shochu is in Japan – but no less interesting.[16]

The idea of shochu being different outside of Japan is an interesting thought. One of the biggest foreign drives I'm seeing is in the development of chuhai, an abbreviation of shochu highball that may be mixed with carbonated water and a variety of flavours like apple, grapefruit, orange, pineapple etc that come in cans. It's an example of mass-produced korui shochu, which some shochu purists frown on as a soulless commercial cash grab. I don't. In some cases, chuhai is lower in ABV than honkaku shochu and can be more accessible and inspire patrons to want to dig deeper into the category.

There have been several attempts to make Western-inspired honkaku, some better than others. UK craft beer brand BrewDog put out their version of a shochu called Inugami, but it isn't honkaku. BrewDog are well-known for their irreverent marketing tactics and that plays into the story of Inugami, which is inspired by the Japanese dog spirit that can possess people and be used to carry out evil deeds. The label features a sinister-looking inugami being held up by wild birds found in Scotland, as a nod to Japan and Scotland's relationship that has existed since the time that Japanese whisky was first produced.

The story behind the bottle is that of a 'revenge' angle, which taps into the history of the Japanese 'appropriation' of Scotch. This is meant to reference Masataka Taketsuru's study of whisky in Scotland from 1918 to 1920 before returning to Japan to establish the Yamazaki Distillery for Suntory. Eventually, Taketsuru left Suntory to establish Nikka, which retained the Scottish style.

You only have to read the back of the bottle to see this revenge played out. 'From now on, shochu will do BrewDog's bidding. Like the fearsome Inugami dog spirit said to possess unsuspecting travellers, we've taken control of Japan's most popular drink.'

Creators of the spirit, head of distillation Steven Kersley and distiller Dzeti Zait, have pointed out that the marketing isn't to do with an 'us-vs-them' mentality, but as a way to stand out in the category. Zait explained:

> it was a maverick move for that person from Japan to take whisky and bring it to an uninitiated crowd, and since then Japanese whisky has gained such popularity and won awards. We'd quite like to do the same with our shochu. So it's not so much about revenge – it's that we want to see how far we can get, and be in the same ranking as the top shochu.

BrewDog has made their shochu by distilling malt barley, malt wheat, molasses and rice. The ingredients are passed through an eight-plate rectification column still and then the drink is infused with rhubarb and ginger.

Bottled at 23% ABV, Inugami falls comfortably into the low-ABV spirits category but can't be considered honkaku because of the the column distillation process and the presence of molasses and rhubarb. Either it's korui, or falls into a third shochu category called konwa, which is a mix of korui and honkaku. Most likely, Inugami is korui because konwa must be clearly labelled under a specific Japanese designation that makes it clear to consumers that they are buying multi-distilled shochu instead of the authentic stuff.

Other Western products have been made to be much more in line with traditional shochu. Los Angeles-based couple Paul and Mai Nakayama were inspired to create a kokuto shochu following a trip they took to the Amami Islands in 2015. They have a few products and Paul explained a few of them to me:

> On the production side, we're the only black sugar shochu that uses 80 per cent black sugar to 20 per cent rice. It's a very expensive ingredient (usually takes about 100kg to make 10kg of black sugar), but it's worth it. Our distillery was also the first to use vacuum distillation for black sugar shochu, which really made it more approachable and more appealing to a global audience.
>
> On the branding side, we're focused on introducing shochu to a brand new audience of drinkers so the look and feel for our bottles is very different from traditional shochu companies.
>
> Nankai Gold is a very special product. Whereas Nankai Shochu is 24% ABV and a single batch shochu, Gold is a blend of five different expressions of black sugar shochu. Different distillation methods, different casks, and different ageing times for each expression. These are then blended together to maximise flavour, complex notes, drinkability, finish and colour. Keeping the flavour and colour consistent is truly a challenge for our master distiller Yoichiro Haseba, but that's why he's a master.

Shochu education is steadily growing throughout the West, with a recent example coming out of Spain with an education programme called Shochu Dō. Brought together by a trio of drink educators and ambassadors, Shochu Dō aims to raise awareness of Japanese spirits across Europe. Co-founder Elvira Aldaz shared more with me:

> I've been working in advertising for more than twenty years but spirits and cocktails have always been my passion. More than ten years ago I established myself as a freelance strategist, so I had more time to pursue my hobby. I started a blog and began educating myself. I studied the Master of Spirits, the WSET2 of Spirits and a lot of other courses regarding cocktails and drinks. I started splitting my time between advertising and drinks-related projects at the Barcelona Rum Congress, editing the magazine *Rumporter,* judging cocktail and spirit competitions and writing for some media outlets.
>
> I discovered shochu and awamori in Spain with the only specialised importer we have so far, Victor from Avihops. I met him at a drinks fest and as I loved Japan, sake and spirits, it was only a matter of time before I fell down that rabbit hole.
>
> With my co-founders Bianca and Francesco, our mission is to help shochu claim their space in cocktail bars and restaurants through education. In Spain, we are at the first steps of this education process. Sake, never mind shochu, is still an unknown beverage for most of the customers, even sommeliers. Bartenders still tend to confuse sake and shochu, and that's if they have heard of them!
>
> But Japanese cuisine is huge here, with a lot of new high-end Japanese restaurants opening every day and being a success. So, a lot of people love Japanese food and it's only a matter of time before they want to learn more about the drinks. Also, the number of Spanish tourists travelling to Japan is growing year on year and that's important for increasing awareness about Japanese drinks generally. Many people who've had an amazing time in Japan come back and talk to their friends about sake and shochu.
>
> At this early stage, we're raising awareness of Japanese drinks through shochu masterclasses and writing about it for different media outlets and are excited about what the future holds.

Of course, shochu education has been an uphill battle across the West, especially in the US. For years, one of the biggest issues was that shochu was confused with Korean soju, due to a bizarre Californian law that failed to make clear cultural differences between the two distinctive drinks.

Pellegrini has a particular axe to grind about this decades old legislation:

> Some shochu makers have taken advantage of a licensing loophole in California that allows 24% ABV (and lower) spirits to be sold on a so-called soft license (what most restaurants have) which allows the sale of fermented beverages such as wine and beer.
>
> If you print the word 'soju' on the front label, then sushi restaurants and other izakaya that don't have a full-blown bar license can still sell your products, and that's where the confusion sets in. It's seeded by the shochu makers that lazily do this, and it's incredibly short-sighted. When consumers in California pick those bottles up, they see both 'soju' and 'shochu' on the label. It's confusing, and a large percentage of Americans think that soju and shochu are one and the same.
>
> And as many have probably discovered, when you're out drinking soju, you often end up imbibing more than you probably should. There's a ton of people out there who have had lost mornings and afternoons due to a few too many green soju bottles, and that experience ends up preventing people from even trying shochu. I've heard it half a million times through meeting tourists in Tokyo.
>
> Unfortunately, the mislabelled shochu bottles don't just stay in California. The same labels are used on bottles that end up getting shipped to other states as well. I'm originally from Vermont, and there's a state liquor store in Burlington that has a half dozen shochu brands, several of which have soju fraudulently printed on the label even though the same soft license loophole doesn't exist in my home state.

Fortunately, these issues were finally solved in October 2023 when Governor Gavin Newsom signed new legislation that allows shochu with an ABV of 24% or less to be classified in the category of beer and wine and be sold under its own name in bars with a Type 41 liquor license. Members of the JSS and many more campaigned for years to see this change be brought in, with Hitoshi Utsunomiya, director of the JSS commenting that it's 'an incredible team effort from distillers, exporters, importers, and especially all members of the Japanese Restaurant Association of America'.[17]

The passing of this law bodes well for the future of shochu and awamori and here are some thoughts on what the next few decades could hold for Japan and Okinawa's indigenous spirits, according to the experts:

> Much like the nihonshu industry, shochu producers are struggling in Japan due to waning domestic demand. It is likely that the industry will have little choice but to develop markets in other parts of the world.
>
> But I see positive signs on the horizon. There are clear trends on consumer groups opting for quality over quantity and shochu should be able to take advantage of that. With bartenders showing ever-increasing excitement about working with the category's immense diversity of flavour and aroma, I don't see anything getting in the way over the next decade. – Christopher Pellegrini

> Considering the future of awamori, I think there is still a long way to go. Many people still don't think about awamori so the upcoming years will be about building awareness. I think those of us who work in the industry can accomplish big things by focusing less on sales and more on making information more readily available. Of course, we eventually want sales growth and to be exporting in bulk, but at the present moment I think we need bottle displays at global trade shows and exhibitions.
>
> I think we can explore ways to grow the small niche of people who are already interested in Asian, specifically Japanese, culture. People who have a strong interest in the

culture of Japan would be more likely to try new products coming from Japan. If we can get new products in front of them via Asian-fusion restaurants and bars for example, or to speciality shows where they already frequent for Asian goods.

Furthermore, there should be more participation in overseas exhibitions as much as possible. This not only includes the big distilleries that currently participate but also the smaller distilleries that may not have as many opportunities or know-how. In fact, part of my mission is to become a bridge for some of the smaller distilleries to reach larger audiences.

Likewise, I would like to see more participation in tasting events and international spirits competitions. Speaking of which, I propose a separate category specific for awamori. Awamori is similar but it's not shochu. To lump it in the same category as shochu – 'Thai rice' or kome shochu is inaccurate. Ryukyu awamori is unique to Okinawa and is capable of standing on its own. – Maurice Dudley

How to Enjoy Shochu

Now we come to the second biggest appeal of shochu – the serving methods. Half the fun of discovering shochu is playing around with the kind of style that works best for you and here are some of the most popular ways to try honkaku:

Mizuwari Mixing shochu with a splash of cold water.

Oyuwari Adding hot water to shochu. Can help to bring out certain aromas in your drink.

Maewari Preparing your own bottle of mizuwari mix twenty-four hours before you plan to drink it. Great for dinner parties!

Hanatare freezing This method is for hanatare (high ABV shochu). Stick it in the freezer and enjoy it ice cold.

More Shochu to Try

To truly appreciate the shochu universe, it's worth checking out at least one bottle from the five main types of sweet potato, barley, brown sugar, rice and buckwheat before venturing off into more adventurous territory. Here are some of my favourite recommendations and because I'm a shochu overachiever (or possibly a functioning alcoholic), there isn't just one bottle per category for you to try.

Sweet potato

Kuro Kirishima is one of the most well-travelled sweet potato shochu on the market. It's produced by the Kirishima Shuzo brewing company in Kyushu and celebrates the legacy of the first shochu made at the brewery by the founder Kichisuke Enatsu in 1916.

Made with black koji, this shochu has a pleasant fruity aroma with hints of melon and citrus. There's a crisp aftertaste and smoky notes that come through on the first sip, a complex, smooth and well-rounded pour. Kuro Kirishima is ideal for cold weather and you can drink it neat or try warming it up oyuwari style with some warm water.

Satsuma Shiranami is a milder and sweeter imo shochu made by the Satsuma Distillery in Kagoshima. It has a musky, woody scent that is deceptive because it disguises that sweetness that will hit your mouth. It's a light beverage with hidden layers.

Sekitoba produced by Hamada Shuzo in Kagoshima has a candy-like bite to it. It's medium-bodied and full flavoured with sugary notes that work their way around your mouth and works well drank neat or with warm water.

Another good sweet potato shochu for the shochu beginner is Satsuma Shima Bijin. It's a sessionable spirit that's a common addition to shochu bars across the world because of its accessibility. It's light, earthy where it counts and gets even better on the second and third sips.

Kaido Blue from the Hamada Syuzou Distillery is an interesting product too because it carries the official Satsuma shochu GI that I talked about earlier in this chapter. The distillery is focused on showcasing the very best of what the sweet potato category is capable of.

Kaido Blue comes in a (you guessed it) bright blue bottle that sports a pair of Japanese wrestlers on the front (perhaps they've been drinking shochu and it put them in a good mood). There's a powerful earthy aroma that comes out as soon as the bottle is opened. Cereal, petrol, nuts. The savouriness carries on in the first sip, with toast and mushroom fighting for attention and then giving way to the flavour of breadsticks in the middle of the mouth.

There's a lot of bite in the mouthfeel, evening out into a smooth and mellow textures with a couple more sips. The finish is dry and lingers at the back of the mouth, bringing to mind a crisp autumn wind that has seasonal appeal in the colder months. In terms of serving styles, you can enjoy Kaido blue neat, with cold or warm water.

Barley

A leading barley shochu you absolutely have to try is Iichiko. With a name that translates to 'it's great', Iichiko has a high level of craftsmanship involved in the distillation process. Produced by the Sanwa Shurai Company in Oita Prefecture, the shochu is created with soft, geothermal-rich water, two-row barley and koji. It's a true expression of Oita Prefecture's impressive natural resources.

The barley is polished to remove impurities and steeped in the water. Then, the barley is steamed and prepared for the starch-to-sugar conversion process that's necessary for producing alcohol. This process is kickstarted by the koji and the mould is essential for preserving the barley's natural flavour through the release of citric acid.

The Sanwa brewery then distils the Iichiko mash using a combination of low pressure and atmospheric techniques. The raw mass is then blended together to create the unique profile of Iichiko.

As for tasting notes, an attractive, fruity aroma escapes from the bottle, setting the stage for what's to come. A mild, pleasant burn builds on the tongue and is accompanied by notes of lychee, walnut and oat. This contrast of sweet and savoury hits on the first sip and grows stronger at the back of the mouth. The next wave of flavour comes in a refreshing tartness that cleans the palate, making way for herbal, astringent qualities.

Whisky drinkers will find a lot to enjoy about the barley category and a good representation of said whisky-like qualities comes with Kannako, which translates to 'river protected by the gods', and is associated with a stream in South Kagoshima. Aged for three years in oak barrels, Kannako has a warm, woody texture that you get in a smooth Scotch.

A more unusual barley shochu is Majo no Itazaura, a playful, potent drink that's ideal for the colder months. Produced by the Yamato Brewery of Saga prefecture, the Majo no Itazura shochu has something of an identity crisis because of its name. Roughly translating to 'witch's kiss' in English, a quick Google search of the Japanese phrase reveals the kind of imagery that would look right at home in a hentai collection. The label has plenty of hex appeal though, showing a witch riding her broomstick against a golden moon. Her ever-faithful black cat clings to the top, looking out into the night sky.

'What the hell am I smelling?' was the first thought that came to mind when I poured the first cup. Pumpkins and roasted vegetables were the answer. A smoky, rich aroma that rushed in like an autumn breeze. Then I was blindsided by a powerful hit of pork scratchings in the mouth. Completely bizarre and completely awesome.

The savoury qualities built up until I was tasting stray notes of Yorkshire pudding and rye bread. They came at the back of the mouth, surrounded by a wall of whisky smoke courtesy of the roasted barley.

The Witch's Kiss also proved to be versatile in how it can be served. I tested it out with a mix of cold water and noticed that the harsher flavours were tamed. I also tried it with hot water and noticed that the whisky flavours cut through. The final verdict? Somewhere between a liquid roast dinner and a whisky lover's dream.

Brown sugar

Tatsugo Gold from Machida Shuzo is a great brown sugar shochu to dip your toe into this category. Named after the city of Tatsugo, the drink is a blend of three different types of shochu, which is matured for at least ten years in different barrels. This includes cognac barrels, stainless steel tanks and white oak barrels. Safe to say this process creates an awesome bouquet of flavour. Tatsugo Gold has a floral scent that reminds me of the light qualities of a good gin. Notes of lychee, strawberry and apple flood into the mouth. This sweetness makes the Tatsugo gold stand apart from savoury shochu like barley.

An aftertaste of vanilla comes in towards the end, silky and smooth. The overall mellowness of the drink is incredible, made even better when sipped on the rocks. Definitely liquid gold.

There's also the beautiful sounding, beautiful tasting Sango, which means coral in Japanese. This is straight from the Amami Islands and is tank-aged for one year and doesn't have any colour compared to its barrel-aged kin. This one is particularly rum-like with the notes that come out of it, mixed with a dryness that cuts in at the end.

Rice

A kome shochu to get you started is Kinjo Shiro from Takahashi Shuzo from the Hitoyoshi Kuma region of Kumamoto Prefecture. Stories point towards Kuma shochu being the oldest known in Japan. This is substantiated by the oldest remaining record of shochu being discovered in the shrine I mentioned earlier where a pissed-off carpenter scrawled graffiti on the wall about the priests being stingy about sharing their shochu.

At the time the message was written the Sagara clan were highly active. Their territory reached beyond the modern day borders that surround Kagoshima Prefecture and Kumamoto, so there is evidence the shochu being referred to by the carpenter was Kuma shochu.

Kinjo Shiro follows in the proud legacy of Kuma shochu. It's been aged in three different barrels: American white oak, cognac and sherry. Vacuum-distilled and bottled at 25% ABV, the shochu comes in an elegant bottle with a beautiful label of the sun shining against a golden backdrop.

On the nose, it smells of cream, yoghurt and bubblegum. It's smooth to the taste, the yoghurty notes ramping up and combining with rye bread, caramel and rice. It's a robust and light product that mixes and matches sweet and savoury flavours.

Another rice shochu to keep an eye out for his Sennen Nebosuke. You'll recognise it by its white logo with a sleepy, smiling face and the name of the bottle loosely translates to 'overslept for a thousand years'. It's a clean and smooth crowd-pleaser, best enjoyed at lower temperatures with ice or mixed with cold water.

Buckwheat

A good introduction to the buckwheat category is Takara Shuzo's Towari brand. As with other bottles, I've experimented with trying Towari in a few different styles. Drinking Towari with ice reveals a mellow, smooth texture that bursts with flavours of rye bread, melon, earth, mushroom and peach. It goes down easily and comes off with a short finish.

When trying the shochu straight, the earthier notes become stronger. The verdict is that Towari is a shapeshifting kind of shochu that'll please beginners and enthusiasts. There's a strong balance of flavours, a sessionable texture and a clean finish that'll leave room for more.

Awamori

Awamori is its own thing and the bottles I've chosen for this section are a reflection of its diversity. Udisan No Sake Awamori is a delicious floral concoction that conjures images of clear skies and tropical beaches.

It's produced by the Miyanohana Brewery, which is located on Irabu Island, a landmass that's roughly 300km southwest of the main island of Okinawa. Founded in 1948, the brewery was named after a flower of Miyako that was meant to represent the beauty of the island.

The brewery is special in the fact that over 80 per cent of the workforce are women. In an industry that's typically male-dominated it's great to see women being able to leave their own mark and produce an awamori that's truly unique. The name 'Udisan' is a Ryukyu word that translates to joy in English and that's really the perfect way to sum up every aspect of the drink. The bottle is beautiful, a bright, luminous blue that's meant to represent a summer sky over Okinawa.

An interesting part of the distillation process is that Udisan doesn't go with the indica Thai rice that awamori is made with. Instead, the Miyanohana brewery decided to throw caution to the wind and do something different. The brewery uses domestic Hinohikari rice that is cultivated in Kumamoto without the use of fertilisers or pesticides. The rice is delivered fresh and has an important effect on the overall taste of Udisan.

The product has a striking smell, yeasty and rich. It's like breathing in the scent of freshly baked bread. The richness carries on through the mouth, with notes of oak, strawberry yoghurt, rice and toasted rye bread standing out.

The strong umami flavours are balanced by a sweetness that appears at the back of the mouth. A bit of bubblegum mixed with liquorice mixed with apple pie. A lovely surprise that reflects the complexity.

Harasume Kari awamori is produced by the tiny Miyazato Distillery that's been making some of the finest Ryukyu awamori for over sixty years. The brewery was founded in 1946 on the tropical island of Naha.

Aged for three years, Harasume Kari has a clean aroma that masks complex flavours. The first sip reveals vivid notes of walnut and hazelnut undercut by traces of sweetness. The taste of fudge and cream burns in the mouth and crashes across the palate like a tsunami. Then, a third wave of flavour kicks in, carrying hints of vanilla and black pepper that leave behind a spicy aftertaste. Lingering notes of mushroom and ginger prickle on the tongue.

Yokka koji awamori is a fascinating spirit. It's made by the Chuko Distillery located in Tomigusuku city next to Naha. Led by the third-generation owner Tsutomu Oshiro, the distillery has a mantra of 'the inheritance and creation of awamori culture'. Oshiro and his team are laser-focused on preserving the tradition of awamori, while passing it on to a new generation.

Chuko has come up with a number of innovations over the years, with perhaps the most famous being the creation of Ryukyu Gusukuyaki kame (clay pots). Designed by Oshiro's father Shigeru in 1989, these pots are specially designed for ageing awamori.

Another innovation is the unique recipe used for making Yokka Koji. Instead of a two-day koji fermentation, the distillery has taken it to the next level with a four-day fermentation, which is where the Yokka (four) name comes from.

According to Oshiro, the four-day fermentation changes 'the amylase, protease and lipases enzymes produced in the fermentation. For ageing the awamori we raise the temperature for the first half of the fermentation and then lower it in the second half.'

By applying this precise level of control, Chuko have instilled some unique flavours into the spirit.

Smelling the Yokka Koji is like breathing in the scent of a forest floor in spring. There's notes of pine, pear, apple and peach in the air. These primal, fruity textures continue in the mouth, with apple and mushroom being the dominant flavours.

Towards the back of the mouth rye bread and green pepper creep in, leaving behind a spicy, spiky aftertaste and a strong finish. An earthy, complex spirit that's sure to grab whisky drinkers from the first sip.

Miscellaneous

As for niche shochu, a brand I recommend is Tantatakatan, which translates to 'flat fish'. Its main ingredient is shisho, a ubiquitous Japanese plant cultivated in Hokkaido. Tantakatan comes from the Godo Shusei company and is made in Asahikawa in Hokkaido. In terms of flavour, this shochu is delicate, fruity and floral. The shiso is the star flavour, backed by notes of blueberry, anise and ginger that leave behind a spicy aftertaste.

There's a great story attached to this shochu based on the Ainu legend of the fish Tan Taka. The Ainu are the native culture of Northeast Honshu and Hokkaido, a culture with a strong attachment to nature. The story begins near Shiranuka in Hokkaido in the sea where the fish lived peacefully.

One day, the sea became polluted and the fish struggled to survive. Tan Taka lived at the bottom of the sea and had the energy to swim. He decided to help the other fish and was persuaded by a wise turtle to fetch a purple herb from the foot of the nearby mountain that could heal the fish.

Tan Taka swam up waterfalls and rivers until he found the herbs. The healing properties cured his fatigue, but he was unable to get the herbs because they were on land. The local animals decided to help Tan Taka and dropped the herbs into the water for him.

Mission accomplished, Tan Taka returned to the sea and cured his friends. The mountain became known as Tan Taka Mountain and the herbs that had been gathered were shiso perilla leaves.

Another niche shochu to try is Beniotome Red Maiden Black, which is made from sesame seeds. The Red Maiden is produced by the Beniotome distillery located in the town of Kurume in Fukuoka Prefecture at Kyushu. The drink is a testament to the hard work and craftsmanship of one woman: Haruno Hayashida.

The wife of a local sake brewer, Haruno lived and breathed the sake production lifestyle, but she wanted to create something that was hers. She experimented tirelessly with shochu production until finally coming up with a unique recipe in 1978 at the age of 65.

Haruno's shochu is made from black sesame, barley, black koji and is aged for three years in steel tanks. Bottled at 25% ABV, the Red Maiden is an award-winning drink that has picked up accolades such as the Best Gold Award at the Monde Selection 2009.

Despite the delicate-sounding name, the Red Maiden has plenty of complexity churning beneath the surface. An aroma of chestnuts, oak and shiitake mushrooms gather on the nose. These savoury notes carry on into an earthy mouthfeel that sticks to the palate, dancing between spicy and sour. Hints of roasted coffee, toast and sesame seeds linger in the mouth for some time. There's an overriding oiliness to the shochu that makes it both light and deceptively filling at the same time.

Chapter 9
Soju

Search any streaming platform and you'll find Korean TV shows consistently ranked as some of the most highly rated among viewers. Go for a walk in a major city and you'll find Korean barbecue restaurants filled with people from all walks of life. Search YouTube and you'll find videos of K-pop music singers and bands with millions of views and subscribers.

This phenomenon is called 'Hallyu', or the Korean Wave that's been sweeping across the world for the past two decades. It's the celebration of various aspects of South Korean culture, including music, television dramas, fashion, film, beauty trends, food and of course alcohol. Specifically, Korean soju is becoming more and more popular at home and in foreign markets.

Commenting on this link between Korean alcohol and the Hallyu phenomenon, writer Hyunhee Park said:

> dramas and advertising often convey scenes of social gatherings in Korean society, where people look natural drinking soju and eating classic grilled meat dishes. The placement of soju in such dramas has dramatically increased overseas demand and export, and this trend will continue as long as the Korean Wave persists.[1]

According to a survey done by *The Korea Times*, soju is the most recognised Korean beverage among international consumers, with 35.1 per cent of people who took part in the survey saying they recognised it because they liked the taste, 16 per cent because of recommendations from others and 15.5 per cent from seeing it in K-dramas and movies.[2]

While well-known brands like Jinro are capitalising on this trend, this popularity can also be a double-edged sword. For soju is sometimes maligned as a soulless, industrial Korean vodka. But it's much more than that and has a history running as deep as the foundations of Korea.

Soju Origins

Soju is a distilled beverage traditionally made from rice but is more likely to be made from grains and starches like barley, sweet potatoes and tapioca in the modern day. The distinctive green bottle soju drunk in Korean restaurants is made from the latter ingredients and is a recent phenomenon, as explained by Bobby Yoon, owner and founder of the New York-based Korean barbecue joint Yoon Haeundae Galbi: 'In the 1950s, when Korean companies were banned from making soju out of rice because it was needed to feed people during the Korean War, companies imported tapioca from Southeast Asia and that's how the green bottle started.'[3] This green bottle stuff makes up 90 per cent of the market, according to Jesse Vida of the Cat Bite Club based in Singapore.[4]

When you trace soju back to its early days, there is fascinating history to discover that starts in Korea's ancient past, with spirits like Chinese baijiu and arak, a spirit popular in the Middle East, Central Asia and the Mediterranean.

The technology needed for making these drinks would have naturally passed over through the cross-cultural exchanges that ancient Korea shared with its neighbours, via the Silk Roads, all of which are corroborated by Chinese and Japanese sources. For example, a Chinese source called the *Youyang zazu* (The Miscellaneous Morsels from Youyang) comments that Koreans had their own distinctive good-tasting booze that could compete with Chinese offerings.

For Korean sources, the two oldest documents on Korean history *Samguk Sagi* (History of the Three Kingdoms) and *Samguk yusa* (Memorabilia of the Three Kingdoms), claim that there were several varieties of Korean alcohol knocking around in the late Koryo period (ad 982–1392) of which these texts were written. The varieties included chiju and mion, high-quality liquor and yorye, a kind of cloudy rice wine.[5] Another early Korean drink that was likely to have been popular is makgeolli, a sparkling rice wine with a milky colour and sweet, bitter taste.

Yet more weird and wonderful varieties of Korean liquor are spoken of with affection by the thirteenth-century poet Yi Kyubo, who could give the legendary drunken Chinese poet Li Bai a run for his money with the amount of alcohol he consumed and wrote about. In Kyubo's poetry there's talk of ihwaju (pear-blossom liquor), chaju (boiled or cooked liquor), hwaju (flower liquor) pip'aju (liquor flavoured with pipa fruit) and paekchu (white liquor).

What this diversity shows is that by the time distillation came to Korea, there was already a wide base for soju to develop from, and this is where the Mongols come in.

The popularisation of soju and arak occurred through the Mongol invasion and domination of the Korean peninsula throughout the thirteenth and fourteenth centuries. Although there is no definitive evidence that the origins of these drinks can be traced directly to the Mongol Empire, it's worth considering the Mongol habit of adapting and assimilating various cultural techniques into their territories and how it influenced the Koryo-era Koreans that they subjugated. Park elaborates further on this connection in her excellent *Soju: A Global History*:

> Some soldiers in the Mongol army came from Southern China, where people distilled grain-fermented alcoholic liquor. Such a method of distilling grain, called shaojiu (Korean soju) by Chinese in the southern part of China, could have worked better in Koryo, and soju made with local grains such as rice and barley could have become popular in Korea.[6]

She goes on to say:

> the fact that soju and arak in Mongol-era Korea were almost identical to shaojiu and arak in Mongol-run China in terms of both of the Chinese characters that compose their written names and also their characteristics as alcoholic beverages, strongly suggests that it developed from an original transference to Korea from China.[7]

This perspective is further backed up by soju being mentioned in the *Koryosa,* the definitive text on the history of the Koryo period. Soju is first mentioned in a biography of the general Ch'oe Yong and introduces a general called Kim Chin under his command who loved soju too much and failed to do his duty:

> Because Kim Chin enjoyed drinking soju, people in the army called him and his men the 'soju group'. And because he assaulted and insulted his soldiers and assistants if they displeased him, they all possessed resentments and grudges against him.[8]

There's another section of the *Koryosa* that details prohibition restrictions and mentions that there was an edict in 1375 that banned the purchasing of soju and other luxury items like gold, silk and jade wares, suggesting that soju was a new and exotic item that Korean nobility wanted to splurge on.

Through these trade systems and cultural swaps laid down by Korea's contact with China and the Mongol Empire, the table was set for soju to rise into being Korea's national drink.

The Rise of Soju

After the ruling Koryo dynasty (which had been allied with the Mongol Empire for decades) fell, the Choson dynasty rose in its place. This officially started the Choson era in 1392 and lasted up to 1897 until it was replaced by the Great Korean Empire.

During this era, Koreans developed practices, systems and beliefs that had been established in the previous era, including the continued development of soju. A prime location for this development was Cheju, an island in the Korean Strait where Mongol occupation had created a lasting Mongol heritage. As the island had a humid environment, it made it difficult for fermented beverages to be preserved and so distillation became necessary.

As was the case in the Koryo period, soju was classified as a range of spirits. Passages from Choson chronicles list chasoju (purple soju), paeksoju (white soju), hongsoju (red soju) made with single and double distillation. Other sources from the period refer to a kind of infused soju that featured ginseng and cinnamon, with all varieties being viewed as a luxury item, a high-value gift for exchange and medicine.

Physical evidence of the exact production volume of Choson-era soju and distilleries is lost to the annals of time, although there is the suggestion that the spirit was produced on a small scale across all aspects of society, from the home to the royal court.

This can be gleaned from a 1459 book called *An Essential Record of Farming Villages* by the distinguished court doctor Chon Sunui (he also wrote a medical text called *A Collection of Various Kinds of Medical Arts* in which he wrote about soju seven times as a solution to different kind of diseases). As the oldest cookbook in the history of Korea, it features recipes for 229 foods and drinks, and Sunui wrote about how to make soju:

> How to get soju
> Pour five bowls of water into a large cauldron and simmer it. Then mix it with 1.5 toe of rice flour and make a porridge [with a consistency] like water made from washing rice. While still warm, put it in a jar and seal it, and after three to four days, it will smell sour and stinky. Steam one mal of glutinous rice and mix it with three toe of qu [yeast, Korean nuruk] powder, put it in the aforementioned jar, and wait it to mature. After that, divide the aged mixture into four pots. From each pot comes four toe of soju.[9]

All in all, Chon Sunui's recipes demonstrate that although soju wasn't as diverse as it would become in later years, it was a staple speciality drink of Korean households and inspired the creation of more cookbooks and soju recipes into the later Choson period.

This is where the development of Andong soju comes in. Made in the southern eastern region of Andong in Korea, this soju is the most famous traditional brand today. This was a region where yangbang, aristocratic Choson families, lived and practised Neo-Confucian principles that meant entertaining guests was an important part of their culture. This led to the advancement of food and drink culture and prompted the writing of more cookbooks to assert family legacy.

The first Andong cookbook was written in 1540 by Kim Yu and featured 121 recipes. The second most notable text, called *Recipes For Tasty Food*, was published in 1670, written by Chang Kyehyang, also known as 'Chang, Lady of Andong'. As the first cookbook ever written by a woman in East Asia, Chang's text has been used as a window into seeing how women lived during this period.

It's safe to assume that women from clans traded food and alcohol recipes but were unlikely to have recorded much. This is possibly because of the patriarchal Confucian culture that frowned on women writing and publishing, or that any books like Chang's were passed down privately between women from generation to generation.

To further understand Choson-era soju, it's worth looking at the type of distillation stills that were being used. At home, the most popular vessel was called a kori. This small, portable still was used to distil fermented liquids. At the Choson royal court, a large silver still was used along with silver pots to make red soju. This method would have been too expensive for regular households. A third kind of still called a kosori became popular on Cheju island. This was a one-piece porcelain vessel different from a two-piece kori.

It was through the continued development of these stills that various types of soju could be created. Red soju became one of the most popular types and a recipe from 1554 states it could be made by distilling,

> three bottles and two pokcha (one pokcha = 450 ml) of hyangonju, a kind of strained wine and then you will get one bottle of liquor. In the course of distillation, cut one nyang of chach'o (Chinese zhicao), into thin pieces and put it in a bowl that receives the alcohol drops. Then you will receive hongnoju that is dyed a rich red colour.[10]

Then there's kamhongno (sweetened soju) that's made after two to three rounds of distillation. The recipe for making it involved spreading honey and chach'o at the bottom of the receiving bowl during the distillation, producing a sweet, high-quality, crimson liquid.

These types of soju flowed through Korean society for their entertainment qualities and supposedly curative qualities. But as with every culture, people were preaching about the dangers of excessive alcohol consumption as much as there were others who 100 per cent believed it to be a curative.

In the influential Korean medical text *Tongui pogam* there are several references to the health hazards of drinking too much soju.

Contrast this with the work of the Choson dynasty creator Kwon Kun, who in his writings recorded an episode of soju being used to cure indigestion. This story involved an Official Kim, who once had a guest that seemed to be dying from severe pain and powerful indigestion. The official told his guest to drink two cups of soju for an easy remedy. After drinking the soju, the guest became drunk, causing him to cough hard and then vomit up chunks of meat filled with live insects. (At least the indigestion symptoms were gone, according to the story.)

Soju's medical properties weren't reserved for the noble class. A diary entry from Yi Munkun, a Choson noble living in the sixteenth century, shows that servants treated soju as a cure-all. Another entry tells of how blind fortune tellers showed up at Munkun's house to offer their services and they received a fee of soju, rice, red beans, paper, fans and booze bowls.

As soju continued to rise in popularity, many writers saw this as a social phenomenon worth commenting on, with the seventeenth-century writer Yi Sungwang saying:

> soju is a liquor that arose in the time of the Yuan dynasty. As it was taken only as a medicine, it was not used haphazardly. Due to this, it became custom that small cups were called soju cups. In the present day, however, those of upper status drink great quantities to their hearts' content; in the summer, they drink much soju from large cups. Drinking their fill and becoming drunk like this has caused many a person to suddenly die.[11]

Despite the warnings from writers and court officials, the overconsumption of soju went on until the introduction of the Liquor Prohibition Law in 1758. A law that was enacted several times, the regulations stipulated the banning of all alcohol and as we've seen from previous chapters, any time an alcohol ban comes along the first card to get played for getting around it is medicinal alcohol. Korean nobility drank yakchu, 'medicinal wine' to get through these rough patches.

Health wasn't the main concern for the Liquor Prohibition Law. The main reason it was introduced was to save grain, meaning soju acted as the main target for the law because the making of it consumed grain.

In the end, this didn't work. Once the genie of soju had been released from the bottle, there was no putting it back in. It had become a drink that the Korean people couldn't do without and its reputation would truly be solidified into the twentieth century.

Modern Soju

The next phase of soju's development arguably didn't start in Korea. It started on the other side of the world with the Industrial Revolution of the eighteenth century which expanded capitalism across Europe and allowed Western superpowers to grow their colonies in Asia.

By the nineteenth century, China and Japan had been forced to open their doors to the West and it was only a matter of time before Korea would have to do the same. At first, the Koreans refused and didn't give in to the pressure from naval attacks in 1866 from France or in 1871 from America. The Japanese finally decided to deal with their stubborn neighbours.

In 1875, a Japanese warship called *Unyo Maryu* attacked the Ganghwado and Yeongjongdo Islands. In no uncertain terms, the Japanese spelt out their demands – that Korea should open its doors to foreign trade missions. With constant pressure, Korea was forced to sign the Gangwha Treaty, a one-sided arrangement that gave the Japanese increasing economic and governing powers over Korea.

Attempting to maintain some level of autonomy, the ruling Korean family changed the name of its regime to the Great Korean Empire and pushed forward with reforms and an open-door policy. However, the writing was already on the wall. Japan had won a series of victories against Russia and the Chinese Qing dynasty, making the Land of the Rising Sun more powerful than it had ever been. By 1910, the Korean Empire had officially been annexed into the Empire of Japan and this would last until 1945.

This changing of the guard had a massive impact on soju. The most notable change being that traditional soju distilling methods established in the Choson period declined in favour of Western industrial distillation the Japanese had adapted for their own use. Instead of a kori being used for distillation, a continuous still became the preferred method.

Jinro, the biggest soju manufacturer in the world, rose out of this machine of mass-produced alcohol. Founded in 1924 in South Pyongan

Province by Chang Hak-yeop, Jinro was a small company that used a monkey as a label because of the animal's association with good luck. In 1950, with the outbreak of the Korean War, the founder's family fled to South Korea and revived the Jinro name four years later.[12]

With this revival came a change in logo and the monkey was replaced with a toad, a sign of prosperity and long life. This label has certainly been auspicious, as Jinro accounts for 65 per cent of the 3.5 trillion won domestic soju market and aims to achieve 500 billion won ($362 million) in overseas soju sales by 2030.[13]

A book that provides deep insight into the sweeping changes that Japanese rule caused in the Korean alcohol industry is 1935's *Choson shuzoshi*. It was written by Japanese scholars who came to Korea to research various fields under the supervision of the Office of the Governor General of Korea and described the general situation of alcohol production in the country before the year it was written.

The overall sentiment of the book is that prior to Japanese practices, the development of soju was inferior and lacked modern technology. The researchers who wrote it made a big song and dance about the lack of hygiene regulation in the making of home-brewed soju, which compelled the Japanese government to introduce taxes and systems to promote hygiene in soju production.

Based on these Japanese changes, Park says that Korean distillers introduced 'new-style' soju:

> Distillers first made high-percentage alcohol (up to 95 per cent) like ethanol spirit from cheaper materials like potatoes or tapioca instead of grains like rice, and then added water and sweeteners such as sugar, glucose, citric acid, saccharin, amino acids and sorbitol to enhance flavour. This event marks the rise of the modern form of industrial soju in Korea, which has remained the country's dominant variety.[14]

Korean independence finally came in 1945, with the US and USSR splitting up the country into two zones ruled over by separate states, the Southern Republic of Korea and the Northern Democratic Republic of Korea. Five years later, the war broke out and people on both sides of the divide experienced horrific poverty and devastation. In these changing circumstances, soju once again went through a metamorphosis.

Throughout the next twenty years, industrial soju remained in the spotlight, thanks to full-scale government involvement. By the 1970s, 300 domestic soju companies were up and running across twenty-four provinces, with each of them being forced to promote a major soju brand that represented the regional style. Otherwise, they would be shut down.

The government rationalised this decision by saying it was for quality control. The real reason was to increase profits collected from tax, creating a state-run monopoly that controlled and distributed ethanol to these distillers. These cartel-like tactics, coupled with the poor conditions that people living in the south were subjected to under the dictatorship of President Park Chung Hee, led to industrial soju being the most widely consumed alcoholic beverage in the country.

It wasn't until the 1980s that the government finally decided to put traditional soju back in the spotlight. Recognising the grief that Koreans felt towards ancestral drinks being suppressed due to strict taxation and government interference, the powers that be launched a campaign to promote a Korean national alcoholic drink called minsokchu, which encouraged the revival of traditional soju methods that had fallen out of favour since Japanese rule.

Two prominent examples of this happened in 1986 at the Asian Games and in 1988 at the Olympics in Seoul. Special licences were handed out to distilleries with the experience to make traditional soju and these products were then sold at high prices and used as gifts, leading to a resurgence of interest. However, it's hard to determine whether this minsokchu was based on authentic recipes from the past. Distillers wanted to secure their position by providing the state with cookbooks they claimed were handed down by ancestors, but these soju recipes were often identical to each other.

Even with the increased production of traditional soju, the industrial stuff has remained at the top of the market because of its price point and accessibility. The 1980s was also the decade in which a distinctive drinking culture of industrial soju developed, namely bomb shots/bomb cocktails. This involved blending beer and soju together, increasing alcohol strength and getting rid of bad tastes in either the beer or the soju. These bomb shots became popular at parties and a hallmark of gatherings at Korean restaurants.

As of the twenty-first century, soju reached new heights with the popularity of Korean culture spreading to the West. Korean restaurants have spread all over the world and a strong association with Korean meat dishes and soju has developed, in the same way consumers might compare Japanese sake with sushi.

There are several reasons for this growing popularity. The first is the 'Korean Wave' of pop culture that has spread far and wide, with savvy soju companies finding ways to get their products advertised by K-pop singers and actors and to appear in films. The second is through the lowering of alcohol content since the start of the millennium.

At one point, it was frowned upon for soju brands to create products of 20% ABV or lower. Since 2000, the domestic alcohol market has been trending towards lower ABV, with 16.5% being the norm by 2009. By dropping the strength, soju brands have been able to appeal to a larger customer base of young drinkers and women.[15]

A third factor is the development of Western soju brands like US-based Tokki (Rabbit). Founder Brandon Hill became interested in the flow of industrial soju that was running through New York and travelled to Korea to learn about it. On his travels, he fell in love with traditional soju and returned to Brooklyn to start a company that used distillation machines similar to the production of whisky to make soju from Choson-era recipes with the inclusion of rice. Tokki took off in the States and even found its way into Korea by way of illegal smuggling.

Tokki's popularity also opened the debate as to what 'traditional' soju is. Oddly, instead of from Korea, it started in the US. An American writer named Joshua Schenkkan wrote a newspaper article questioning whether Tokki can be called traditional if it's made in Brooklyn with modern machinery. Schenkkan interviewed various industry people, getting a range of opinions. Naturally, this is a complex subject with many perspectives and there will always be interesting points on both sides of the fence no matter what spirit we're talking about. The most important thing in my opinion is that one should respect the traditions of a culture while not being afraid to put one's own spin on something, especially in the pursuit of raising more awareness of a category.

Another soju created in the cauldron of Korean and American fusion is Yobo. Founder Carolyn Kim wanted to celebrate her heritage while creating a spirit that would be a hit with Western consumers. Her flagship product was made with wine grapes and comes in an elegant bottle that differentiates itself from industrial soju.

Kim had this to say about her project, which has since grown into a wide range of soju varieties, like Yobo Original and Luxe under the Yobo Spirits banner:

> I wanted to push the envelope and make soju from a raw material that had never been used for soju – grapes made sense because they have a natural elegance. I also wanted to create something native to New York State, which I consider my second home … Moving away from 100 per cent grapes for Yobo Luxe was a hard choice. But adding wheat and rice felt like a homage to traditional soju, which was made from grain. The wheat adds a layer of softness to the formula and the rice brings a little funk and character that I love.[16]

Kim has also been candid with her thoughts on how the Korean Wave is impacting soju and what an American influence for the category means:

> One of the most eye-opening things about this journey is experiencing how quickly people embrace new preferences for music, movies, food, and drink. Before *Parasite* and *Squid Game* were on the map … we felt a lot of resistance within the American and Korean drinks industries on the viability of an American-made soju that did not emulate tradition. Korean cuisine was experiencing a big surge in popularity in the US, so we had a sense that drinks would follow. Still, we could not imagine the way that different Korean cultural phenomena took centre stage in pop culture and also helped generate curiosity about Yobo …
>
> My spin on soju comes from wanting to create something that is rooted in Korean culture but is also an expression of my Korean-American-ness – a layered identity. Yobo is definitely not a traditional Korean soju. As far as I know, Yobo was the first soju made from grapes, possibly even fruit. And it continues to evolve, all while using natural base ingredients that create a clean yet aromatic flavour.[17]

Americans aren't the only ones putting their spin on Korea's national spirit. Australians Paul Wheatley and Damian Kent decided to create a soju brand called Hoju (Australia) out of a love of Korean culture and to celebrate their own culture too. The co-founders embarked on a journey of research in the making of their soju:

> Several years ago, we stumbled across this cool little Korean BBQ place that was bustling with energy and excitement. They had soju on the menu – something we had only heard about but never tried before. We really enjoyed the non-flavoured version and not realising at the time, the seed was planted.
>
> Fast forward to the COVID-19 lockdown, we toyed around with a few product ideas – but kept circling back to soju and that memorable experience at the Korean BBQ. We saw an opportunity to produce a larger, premium version, using only locally sourced ingredients.
>
> Putting a premium and more responsible spin on how people can consume soju, it was important it looked great in a bottle, on-shelf or behind the bar and was large enough to share with friends at a party. Hoju Soju is one of the most versatile spirits around. Being lower in ABV at 17%, it's delicious, chilled or neat and perfect for cocktails.
>
> We compared as much non-flavoured soju as we could find. From there, we conducted a blind tasting to decide if our own flavour palate aligned before searching for someone who could help us create our own version. We delivered our research notes to several distillers around the basic constituents and traditional production methods. Soju … should start with a grain-based ferment and be traditionally made with rice. We started (and failed) using rice and grains, before eventually landing on locally grown wheat grain as the best option.
>
> Once we had a liquid that we were happy with, we carried out tastings with a group of experts that included chefs, sommeliers, bartenders, Korean businessmen, distillers, family, friends and more.[18]

Then there's Isae soju, Germany's only soju brand which is made from winter wheat and organic rice. The name means 'second generation' and is a nod to the family of the founders who immigrated to Germany in the 1960s. A major selling point of the brand is that it rejects flavour additives found in industrial soju and aims to put the traditional variety back on the map in small batches.

These examples are just a handful of the soju range that's out there waiting to be discovered by you. What began as an obscure drink in Korea has exploded into an international movement I predict will continue to go from strength to strength, long after the Korean Wave has died down and the next one rises up.

Soju is here to stay.

Chapter 10

Bartenders

Friend at the bar. Counsellor. Shoulder to cry on. Stranger to share good news with. Interlocutor. These are some of the roles your local bartender might fulfil for you, along with the job of making and serving drinks. The fact is the hospitality industry can't work without them and there wouldn't be any creativity or innovation in any drinks category. Bartenders have always been at the centre of drink revolutions, developing cocktails that have stood the test of time and running bars that have become the stuff of legend.

In this chapter, we'll look at the lives of some of the most influential bartenders in history and examine their contributions to the spirits zeitgeist. A fitting place to start is with the godfather of cocktail making.

The World's First Mixologist

> JERRY THOMAS DEAD – New York's Famous Old Barkeeper a Victim of Apoplexy[1]

Splashed across the front page of the New York paper *The World* on 15 December 1885, this headline signalled the end of an era and the beginning of a new one. Jerry 'The Professor' Thomas, the founding father of American cocktail culture, had died not long after leaving New York's Hotel Brighton at Broadway and 42nd Street. When Thomas got through the door of his home, he collapsed and died of a stroke, aged 55.

It was an ignoble end for a man who had lived an iconic American life long before he became famous behind the bar. A journeyman sailor, gold prospector, art collector, gambler and theatrical impresario, Thomas was a man of many professions and contradictions. He also set the gold standard for cocktails, serving etiquette and American bar styles all over the world, cementing his legacy in the first bartender's guide: *How to Mix Drinks/The Bon Vivant's Companion* in 1862.

Born in 1830 in Sacketts Harbour, New York, Thomas got a taste for travelling early when his family moved out to New Haven, Connecticut. At 15, Thomas was plying his craft as an assistant bartender at a leading hotel in the city called the Park House, under the watchful eye of his older brother David, serving the young men of Yale who rubbed shoulders with mercurial bankers and hard-bitten sailors.

After a few years, Thomas' thirst for fortune and quest to slake his creativity sent him out west and he boarded a boat at 19 years old in 1849. His final destination on this trip was San Francisco, a city caught up in the mania of the Gold Rush, and instead of breaking his back in the dirt like so many other prospectors, Thomas saw there was golden opportunity to be found in what he'd always done best.

Joining the El Dorado hotel in Portsmouth Square, Thomas settled in and this is where many of the legends about his life first began. In an era of gunslingers, Thomas was a drink slinger who was as quick with his mind as he was with his mouth and fists.

One story claims that a gang of desperados came into the El Dorado bar to steal everything that wasn't nailed down. Thomas offered them a drink of lethally mixed ingredients that knocked them on their asses. Because of Thomas' quick thinking, the local militia were able to arrest the gang and sentence them to death.

Another story tells of how Thomas put his reputation on the line when a giant gold miner demanded he make a drink to remember. Telling the man to come back in an hour, Thomas poured out a full tumbler of Scotch, filled another with near-boiling water and grabbed a sulphur match. He lit it, ignited the whisky and passed the flaming liquid into the other tumbler, creating a blue firestorm that settled into a glass. To top off the still-smoking drink, Thomas put in a dash of sugar and lime and presented it to the gobsmacked miner, who took a swig and keeled over. And so, the legendary Blue Blazer cocktail was born.[2]

Thomas' mad genius sparked 'the first American culinary art' of mixing drinks, according to *Imbibe!* author David Wondrich; 'It was the first American cultural product to catch the world's imagination,'[3] a product Thomas doubled down on with the flair and panache of a salesman magician.

In 1851, he went into show business, organising some of the earliest touring musicals in California. Dressed in flashy jewellery and never seen without his bar tools and cups embellished with precious stones and metals, Thomas went back to New York to open a saloon beneath Barnum's American Museum, the first of the four New York establishments he would run. Around this point, Thomas was earning $100 a week – more than the Vice President of the US.

But for all his grandstanding and flair, Thomas could never hold on to his wealth. He was a man who loved 'the sporting life' – owning and betting on fast horses, bare-knuckle fights and any other speculative activity he could turn his hand to. He was a member of the tribe of men who flaunted a veneer of wealth to disguise their poverty, who could win big one day and be broke again the next.

Still, no one could ever say the life of a sporting man wasn't adventurous. Thomas carried on building his bar empire, opening another New York tavern in 1860. Here he served distinguished guests like Queen Victoria's son, Edward Prince of Wales. So eager to be served by the 'Napoleon of Bar Keepers', Edward snuck out of his hotel one night to drink Mint Juleps by the one and only Thomas. In the morning, he was found stumbling alone in the streets.

In 1862, Thomas distilled his teachings and recipes into the first-ever drinks book published in the US. *How To Mix Drinks* contained knowledge that until that year had only been passed down through oral traditions on the early days of cocktails. Thomas included many of his own recipes and might have been able to grow fat and rich off his reputation and position at the Occidental Hotel in San Francisco. After all, he'd well and truly established himself as 'the Jupiter Olympus of the bar' and had nothing to prove.

Alas, the sporting life forever beckoned and Thomas returned to his rambling ways. His next stop? Virginia City, Nevada.

According to Wondrich:

> The fortunes of Thomas' book were likely affected by the Professor's next move: rather than stay at the Occidental (SF), where he could have passed the volume along to the steady stream of clay-moistening literati who stopped in at his bar, he pulled up stakes yet again and headed east to witness the vast and vulgar spectacle that was unfolding 200

> miles away in Virginia City, Nevada where a city of 30,000 had sprung up overnight on top of the massive mountain of silver known as the Comstock Lode. By 1864, Thomas was there, either (as local legend has it) at the famous Delta Saloon or at the Spalding Saloon on C Street, where the city directory found him – or, of course, at both.[4]

Towards the end of his life, Thomas tried speculating on Wall Street and was left broke because of bad decisions. Forced to sell off an impressive art collection he'd made over the years, the father of mixology's star had dimmed, evident from his struggle to open a new bar that didn't reach the popularity of his previous venues.

Then came his unceremonious stroke, but The Professor would not be forgotten. An outpouring of obituaries came out around the country for Thomas and there would never be another like him. His flair for bartending kicked open the door for countless others to follow in his footsteps.

The Cocktail Grifter

After Jerry Thomas ushered in the half-high art, half-money-making machine of mixing drinks, the First Golden Wave of cocktails swept the US and hopped aboard passenger ships and planes to Europe and beyond in a fever pitch of excitement that reached a peak in the 1920s and '30s. Iconic cocktails like the Mint Julep, Old Fashioned, Martini, Negroni and Daiquiri were all forged in a crucible of bartenders regularly pushing the envelope.

William 'Cocktail' Boothby was another giant who made all this possible. Sometimes called the patron saint of California bartenders, Boothby's talent for making drinks was matched only by the size of his ego.

Born into a family of Forty-Niner hustlers in 1862, Boothby learned from the can-do spirit of his parents early on. In his twenties, he went through a string of colourful jobs, including vaudeville jig dancer, tailor, real estate agent and 'patent medicine' salesman. Once, he spoke of the virtues of a magical remedy called Dr McConkey's Vigour of Life liver pills and as you can imagine, local journalists had a field-day whenever they caught him spinning a yarn or hucking another miracle cure-all.[5]

By the time he was 30, Boothby had also worked up some experience behind a bar and published the first edition of his book *Cocktail Boothby's American Bartender.* But not *that* much experience – he'd only worked at the Silver Palace on Geary Street in San Francisco and a few out-of-town resorts.

Despite being a greenhorn to the back bar, Boothby never wavered in confidence. He was prone to advertising his book whenever he could, using a favoured ad line of: 'Bar-Keepers – You're Not In It If You Don't Read Cocktail Boothby's American Bartender.'[6] By the time the book had come out in 1891, Boothby had taken to calling himself 'the Presiding Deity' of the glamorous Hotel Rafael in San Rafael.

After another decade, Boothby brought out the second edition of the book with some additional drink recipes and was busy plying his god-like powers in San Francisco's iconic Parker House. He'd also earned himself the name of the Honourable William T. Boothby by serving as a Republican candidate for the 43rd Assembly District for a year. It was a title he would carry with him for the rest of his life and contributed to his image as a local celebrity at the Parker House. He even hung a picture of himself dressed like a rooster on the outside wall of the bar.

Then came the earthquake and fire of 1906 that devastated San Francisco, which destroyed the Parker House and the printing plates of Boothby's books. This meant Honourable Bill had to start from scratch and so the third edition in 1908 contained more new recipes, making sure the work of various bartenders wouldn't be lost to history.

Boothby was so cheery about the third edition that he dedicated it 'to all the liquor dealers of San Francisco who unanimously assisted in my election to the Legislature by an unprecedented majority'. In context, the San Francisco of the time was awash with booze and the man who had the city in a chokehold was J.C. 'Fat Jack' O'Connor, who organised his brigade of 'saloon men' like they were a political outfit.[7] Boothby went out of his way to support all initiatives that would increase drinking in the city.

In 1914, Boothby climbed to the bartender's equivalent of Mount Olympus as head of the Pied Piper bar in The Palace Hotel. An interesting story from his time here involved stopping a fight between French and German customers by creating a Peace Cocktail with ingredients from across Europe as a panacea against the oncoming war.

Boothby wasn't one to let a war stop him from serving drinks, any more than he'd allow a complete ban on alcohol to get in his way. Unlike so many other bartenders who moved to Pasture's new or changed careers when the Volstead Act hit in 1919, Honourable Bill stayed put and kept right on pouring and serving alcohol until he couldn't anymore. In 1922, he was finally arrested for breaking the Act. With the help of friends, Boothby got a job mixing soft drinks.

Boothby died of cancer in 1930, and at his funeral on 4 August roughly 100 bartenders from all over America came to pay their respects. From one account, the mourners drank to his memory with a Boothby classic, a Manhattan with a punch of champagne. In the words of that person, it was 'a drink that never gods on high Olympus quaffed'.[8]

The Gentleman Bartender

While showmen like Thomas and Boothby were known for their colourful antics and personalities, arguably the first bartender to be recognised more for the strength and crafting of his cocktails was a man called William Schmidt. Born in Heide, Germany, Schmidt was a gentleman bartender with an elaborate moustache, fine manners and an even finer manner of speech.

Schmidt came to America at some point in 1868, leaving behind – according to him – a life of wealth. He settled in Chicago and ended up as the bar manager at the Tivoli Garden, the Windy City's biggest, glitziest beer hall until it shut in 1882. While working at the Tivoli, Schmidt was known for crafting pyramids of glasses festooned with fruits and flowers that brought people to the bar so he could knock their socks off with beautifully made drinks.[9]

After his stint in Chicago, Schmidt moved out to New York where he worked in a saloon called George Hillen's Bridge Exchange next to Brooklyn Bridge. Here, he caught the attention of a reporter from the *New York Sun* in 1888, who got a front-row seat to Schmidt's bartending style that consisted of an elegant simplicity that didn't need the flashiness of a contemporary like Jerry Thomas to draw someone in.

From this display, Schmidt had several articles written about him for the *Sun* and *New York World*, establishing his reputation under names like 'William of the Bridge', 'William the Learned' and his most enduring nickname, The 'Only William'.[10]

In 1889, Schmidt returned to Hamburg to visit his parents. In another life, he might have stayed in Europe, as he was offered many jobs that piqued his interest, with the most notable being the directorship of the bar in the newly constructed Eiffel Tower. Yet New York beckoned him back and he opened his own bar on Broadway, above Park Row.

Unfortunately, the bar failed and had to be sold. Though Schmidt couldn't just walk away from what he'd created. He stayed on as head bartender, plying his trade as he always did, chatting to patrons with his grand and eloquent speech, mixing unusual drinks and courting the attention of the press.

By 1892, The Only William had a hankering to put his recipes down in print and published *The Flowing Bowl*, a cocktail book that cemented his legacy with its intriguing content on historical beverages, Greco-Roman banquets and sample menus with drink pairings. Wondrich recalls his experience of reading the book for the first time:

> It was like reading a cookbook from ancient Rome. There were splashes of crime de roses, Calisaya, tonic phosphate and all kinds of other oddball things ... And plenty of recipes with ten ingredients, and others that required you to stencil on nutmeg garnish. And the names! Nothing simple like 'Aviation' for him; think instead 'The Broker's Thought' and 'Absinthe aux Dieux.'[11]

Schmidt saw every cocktail he made as a musical number to be served with harmony, putting this philosophy into his book: 'Mixed drinks might be compared to music: an orchestra will produce good music, provided all players are artists; but have only one or two inferior musicians in your band and you may be convinced they will spoil the entire harmony.'[12]

At the turn of the twentieth century, Schmidt found himself among the last of a dying breed. His type of mixology was being replaced by minimalist aesthetics. Nevertheless, the Gentleman Bartender soldiered on. He never stopped believing that a 'man in my profession should never forget that he is a gentleman. However well-mixed a drink is, much of the flavour will be lost unless politeness is added. A true artist should infuse courtesy and quality into all his liquid pictures.'[13]

He kept going until his employer forced him out of the bar he'd once owned; he died of dementia in 1904. But Schmidt wouldn't be consigned to obscurity; after reading an obituary that said Schmidt had no family in the US to claim his remains, loyal customers and friends retrieved his body from the Manhattan hospital where he'd died. They raised funds and gave him a send-off with a proper funeral, ensuring Schmidt's legacy as one of the most talented bartenders of all time would be honoured.

The Dean of Cocktail Shakers

William Schmidt wasn't the only foreigner to make a mark on the world of American bartending. A white-jacketed English dynamo by the name of Harry Craddock, who worked a bar like a preacher does a pulpit, became a legend in his own right, transplanting American cocktail culture into an English aesthetic and transforming the hospitality scene in London forever.

Born in 1875 in Stroud, Gloucestershire, Craddock moved to the US in 1897, taking up his bartending apprenticeship at the Hollenden Hotel in Cleveland, Ohio, and the Knickerbocker Hotel in New York. These early experiences instilled a powerful work ethic in Craddock and an American accent that would stay with him for the rest of his life. By 1916, Craddock had become a naturalised American citizen and stayed until 1920, when he packed up his bags in the chaos of Prohibition, poured and served the last legal cocktail in New York (according to legend) and returned to England.

Craddock's homecoming was well-timed. The UK hospitality scene, especially in London, seemed trapped in stagnation. Dusty bars felt like mausoleums and some customers longed for the excitement and liveliness they heard in stories coming over from the Atlantic about speakeasies and illicit drinking activities, even though alcohol was perfectly legal in England.

There was one reliable place in the capital for sating thirst, curiosity and adventure. The American Bar at the Savoy Hotel, an art-deco paradise, was the beating heart of a new wave of drinking culture. With his American accent, bartending skills and old-world charm, Craddock was the perfect addition to the Savoy, quickly rising to the head honcho of The American Bar.

Here, Craddock would build his name as 'The Dean of Cocktail Shakers', serving royalty and pouring for movie stars like Ava Gardner,

Charlie Chaplin and Errol Flynn. He epitomised a hospitality mindset that 'went beyond the call of duty' according to drinks historian Jared Brown. In his biography of Craddock, Brown recalls a story about him spending $60 on a transatlantic call to supply a loyal customer with a favourite cocktail recipe. 'That is the essence of being a hotel bartender. You extend the caring for your guests beyond the time they are under your roof.'[14]

Craddock was a man on a mission. He was determined to promote the culture of the Savoy and the beauty of cocktails far and wide and to do that he'd publish arguably the most well-distributed bartender's book in the world, *The Savoy Cocktail Book*. Containing all of Craddock's drink wisdom, wry wit and cultural observations, the book has remained in publication to this day, serving as an inspiration for bartenders of all backgrounds.

In promoting the book, Craddock showed himself to be a master publicist. Once, a government commission voiced their dislike of the growing cocktail culture. Craddock put out an editorial piece, offering £50 to any committee member who could try one of his drinks and not find their lunch and dinner greatly enhanced. On a return visit to New York, Craddock got in touch with as many of the city's luminaries as he could so they could form a group that would show him around New York's best watering holes. The press picked it up and his book was covered extensively. Unfortunately, he never earned any money from it.[15]

Craddock's cocktails were as lively and memorable as the man himself. Two of the most iconic recipes he committed to his book were: the Corpse Reviver No.2, a heady combo of gin, lemon juice, Lillet Blanc, triple sec and a splash of absinthe; and the White Lady, a mix of gin, lemon juice and Cointreau, which was possibly a precursor to the Cosmo. The White Lady is especially legendary, perhaps because it's the cocktail most associated with Craddock's habit of burying booze-filled shakers in the walls of the bars he worked at. In 1927, he entombed a White Lady shaker in the American Bar that has never been found.

After Prohibition was repealed, Craddock was invited back to the US and he refused. He was content where he was. London needed him and he needed London. His next project was to set up the UK Bartenders Guild in 1934, introducing the novel concept of bartender training infused with the spirit of American hospitality. This was a revolutionary idea that helped change the face of England's bar scene forever, turning stuffy venues into world-class cocktail destinations.

By 1938, Craddock wanted to spread his wings. He moved from the Savoy to the Dorchester Hotel, where he served the likes of President Eisenhower when the hotel became the American military headquarters in the Second World War.

The Dean of Cocktail Shakers finally decided to hang up his bar tools in 1947 and retired. On his death in 1963, Craddock didn't get the send-off he deserved, or perhaps it was his wish to shuffle off this mortal coil without pomp and circumstance, to let his drinks be the testament of his memory. He was buried in a pauper's grave in Gunnersbury cemetery in West London.

Still, Craddock has maintained his larger-than-life persona at the epicentre of cocktail culture in England and the US. A cocktail time capsule of his work can be found at the Savoy Museum next to The American Bar, with instructions for it to be opened in 2063.

He will forever remain an influence on mixologists and bartenders looking to leave their own mark. As Peter Dorelli, the head bartender of the American Bar from 1985 to 2003 observed:

> As a bartender at the Savoy, you must always remember you are part of the bigger picture; you are carrying on a legacy. When a person arrives at a hotel, one of the first things they do is go to the bar, so you are the first point of contact, the ambassador.[16]

Craddock was the embodiment of this ambassadorship, a valuable lesson to learn no matter the style of bar or venue.

The First Lady of Bartending

For all the men that have earned their stripes as bartending legends, there's no shortage of women breaking down barriers and doing incredible things with cocktails.

There's a long list of talented women changing the face of the industry today like Mia Kumari, winner of the 2023 International Wine and Spirits Competition Emerging Talent competition; Chelsie Bailey, mixologist master and former head of The Savoy's American Bar; Kat Stanley-Whyte, agave spirits maestro; Monica Berg, Norwegian bartending extraordinaire; Joy Perrine, Kentucky Bourbon Hall of Fame alumni; Pamela Wiznitzer, powerhouse drinks consultant out of New York; Erika Haigh, owner of the UK's first sake bar Moto, and so many others.

The foundations for empowerment of women in the bartending industry can arguably be traced back to a firebrand from London who not only broke the mould of what a 'barmaid' could and should be, but she defined the cocktail-making culture of the UK, long before Harry Craddock set foot in The Savoy. Her name was Ada Coleman and she was the First Lady Of Bartending.

Born in 1875 to a steward who worked at a golf club owned by the famous hotelier Rupert D'Oyly Carte, 'Coley' as she would affectionally be known by her patrons, entered bartending in her early twenties. Her father had died and she needed to supplement her income and was given a job by Carte at the Claridge's Hotel. At 24, Coleman had almost hit the age-ceiling for entry level women bartenders, or barmaids in the common parlance of the time. Anyone older than 25 would likely have been turned away and this sheds some light on the inequality and prejudice that women faced at the bar (and still do).

In the early twentieth century, the typical image of a barmaid was the daughter of a tradesman or a young woman who came from a higher class that had needed to rely on themselves to earn a living. Many women saw bartending as a more lucrative job than what was generally available for them at the time. They wanted to be involved in the industry, even as campaigns tried to restrict them on the grounds that the job was bad for them physically and that it was a sign of moral decay.

Coleman didn't let any preconceived notions stop her, even though 'her fame behind the bar came about with more serendipity than use of any conventional professional inroads for the ladies',[17] according to writer Emily Bell. She proved to be a quick study, learning to mix drinks with the help of the Claridge's wine butler. By Coleman's admission, the first cocktail she ever made was a Manhattan.

It wasn't long before her diligence caught the attention of the Savoy and she was set up at the American Bar, becoming head bartender in 1903. The reason was likely a combination of her natural charm and drink-making ability. Coley was known as the life of the party, with a personality that bordered on the theatrical. The party didn't stop at the American Bar. Ever the hostess, Coleman held get-togethers at her home and served famous names like Mark Twain, Marlene Dietrich and Charlie Chaplin when she was at the bar.

And while Coleman made memorable cocktails, the one she'll be remembered for the most is the Hanky Panky, a mix of gin, sweet vermouth and fernet-branca topped with an orange peel. Coleman said she made it for the comic actor Charley Hawtrey (not the one of *Carry On* fame), calling him 'one of the best judges of cocktails that I knew. Some years ago, when he was overworking, he used to come into the bar and say 'Coley, I am tired. Give me something with a bit of punch in it.' When Hawtrey next came to the bar, she had a new drink for him to try, exclaiming 'By Jove! This is the real hanky panky!'[18]

Coleman's time at The American Bar wasn't all sunshine and rainbows. She had to put up with her fair share of sexism. There's been many rumours of Coleman's working relationship with Harry Craddock, who came into The American Bar to either work under her initially, or replace her altogether as the head bartender.

And with Coley's fame, it's all too easy to forget that there was another woman working at The American Bar alongside her called Ruth Burgess. Reports from the time claim that Burgess was as popular with patrons as Coleman and the main reason why Coleman is remembered most is because she was asked to be interviewed by the media when she retired.

One newspaper account reveals that they worked different shifts for twenty years without speaking to each other and there was an intense rivalry between them:

> For over twenty years they have worked in the same little corner, handled the same bottles and beamed on the same good friends – without speaking to each other … Men have long been puzzled over this unhappy state of affairs. Each was so jolly and sympathetic, each had such a pleasant personality that it was hard to realise they could never be friends … they kept their own hours, totalled their own accounts and when on duty at the same time could scarcely take two steps without brushing each other, but there never came a sign of recognition.

In the same account, it's claimed that the animosity between Burgess and Coleman was because Burgess didn't know how to make her cocktails. 'She asked Coley to give her the ingredients and Coley, with perhaps justifiable professional pride, refused.'[19]

Could this feud have been fanned by male colleagues or blown out of proportion? It's possible. Both Coleman and Burgess were made to retire from the Savoy around the same time and then Craddock moved into the position of head bartender.

Whatever happened, Coleman took the news gracefully and stepped down, with a popular theory being that she moved to the Savoy's flower shop, though no staff at the hotel have found any evidence of that ever being the case. She lived to be 91, passing away in 1996 as another wave of mixology was gearing up.

Today, Coleman is rightfully celebrated as a pioneer and symbol of a woman's right to work in hospitality. A recent example of her legacy in action is the launch of The Ada Coleman Project by Kristine Bocchino and Kaitlin Wilkes. This digital space has been designed to empower women through mentorship opportunities, networking and workshops in hospitality. As both have explained:

> The platform aims to foster gender equality and diversity within the industry while offering an array of essential resources, including educational content, health resources and job listings. However, the standout feature of The Ada Coleman Project is its rotating database of accomplished women in the drinks industry. Updated biannually, the database showcases both veteran and rising stars from diverse backgrounds and areas of expertise. Presented alphabetically to avoid ranking, it serves as a valuable tool for event organisers, competition hosts, bar owners and writers seeking to diversify their talent pool for collaborations and editorials.[20]

The creation of this initiative is another step in the right direction for gender equality in hospitality, a path forged by Coleman and every other female bartender doing their thing.

The Ideal Bartender

When discussing the early history of spirits and cocktails, it's easy to fall into the trap of seeing it being shaped by a bunch of dead white guys. This is the furthest thing from the truth, as there have been many bartenders in the African American community that have defined the culture. One of the loudest voices was a man named Thomas Bullock.

Born in Louisville, Kentucky in 1872, Bullock wasn't the first black bartender to be recognised for his skills. Across the history of slavery in the United States, there would have been generations of black people serving drinks that have been forgotten, but are no less important. Bullock was the first black bartender to publish a cocktail book called *The Ideal Bartender.*

As the son of a former slave who fought for the Union Army in the Civil War, Bullock's trajectory into bartending can be contextualised through the area and culture in which he grew up. During the war, Louisville had been a Union stronghold and after it was over the city attracted ex-Confederates. With so many rebels flooding into the city, it wasn't only a matter of time before they came to define Louisville's culture.

According to historian George C. Wright, 'It seems that a part of the rite of passage into the business world of the city was to have been an officer of the Confederacy. Nearly all of Louisville's journalists, lawyers, realtors and merchants were former rebels.'[21]

A tradition that came out of this culture was the common use of black bartenders. This was in direct contrast with Northern cities that barred black people from serving in drinking establishments that weren't catering to black patrons. Competition was fierce in bartending. It was a great opportunity for enterprising young men to rub shoulders with well-connected people in luxurious venues, and so the position was limited to white men in major northern cities.

Cocktail historian David Wondrich adds: 'in the North, black bartenders were seen as competition and shut out entirely. In Southern-leaning cities like Louisville and St Louis, the situation was different. They had a history of using African Americans in all types of serving positions.'[22]

An inquisitive, energetic man, Bullock seized on any opportunity he could to create a better life for himself. His first job in hospitality was as a bell boy at the prestigious Pendennis Club, perhaps Kentucky's finest gentleman's club, where the country's elite broke bread and drank together. Bullock worked his way up to the bar, developing his craft to the point where the Southern businessman George Walker Bush, whose descendants would serve as Presidents of the United States, wrote an introduction in Bullock's cocktail book that said 'Tom, than whom there is no greater mixologist of any race, colour or condition of servitude.'[23]

This book was *The Ideal Bartender*, a window into Pre-Prohibition drinking culture and cocktail recipes that have become fused into myth and legend. For example, the Old Fashioned recipe that Bullock featured in the book has been called the first Old Fashioned in some circles. The legend goes that Bullock had a hand in developing the recipe alongside a Pendennis Club member called James E. Pepper. However, there have been Old Fashioned recipes that pre-date the Pendennis Club version.[24]

Another cocktail Bullock became famous for was Mint Juleps. There are two recipes in his book – St Louis style and Kentucky style. The former was probably perfected during Bullock's time at the St Louis Country Club, a mixture of gin, lemon, lime juice and Grenadine. The latter was likely made while he was still working at the Pendennis.

Interestingly, *The Ideal Bartender* might never have made it to publication without the controversy of one President's drinking habits. In the election of 1912, Theodore Roosevelt had to deal with rumours that he was a closeted drunk. A newspaper editor George Newett decided to stir the pot by writing an article about Roosevelt's drunkenness after hearing a speech. Newitt wrote: 'Roosevelt lies and curses in a most disgusting way. He gets drunk too and that not infrequently and all of his intimates know about it.'[25]

Roosevelt sued for libel, eventually admitting that he had only taken a couple of sips of Mint Juleps at the St Louis Country Club. Another journalist decided to have fun at Roosevelt's expense, penning an article that referred to Bullock's Mint Juleps being so good that Roosevelt surely had to be lying and that he'd drank all the cocktails when they were served to him. In the end, Roosevelt won his libel case and that put Bullock and his juleps on the map, aiding in the publication of *The Ideal Bartender*.

By 1917, Bullock was as popular as he was ever going to be. Prohibition damaged his career, though it's thought he stayed on at the St Louis Country Club for several years, even if his duties aren't known. Bullock disappeared from the public record after Prohibition, with it generally being believed that he died in 1964.

Bullock and his book might never have been rediscovered if not for writer Dianna Seay, who published two books inspired by *The Ideal*

Bartender in the early 2000s called *173 Pre-Prohibition Cocktails: Potations So Good They Scandalised A President* and *Classic Cocktails: Over 170 Drinks From Yesteryear that You Can Enjoy Today.*

Since then, a renewed interest in Bullock and his career has blossomed across the bar scene. In 2013, D'USSE Cognac created the Tom Bullock Award for Distinguished Service in Washington. In 2017, Louisville brandy distillery Copper & Kings started The Ideal Bartender School, a hub of spirits and cocktail education for young bartenders. In 2019, a Bullock mural was painted on a restaurant of a major Urban Bourbon Trail restaurant down the street from the site of the original Pendennis Club.

Henderson Spirits Group have also created a bourbon and gin line called Tom Bullock's. The brand story and copy taps into Bullock's life. Written in the first person, there's a passage on the website that does a decent attempt at summarising Bullock's importance to bartending:

> At a time when a black man could hardly walk into a 'white' bar, I was the reigning king. I was not only allowed IN the bar, but people came to the bar FOR me – in order to sample my cocktails, shake my hand and get me to sign my book for them … I realised a few things behind the bar … Superb cocktails inspire all types of people to congregate … Being a true Tastemaster is about breaking down preconceived ideas and bringing new flavours together … the same is true for bringing people together.[26]

Bonus Chapter

A Night In Manchester

For anyone who's read this far into the book, thank you. Think of this bonus chapter as part bar guide, part educational resource for my home city of Manchester. You'll find commentary on some of my favourite bars and pubs along with insights from industry folks in the city who're doing amazing things for alcoholic drinks of all categories. (Given the fast-moving nature of hospitality, not every bar mentioned here may still be open when you read this. But they will live on in spirit).

Deansgate

I like to think of this section of the city as the most generally accessible to casual drinkers looking for a pint at cheap prices. Within this area, you'll find pub chains like Wetherspoons to wet your whistle. Of course, there are various historical pubs to check out like The Briton's Protection, a venerable old boozer with one of the most impressive whisky collections in the city. Down the road from The Briton's is Peveril of the Peak, a stunning pub that you can't miss with its stained-glass windows and bright brickwork.

Heading past St Peter's Square where the Central Library is located, you'll come across two of the best cocktail bars in the city. The first is Schofield's Bar, an art deco masterpiece of a bar run by brothers Joe and Daniel who've been recognised as two of the best cocktail makers in the world. The second cocktail bar to check out is Blinker, another venue that calls back to the decadence of the 1920s with cocktails that taste as if they've been pulled from the minds of legendary bartenders like Harry Craddock and Ada Coleman.

One of the most underrated parts of Schofield's and Blinker is the ice they use. Local ice supplier Chas Ayres shared his insights on this as I drank an Old Fashioned served with ice he'd crafted at Schofield's. As the founder of craft ice supplier Black Ice, Ayres' passion for his subject matter is infectious and he had plenty to say on the importance of using ice in cocktails:

> There's a lot of trends with ice making in hospitality. The two that never go away are luxury and niche. This might involve sipping a perfectly crafted cocktail with an intriguing garnish, primo glass and a top-shelf spirit and piece of ice that complements the drink.
>
> This also ties into the cyclical trend of the big four spirits: vodka, gin, whisky and rum. Vodka was big in the 1990s, then you have a rotating door of people moving to whisky, the massive gin boom of the 2010s and now we're seeing rum come back along as a premium spirit.
>
> Ice has had an important role in the popularity of the big four from an aesthetics and tasting perspective. I also see it having a positive impact on the emerging no and low movement. Imagine you're in a bar with someone who doesn't drink and they see a fancy, colourful mocktail with a beautifully crafted piece of ice in it.
>
> From my experience, most speciality ice providers worldwide have six to eight styles of ice available. A couple of rocks, a couple of highballs, a couple of balls and one other style.
>
> Finding out what the client wants is always my first question with any prospective ice programme. Establishing the budget is the second question and then it's about getting into the nuts and bolts of the drink. It isn't a fluke when someone has a drink presented to them that has a piece of ice that sits perfectly between the rim and the wash line and bartenders can execute it time after time, getting the same volume into the vessel.
>
> And you also have to consider how shape impacts the quality of a drink. Drinking a Martini is different to drinking a Long Island iced tea. The ice in a drink, whether out of a

machine or a piece cut by a human, should complement and elevate that particular serve.

A couple of examples come to mind. Most drinks in Tiki bars are served over crushed ice, generally because they (historically) contained more than the standard 50–60ml of alcohol. The crushed ice adds to the dilution and was probably a cool (no pun intended) factor that Donn Beach, the founder of Tiki bar culture in the US had in mind when he opened his gaffs in the 1950s.

On the other hand, a negroni served over crushed ice may or may not work as well and the essence of the cocktail could be lost. That strong, sharp, short experience would be radically altered.

For the operators that think about this deeply, form follows function. If we continue by looking at the Negroni, let's look at it two ways: in the first establishment there's no fancy ice programme and the drink is ordered, and then built in the glass. Ice. Equal parts Gin/Vermouth/Campari over. Stirred, garnish in and sent out. The drink will continue to develop and dilute in that glass.

The second establishment uses fancy ice. The drink is ordered, the glass with fancy ice gets put on the counter. The equal parts go into a mixing glass and are stirred down for a few moments with machine-made ice poured over. Garnish in and sent out.

For the vast majority of those serves, that drink will not change in flavour. Anything up to about fifteen minutes (and that's a long time for the average person to imbibe a short drink) and the ice will add practically no dilution into the drink but will maintain the temperature of the serve. High-quality bars understand what they want to achieve and will use different pieces of ice to achieve different results. The best ones even monitor the drinks in their programme and change a variable if they aren't achieving the result they want.

Deansgate also has niche offerings for category-specific drinkers. One of my favourite Japanese bars can be found in Deansgate in the Radisson Blu hotel. The Rikyu bar has a wide range of Japanese sake to try.

Northern Quarter

I like to think of the Northern Quarter as the 'hipster' part of Manchester. But don't let that put you off. There's an amazing range of quirky bars to discover as you walk through the graffiti-decorated streets and back alleys reminiscent of New York.

At the top of my list is Manchester's premier whisky bar, the Whiskey Jar. The back shelf is packed with bottles from all over the world, so you're bound to find something that meets your taste. Hop next door to Northern Monk, a craft beer boozer that regularly knocks out mad and delicious concoctions like Eternal, Heathen and Striding Edge.

Talk a stroll through Stevenson Square and into the covert Dusk Til Pawn, a hidden cocktail bar disguised as a pawn shop. Listen to indie music in the historic Night & Day Café which has seen hallowed bands like The Arctic Monkeys, Kasabian and The Manic Street Preachers roll through the door and play on stage. After that, you could drop by Lost in Tokyo, a Japanese-inspired club that knocks out decent cocktails. Or spend time in Gulliver's, one of the top Irish pubs in the city that knocks out Guinness (read on to discover where I think the best Guinness can be found in Manchester …).

An alternative to Gulliver's is to walk across the road to the Castle Hotel, which is owned by the same group. The Castle itself has a storied 200-year history that goes back to 1776 when it started life The Crown and Sceptre. Over the years, the pub changed names to The Crown and Anchor and The Clock Face, eventually becoming The Castle Hotel in the late nineteenth century.

Finally, fans of jazz, soul and funk will want to stop at Matt and Phred's, which features upcoming and established acts in their respective genres most nights.

Ancoats

Once upon a time, Ancoats was one of the most run-down and derided sections of Manchester. Now, it's regularly featured in travel guides and columns as one of the trendiest places to visit and live in the world. With its Industrial Revolution era red brick mills turned into offices and apartments, street art and brunch venues on every corner, Ancoats' makeover is a far cry from the decaying buildings and rough streets left to fester in the 1990s. And yet, it still retains a small community-like charm that is best represented by its bars and restaurants.

Your first port of call should be the Edinburgh Castle, a cosy Londonesque pub sequestered on the corner of the Cutting Room Square. In this warm environment, you'll find what I believe to be the best Guinness in Manchester. (You're welcome to challenge me on this after you've sampled the Guinness at Gulliver's in the Northern Quarter, Mulligans on Deansgate and O'Sheas near Canal Street).

Once you're done at the Edinburgh Castle you might stop next door at the Seven Bro7hers beer house, a chain of bars that really is owned by seven brothers who also have four sisters who run a gin distillery called Four Sis4ers. The McAvoy siblings have been taking the UK alcohol industry by storm since 2014, making them one of the biggest modern alcohol-producing dynasties in the country.

According to Keith McAvoy, the bar empire began for the brothers in childhood and became a reality after a trip to Norway:

> Our dad was a really keen home brewer, and we all got involved helping him as we grew up. We enjoyed that aspect with him, and it was great. We didn't always get it right, there was the odd explosion when he was attempting things, but some of us got into it more than others. When we got older, most of us got more interested in drinking it rather than making it.
>
> I was out working in Oslo with an offshore pipeline company and while living out there for just over a year I became completely blown away by the craft beer scene there. It was so cool, I'd never seen anything like that in Manchester. It was really contemporary. Bars were having their brew kit installed in the bar and it was right there front of house instead of being in the cellar of the pub which is quite traditional.
>
> Everything that drives the decisions we make is around the community. We try to embody that in the bars that we own and operate. Pubs are an essential part of the British mentality and we are a craft brewer, but I wouldn't say we are a craft beer for the beer geeks as such. We're a craft beer

brewery for the masses. Our beers are open and accessible, they're not confusing with names that don't relate to the product we've produced.[1]

The McAvoy sisters are just as keen to further the renown of their family with their gin distillery. Lucy McAvoy, the sales and marketing director of the distillery said:

> The brothers were about three years ahead of us. I had an events management company at the time and they approached me to help with their first crowdfunding campaign. That gave me an insight into what they were doing.
>
> We thought joining the brothers in the same industry would not only give us a great story, but we would have a bit of a springboard into the industry at the same time because the brothers were starting to establish themselves and we would have had a lot of experience to gain from them but we didn't want to step on their toes. Spirits were obviously the next best choice to craft beer, and in 2017 we were going through a real gin resurgence. It was also our mum's favourite drink.[2]

Of course you'll find other pubs in Ancoats that reflect the history of the place. An example is the Marble Arch Inn, an iconic Manchester institution built in 1888. The centrepiece of the Marble Arch is the mosaic-sloping floor that leads straight to the bar.

You can grab a pint down the road at another iconic pub called The Angel. Situated near Angel Meadow, this pub had the misfortune of taking its name from arguably the worst slum in the city back in the Industrial Revolution. The German philosopher and historian Friedrich Engels once called Angel Meadow 'hell on earth'. This definitely isn't the case today, as the area and the rest of Ancoats is a beer and spirit lovers paradise.

Endnotes

Introduction

1. *Quote Origin: Truth Is Stranger than Fiction, But It Is Because Fiction Is Obliged to Stick to Possibilities; Truth Isn't,* https://quoteinvestigator.com/2015/07/15/truth-stranger/
2. Ian Russell, *Famous Whisky Drinkers: Mark Twain*, https://Scotchwhisky.com/magazine/famous-whisky-drinkers/6110/famous-whisky-drinkers-mark-twain/

An Overview of the Distillation of Alcoholic Spirits

1. *History Of Alcohol Distillation*, https://www.copper-alembic.com/en/page/history-of-alcohol-distillation
2. Hyunhee Park, *Soju: A Global History* (Cambridge University Press, 2021), p.33
3. *History Of Alcohol Distillation*
4. Ufuk Necat Tasci, *Hayyan: the 9th-century polymath who brought scientific temper to alchemy,* https://www.trtworld.com/magazine/hayyan-the-9th-century-polymath-who-brought-scientific-temper-to-alchemy-12738769
5. Marco Pierini, *The Origins of Alcoholic Distillation in the West: 4. The Medical School of Salerno,* https://www.gotrum.com/the-rum-university/rum-in-history/the-origins-of-alcoholic-distillation-in-the-west-4-the-medical-school-of-solerno/
6. Pierini

Chapter 1

1. *To the mortal memory of Madam Geneva*, https://www.britishmuseum.org/collection/object/P_1868-0808-3580
2. Simon Difford, *History of gin (1728 – 1794) – London's gin craze*, https://www.diffordsguide.com/g/1108/gin/history-of-gin-1728-1794

3. Wayne Curtis, *And A Bottle Of Rum: A History Of The New World In Ten Cocktails* (Broadway Books, 2018), p.197
4. Patrick Dillon, *Gin: The Much Lamented Death of Madam Geneva: The Eighteenth Century Gin Craze,* https://bookreadfree.com/389374/9576675.amp
5. Henry Fielding, *An Enquiry into the Causes of the late Increase of Robbers*
6. Dillon
7. Fiona Halsam, *Hogarth and the Art of Alcohol Abuse,* https://www.rcpe.ac.uk/heritage/hogarth-and-art-alcohol-abuse
8. Eliza Fowler, *A Present for Women Addicted to Drinking Adapted to all the different Stations of Life, from a Lady of Quality to a Common Servant*
9. Angela Youngman, *The Weird & Wonderful Story Of Gin: From The seventeenth Century To The Present Day* (Pen And Sword History, 2022), p.31
10. Dudley Bradstreet, *The Life and Uncommon Adventures of Captain Dudley Bradstreet,* https://www.chanticleersociety.org/index.php?title=The_Life_%26_Uncommon_Adventures_of_Captain_Dudley_Bradstreet
11. *Welcome to Smugglers' Town,* https://www.yorkshire.com/inspiration/features/welcome-to-smugglers-town/
12. *Smugglers' Britain: Guide-Book: South-East England,* http://www.smuggling.co.uk/gazetteer_se_12.html
13. Greg Mays, *Meet Charles Tanqueray: History in a Bottle,* https://www.burn-blog.com/8554/meet-charles-tanqueray-history-in-a-bottle/
14. Youngman, p.57
15. *Meet The Distiller: Lesley Gracie, Hendricks Gin,* https://www.theginguild.com/ginopedia/gin-distillers/lesley-gracie-hendricks-master-distiller/
16. *KI NO BI – A Kyoto-style Pursuit of Perfection,* https://theabsolutgroup.com/story/ki-no-bi-a-kyoto-style-pursuit-of-perfection
17. Youngman, p.173
18. Albert Camus, *The Fall*

Chapter 2

1. Robert Burns, *Scotch Drink,* https://www.nts.org.uk/stories/Scotch-drink
2. Tom Bruce-Gardyne, *Scotch Whisky: The Essential Guide for Single Malt Lovers* (Wellbeck Publishing, 2018), p.14
3. Gardyne, p.17
4. *Highland Single Malt Scotch Whisky,* https://www.thewhiskyexchange.com/c/313/highland-single-malt-Scotch-whisky
5. *Whisky Making,* https://www.Scotchwhiskyexperience.co.uk/about/about-whisky/whisky-making
6. Gardyne, p.17

7. *Haig Whisky & Jameson – The Story Of The Whisky Cousins*, https://www.haigwhisky.com/haig-whisky-jameson-history-whisky-cousins/
8. Gardyne, *Sweet Juice Of Success,* https://whiskymag.com/articles/sweet-juice-of-success/
9. Gavin D Smith, *Whisky Heroes: Tommy Dewar*, https://Scotchwhisky.com/magazine/whisky-heroes/11735/tommy-dewar/
10. *Chivas Brothers Holdings Profile*, https://Scotchwhisky.com/whiskypedia/2580/chivas-brothers-holdings
11. Smith, *Whisky Heroes: James Buchanan*, https://Scotchwhisky.com/magazine/whisky-heroes/10632/james-buchanan/
12. *Highland Park*, https://Scotchwhisky.com/whiskypedia/1867/highland-park/
13. Ellie Forbes, *Bessie Williamson: The woman behind Laphroaig distillery,* https://www.scottishfield.co.uk/food-and-drink-2/bessie-williamson-the-woman-behind-laphroaig-distillery/

Chapter 3

1. Curtis, p.173
2. Adam O'Connell and Jake Mountain, *How is Rum Made?,* https://www.masterofmalt.com/guides/rum-guides/how-is-rum-made/
3. Curtis, p.29
4. Curtis, p.29
5. Curtis, p.81
6. *A Brief History Of Rum*, https://thecraftycask.com/craft-spirits-liqueurs/history-rum/
7. *A Brief History Of Rum*
8. Curtis, pp.43 – 44
9. *The History Of Grog*, https://sailorjerry.com/en-gb/blog/post/the-storied-history-of-the-drink-we-call-grog
10. Captain Daniel A. Laliberte, *The Real McCoy*, https://www.usni.org/magazines/naval-history-magazine/2020/february/real-mccoy
11. Gertrude Lythgoe, *The Bahama Queen,* (Flat Hammock Press, 2006)
12. *Who was Cleo Lythgoe?,* https://lythgoebourbon.com/who-was-cleo/
13. Joseph Piercy, *A Rum Tale: Spirit of The New World* (The History Press, 2019)
14. *History of the Song: 'Rum and Coca-Cola'*, https://www.swingcityradio.com/2020/07/history-of-song-rum-and-coca-cola.html
15. Curtis, p.250
16. *Maggie Campbell | Head Distiller, Privateer Rum*, https://punchdrink.com/lookbook/maggie-campbell-head-distiller-privateer-rum/

Chapter 4

1. Fred Minnick, *Bourbon: The Rise, Fall And Rebirth Of An American Whiskey* (Voyageur Press, 2016), p.18
2. Audrey Morgan, *What Is Bourbon? A Guide to America's Original Whiskey*, https://www.liquor.com/bourbon-whiskey-guide-7369244
3. Minnick, p.20
4. Minnick, p.25
5. Minnick, p.23
6. Timothy Reeves, *Grant, Babcock and the Whiskey Ring,* https://www.archives.gov/publications/prologue/2000/fall/whiskey-ring-1
7. Minnick, p.55
8. Tyler Zielinski, *What Does Bottled-In-Bond Mean?,* https://www.foodandwine.com/cocktails-spirits/what-does-bottled-in-bond-mean
9. William Howard Taft, *Decision on the Meaning of the Term 'Whisky' Under the Pure Food Act and the Proper Regulations for Branding Various Kinds of Whisky Under the Internal Revenue Act,* https://www.presidency.ucsb.edu/documents/decision-the-meaning-the-term-whisky-under-the-pure-food-act-and-the-proper-regulations
10. Taft
11. Minnick, p.90
12. Laura Fields, *Mexican Bourbon History*, https://www.dramdevotees.com/mexican-bourbon-history/
13. Minnick, p.129
14. *The Big Four Distilling Companies,* https://bourbonveach.com/2020/06/08/the-big-four-distilling-companies
15. Minnick, p.167
16. *Flashback Friday – Frost 8/80 Dry White Whisky*, https://bourbonveach.com/2020/11/06/flashback-friday-frost-8-80-dry-white-whisky/
17. Minnick, p.192
18. Minnick, p.216
19. Stuart Ramsay, *Booker Noe*, https://whiskymag.com/articles/booker-noe/
20. Hudson Lindenberger, *CaskX Founder Jeremy Kasler On The Future Of Bourbon Investing*, https://www.forbes.com/sites/hudsonlindenberger/2024/03/19/jeremy-kasler-the-founder-of-cask-x-discusses-bourbon-investing/?sh=22d2b744222c
21. Linderberger

22. *The Future of Sustainable Bourbon*, https://www.wired.com/sponsored/story/the-future-of-sustainable-bourbon/
23. Michael Veach, *The Future Of New Distillers,* https://bourbonveach.com/2024/05/13/the-future-of-new-distilleries/

Chapter 5

1. *The Captivating History of Smirnoff Vodka: From Russia to Global*, https://junosliquor.com/f/the-captivating-history-of-smirnoff-vodka-from-russia-to-global
2. Minnick, p.176
3. Scott Simpson, *History and Mythology of Polish Vodka: 1270 – 2007*
4. *The History of Vodka: From Rough Spirit To Refined Future*, https://www.greygoose.com/en-gb/stories/vodka-essentials/history-of-vodka.html
5. Simpson
6. Simpson
7. Simpson
8. *History of Vodka in Russia*, https://homedistiller.org/wiki/index.php/History_of_Vodka_in_Russia
9. *History of Russian Vodka,* https://www.bbc.co.uk/dna/mb6music/A871995
10. Vladimir Shiltsev, *Dmitri Mendeleev and the science of vodka,* https://pubs.aip.org/physicstoday/online/5317/Dmitri-Mendeleev-and-the-science-of-vodka
11. Shiltsev
12. Patricia Herlihy, *The Alcoholic Empire: Vodka & Politics In Late Imperial Russia,* https://academic.oup.com/book/47706
13. Herlihy
14. Herlihy
15. Natasha Frost, *How America Fell in Love With Vodka*, https://www.atlasobscura.com/articles/how-america-fell-in-love-with-vodka-smirnoff
16. Frost
17. *The Absolut Company (Destilleriet Nobbelov)*, https://www.diffordsguide.com/producers/214/the-absolut-company-destilleriet-nobbelov
18. *The Story of the Absolut bottle and brand*, https://theabsolutgroup.com/legacy/post/lo-smith-english/the-story-of-the-absolut-bottle-and-brand/
19. Seth Stevenson, *The Cocktail Creationist,* https://nymag.com/nymetro/news/bizfinance/biz/features/10816/

20. Lauren Eads, *The reinvention of vodka*, https://www.thespiritsbusiness.com/2024/04/the-reinvention-of-vodka/
21. Eads

Chapter 6

1. *MezcalHistory*,https://www.pensadormezcal.com/blogs/journal/the-making-of-pensador-ensamble-batch-1
2. Tom Bullock, *The Mezcal Experience: A Field Guide To The World's Best Mezcals And Agave Spirits* (Jacqui Small, 2017), p.24
3. Bullock, p.26
4. *The History of Tequila in North America Part 1: Pre-Hispanic Era – 1700,* https://www.casamexicotequila.com/the-history-of-tequila-in-north-america-part-1
5. Bullock, p.29
6. Kevin Wilkerson, *How Prohibition Helped Tijuana Become A Nightlife Boomtown*, https://www.pubclub.com/destinations/mexico/tijuana/how-prohibition-helped-tijuana-become-a-nightlife-boomtown/
7. David Wondrich, *Tequila Daisy*, https://www.liquor.com/recipes/tequila-daisy/
8. *The History of Tequila in North America Part 2: 1700 – Present Day,* https://www.casamexicotequila.com/the-history-of-tequila-in-north-america-part-2
9. Bullock, p.30
10. Kate Malczewski, T*he big interview: Dwayne 'The Rock' Johnson, Teremana Tequila,* https://www.thespiritsbusiness.com/2022/01/the-big-interview-dwayne-the-rock-johnson-teremana-tequila/
11. Malczewski
12. *The legend of tequila with worm*, https://www.beverage-world.com/en/newsdetail/the-legend-of-tequila-with-worm
13. Lou Bank, *Uncovering the Real Reason Behind the Mexican Mezcal Worm*, https://www.insidehook.com/drinks/reason-mezcal-worm-history
14. Patrick Reed, *Vintage Ad Archive: Tequila For All!,* https://www.alcoholprofessor.com/blog-posts/blog/2014/08/22/vintage-ad-archive-tequila-for-all
15. John McCarthy, *Art, Love, And Mezcal: How Ron Cooper Sparked A Revolucion For Oaxaca's Smoky, Mysterious Spirit,* https://www.forbes.com/sites/johnmccarthy12/2018/04/16/art-love-and-mezcal-how-ron-cooper-sparked-a-revolucion-for-oaxacas-smoky-mysterious-spirit/

16. McCarthy
17. Brad Japhe, *After 20 Years Of Illegal Mezcal, Founder John Rexer Talks What's Ahead,* https://www.forbes.com/sites/bradjaphe/2023/07/12/after-20-years-of-ilegal-mezcal-founder-john-rexer-talks-whats-ahead/
18. Japhne
19. Anna Bruce, *Siete Misterios looks to the future*, https://www.mezcalistas.com/siete-misterios-looks-to-the-future/
20. Elise Taylor, *How Yola Jimenez Is Making Mezcal With Women's Empowerment in Mind,* https://www.vogue.com/article/yola-jimenez-yola-mezcal
21. *Mezcal Story*, https://mezcaldonavega.com/mezcal-story/
22. *Mezcal Market Outlook from 2024 to 2034*, https://www.futuremarketinsights.com/reports/mezcal-market
23. *Mezcal Market Outlook from 2024 to 2034*
24. *Mezcal Market Size, Share, and Industry Analysis, By Age (Mezcal Joven, Mezcal Reposado, and Mezcal Anejo), By Distribution Channel (On-premise and Off-premise), and Regional Forecast, 2024 – 2032,* https://www.fortunebusinessinsights.com/mezcal-market-102652
25. *Mezcal Market Size, Share, and Industry Analysis, By Age (Mezcal Joven, Mezcal Reposado, and Mezcal Anejo), By Distribution Channel (On-premise and Off-premise), and Regional Forecast, 2024 – 2032*

Chapter 7

1. Yuan Ren, *5 Drunken Poems To Read While Drinking Chinese Liquor,* https://theculturetrip.com/asia/china/articles/5-drunken-poems-to-read-while-drinking-chinese-liquor
2. Derek Sandhaus, *Baijiu: The Essential Guide To Chinese Spirits* (Viking Australia, 2015), pp. 22 – 23
3. Sandhaus, p.11
4. *All you need to know about baijiu in a nutshell*, https://spiritsfully.com/all-spirits/baijiu/
5. *The fall of the Qing dynasty*, https://www.bbc.co.uk/bitesize/articles
6. *The Chinese Revolution of 1911*, https://history.state.gov/milestones/1899-1913/chinese-rev
7. *Expo 1915 in San Francisco, USA*, http://www.bjreview.com.cn/expo2010/2010-04/27/content_267377.htm
8. Sandhaus, *The Panamanian connection*, https://300shots.wordpress.com/2012/01/31/the-panamanian-connection/
9. *The Panamanian connection*

10. *Who shaved $250bn from Kweichow Moutai's market value?* https://www.economist.com/business/2024/06/27/who-shaved-250bn-from-kweichow-moutais-market-value?giftId=86f576fe-126d-4b96-b122-31aee482c795
11. *Drunken Poems to Read While Drinking Chinese Liquor*

Chapter 8

1. Michael Huband, *Sake exports show progress towards key targets, according to JSS,* https://www.thedrinksbusiness.com/2024/02/sake-exports-show-progress-towards-key-targets-according-to-jss/
2. Abby Stern, *Japanese Liquor Aren't Just A Splashy Cocktail Trend,* https://www.thezoereport.com/living/japanese-liquor
3. *Feeding the UK's growing taste for Japanese cuisine*, https://www.independent.co.uk/news/business/business-reporter/japan-supermarkets-food-cooking-sushi-b2372381.html
4. Christopher Pellegrini, *The Shochu Handbook: An Introduction To Japan's Indigenous Distilled Drink* (Telemachus Press, 2020), p.13
5. Pellegrini, pp.35 – 36
6. Stephen Lyman & Chris Bunting, *The Complete Guide to Japanese Drinks: Sake, Shochu, Japanese Whisky, Beer, Cocktail and Other Beverages* (Tuttle Publishing, 2019), https://www.everand.com/book/415327522/Complete-Guide-to-Japanese-Drinks-Sake-Shochu-Japanese-Whisky-Beer-Wine-Cocktails-and-Other-Beverages
7. *The History of Shochu,* https://honkakushochu-awamori.jp/english/basic/history-of-shochu
8. *Sake Kasu Shochu*, https://honkakushochu-awamori.jp/english/professional/shochu-production-method/sake-kasu-shochu/
9. *Satsuma Sweet Potatoes and the Man who Inadvertently Became a God*, https://www.morethantokyo.com/satsuma-sweet-potatoes-man-became-god/
10. Pellegrini, p.49
11. *The Fascinating History of Amami Kokuto Shochu,* https://amamikokutoshochu.jp/history
12. Gavin Yeung, *Why Is Shochu Suddenly Everywhere?,* https://www.tatlerasia.com/dining/drinks/the-new-age-of-shochu
13. Yeung
14. Yeung
15. Yeung
16. Yeung

17. Eloise Feilden, *Japanese shochu sold in California under its own name for the first time,* https://www.thedrinksbusiness.com/2023/12/japanese-shochu-sold-in-california-under-its-own-name-for-the-first-time/

Chapter 9

1. Park, p.187
2. KwonMee-yo,*Sojuisthemostrecognised Koreanalcoholicdrink,surveyshows,* https://www.koreatimes.co.kr/www/culture/2024/07/135_374380.html
3. Lane Nieset, *Soju Explained: What Is It and How Do You Drink It?,* https://www.foodandwine.com/cocktails-spirits/korean-soju
4. Nieset
5. Park, p.71
6. Park, p.108
7. Park, p.85
8. *Koroysa: The History of Koryo, annals of kings, 918 – 1095,* p.26
9. Park, p.134
10. Park, p.147
11. Michael J Pettid, *Korean Cuisine: An Illustrated History* (London: Reaktion Books, 2008), p.119
12. *Hite Jinro,* https://en.namu.wiki/w/%ED%95%98%EC%9D%B4%ED%8A%B8%EC%A7%84%EB%A1%9C?from=%ED%95%98%EC%9D%B4%ED%8A%B8%20%EC%A7%84%EB%A1%9C
13. *Hitejinro targets $362 mil. In overseas soju sales in 2030*, https://www.koreatimes.co.kr/www/tech/2024/08/129_376851.html
14. Park, p.173
15. Cho Songgi and Yu Kimok, *A Study of the Establishment of the Identity of Soju's Alcohol Content* (Korea Alcohol Research Centre, 2010), p.9
16. *Toasting a Korean-American Renaissance with Yobo Soju*, https://www.linkedin.com/pulse/toasting-korean-american-renaissance-yobo-soju-/
17. Asonta Benetti, *Carolyn Kim Crafts Soju Her Way – With American Spirit and Korean Soul*, https://vinepair.com/articles/vp-pro-qa-carolyn-kim/
18. *The making of ... Hoju Soju*, https://hunterand.co/blog/the-making-of-hoju-soju

Chapter 10

1. Theodora Sutcliffe, *Jerry Thomas*, https://www.diffordsguide.com/encyclopedia/2882/people/jerry-thomas

2. Colin M. Caplan, *Jerry Thomas, Father of American Mixology*, https://tasteofnewhaven.com/2018/10/10/jerry-thomas-father-of-american-mixology/
3. *Meet Jerry Thomas*, https://www.newyorkcity-eats.com/jerry-thomas
4. David Wondrich, *IMBIBE!* (Penguin Group, 2007)
5. Sutcliffe, *William T. Boothby*, https://www.diffordsguide.com/encyclopedia/2963/people/william-t-boothby
6. Sutcliffe
7. Sutcliffe
8. Sutcliffe
9. Sutcliffe, *'The Only William' Schmidt*, https://www.diffordsguide.com/encyclopedia/2964/people/the-only-william-schmidt
10. Wondrich, *Schmidt, William*, https://spiritsanddistilling.com/dictionary/id/acref-9780199311132-e-77/
11. Wondrich, *Masters of Mixology: William Schmidt*, https://www.liquor.com/articles/masters-of-mixology-william-schmidt/
12. *The Flowing Bowl By The Only William (1892*), http://euvslibrary.com/?p=341
13. Sutcliffe
14. Alice Lascelles, *Being Harry Craddock*, https://punchdrink.com/articles/being-harry-craddock/
15. Sutcliffe, *Harry Craddock*, https://www.diffordsguide.com/encyclopedia/2345/people/harry-craddock
16. Lascelles
17. Emily Bell, *Ada Coleman: One Of History's Most Famous Female Mixologists*, https://vinepair.com/wine-blog/ada-coleman/
18. Bell
19. Minnot Sanders, *Famous Bar Maids Who Worked at the Same Bar Twenty Years Without Speaking, Retire* https://www.coloradohistoricnewspapers.org/cgi-bin/colorado?a=d&d=ADT19260216.2.2
20. *Give it up for The Ada Coleman Project, the new initiative for women+ to help the entire industry,* https://thecocktaillovers.com/give-it-up-for-the-ada-coleman-project-the-new-initiative-for-women-to-help-the-entire-industry/
21. Michael Jones, The Life and Legacy of Tom Bullock, https://www.gotolouisville.com/blog/the-life-and-legacy-of-tom-bullock/
22. Jones
23. Sutcliffe, *Tom Bullock*, https://www.diffordsguide.com/encyclopedia/2953/people/tom-bullock

24. Jones
25. Jones
26. https://tombullocks.com/#about

Bonus chapter

1. Patrick Hollis, *'Hopefully we'll open a few more bars soon' – Salford success story Seven Bro7hers on 10 years in business*, https://www.manchesterworld.uk/business/greater-manchester-beer-brewery-family-salford-interview-4655060
2. Bethany Whymark, *The gin-making siblings who built Sis4ers Distillery*, https://gin-mag.com/2021/03/25/sis4ers-distillery-founders-are-doing-it-for-themselves/

Bibliography

A Brief History Of Rum, https://thecraftycask.com/craft-spirits-liqueurs/history-rum/

All you need to know about baijiu in a nutshell, https://spiritsfully.com/all-spirits/baijiu/

Bank, Lou, *Uncovering the Real Reason Behind the Mexican Mezcal Worm*, https://www.insidehook.com/drinks/reason-mezcal-worm-history

Bell, Emily, *Ada Coleman: One Of History's Most Famous Female Mixologists*, https://vinepair.com/wine-blog/ada-coleman/

Benetti, Asonta, *Carolyn Kim Crafts Soju Her Way – With American Spirit and Korean Soul*, https://vinepair.com/articles/vp-pro-qa-carolyn-kim/

Bradstreet, Dudley, *The Life and Uncommon Adventures of Captain Dudley Bradstreet*, https://www.chanticleersociety.org/index.php?title=The_Life_%26_Uncommon_Adventures_of_Captain_Dudley_Bradstreet

Bruce, Anna, *Siete Misterios looks to the future*, https://www.mezcalistas.com/siete-misterios-looks-to-the-future/

Bullock, Tom, *The Mezcal Experience: A Field Guide To The World's Best Mezcals And Agave Spirits* (Jacqui Small, 2017)

Burns, Robert, *Scotch Drink*, https://www.nts.org.uk/stories/Scotch-drink

Camus, Albert, *The Fall* Penguin Classics, 1956

Caplan, M. Colin, *Jerry Thomas, Father of American Mixology*, https://tasteofnewhaven.com/2018/10/10/jerry-thomas-father-of-american-mixology/

Chivas Brothers Holdings Profile, https://Scotchwhisky.com/whiskypedia/2580/chivas-brothers-holdings

Curtis, Wayne, *And A Bottle Of Rum: A History Of The New World In Ten Cocktails* (Broadway Books, 2018)

Dillon, Patrick, *Gin: The Much Lamented Death of Madam Geneva: The Eighteenth Century Gin Craze,* https://bookreadfree.com/389374/9576675.amp

Difford, Simon, *History of gin (1728 – 1794) – London's gin craze*, https://www.diffordsguide.com/g/1108/gin/history-of-gin-1728-1794

Eads, Lauren, *The reinvention of vodka*, https://www.thespiritsbusiness.com/2024/04/the-reinvention-of-vodka/

Expo 1915 in San Francisco, USA, http://www.bjreview.com.cn/expo2010/2010-04/27/content_267377.htm

Feeding the UK's growing taste for Japanese cuisine, https://www.independent.co.uk/news/business/business-reporter/japan-supermarkets-food-cooking-sushi-b2372381.html

Feilden, Elois, *Japanese shochu sold in California under its own name for the first time,* https://www.thedrinksbusiness.com/2023/12/japanese-shochu-sold-in-california-under-its-own-name-for-the-first-time/

Fielding, Henry, *An Enquiry into the Causes of the late Increase of Robbers*

Fields, Laura, *Mexican Bourbon History*, https://www.dramdevotees.com/mexican-bourbon-history/

Flashback Friday – Frost 8/80 Dry White Whisky, https://bourbonveach.com/2020/11/06/flashback-friday-frost-8-80-dry-white-whisky/

Forbes, Ellie, *Bessie Williamson: The woman behind Laphroaig distillery,* https://www.scottishfield.co.uk/food-and-drink-2/bessie-williamson-the-woman-behind-laphroaig-distillery/

Fowler, Eliza, *A Present for Women Addicted to Drinking Adapted to all the different Stations of Life, from a Lady of Quality to a Common Servant*

Frost, Natasha, *How America Fell in Love With Vodka*, https://www.atlasobscura.com/articles/how-america-fell-in-love-with-vodka-smirnoff

Gardyne-Bruce, Tom, *Scotch Whisky: The Essential Guide for Single Malt Lovers* (Wellbeck Publishing, 2018)

Gardyne-Bruce, Tom, *Sweet Juice Of Success,* https://whiskymag.com/articles/sweet-juice-of-success/

Give it up for The Ada Coleman Project, the new initiative for women+ to help the entire industry, https://thecocktaillovers.com/give-it-up-for-the-ada-coleman-project-the-new-initiative-for-women-to-help-the-entire-industry/

Haig Whisky & Jameson – The Story Of The Whisky Cousins, https://www.haigwhisky.com/haig-whisky-jameson-history-whisky-cousins/

Halsam, Fiona, *Hogarth and the Art of Alcohol Abuse,* https://www.rcpe.ac.uk/heritage/hogarth-and-art-alcohol-abuse

Herlihy, Patricia, *The Alcoholic Empire: Vodka & Politics In Late Imperial Russia,* https://academic.oup.com/book/47706

Highland Park, https://Scotchwhisky.com/whiskypedia/1867/highland-park/

Highland Single Malt Scotch Whisky, https://www.thewhiskyexchange.com/c/313/highland-single-malt-Scotch-whisky

History Of Alcohol Distillation, https://www.copper-alembic.com/en/page/history-of-alcohol-distillation

History of Russian Vodka, https://www.bbc.co.uk/dna/mb6music/A871995

History of the Song: 'Rum and Coca-Cola', https://www.swingcityradio.com/2020/07/history-of-song-rum-and-coca-cola.html

History of Vodka in Russia, https://homedistiller.org/wiki/index.php/History_of_Vodka_in_Russia

Hite Jinro, https://en.namu.wiki/w/%ED%95%98%EC%9D%B4%ED%8A%B8%EC%A7%84%EB%A1%9C?from=%ED%95%98%EC%9D%B4%ED%8A%B8%20%EC%A7%84%EB%A1%9C

Hitejinro targets $362 mil. In overseas soju sales in 2030, https://www.koreatimes.co.kr/www/tech/2024/08/129_376851.html

Hollis, Patrick, '*Hopefully we'll open a few more bars soon' – Salford success story Seven Bro7hers on 10 years in business*, https://www.manchesterworld.uk/business/greater-manchester-beer-brewery-family-salford-interview-4655060

Huband, Michael, *Sake exports show progress towards key targets, according to JSS,* https://www.thedrinksbusiness.com/2024/02/sake-exports-show-progress-towards-key-targets-according-to-jss/

Japhe, Brad, *After 20 Years Of Illegal Mezcal, Founder John Rexer Talks What's Ahead,* https://www.forbes.com/sites/bradjaphe/2023/07/12/after-20-years-of-ilegal-mezcal-founder-john-rexer-talks-whats-ahead/

Jones, Michael, *The Life and Legacy of Tom Bullock*, https://www.gotolouisville.com/blog/the-life-and-legacy-of-tom-bullock/

KI NO BI – A Kyoto-style Pursuit of Perfection, https://theabsolutgroup.com/story/ki-no-bi-a-kyoto-style-pursuit-of-perfection

Koroysa: The History of Koryo, annals of kings, 918 – 1095

Laliberte, A Daniel Captain, *The Real McCoy*, https://www.usni.org/magazines/naval-history-magazine/2020/february/real-mccoy

Lascelles, Alice, *Being Harry Craddock*, https://punchdrink.com/articles/being-harry-craddock/

Lindenberger, Hudson, *CaskX Founder Jeremy Kasler On The Future Of Bourbon Investing*, https://www.forbes.com/sites/hudsonlindenberger/2024/03/19/jeremy-kasler-the-founder-of-cask-x-discusses-bourbon-investing/?sh=22d2b744222c

Lythgoe, Gertrude, *The Bahama Queen,* (Flat Hammock Press, 2006)

Lyman, Stephen, & Bunting, Chris, *The Complete Guide to Japanese Drinks: Sake, Shochu, Japanese Whisky, Beer, Cocktail and Other Beverages* (Tuttle Publishing, 2019), https://www.everand.com/book/415327522/Complete-Guide-to-Japanese-Drinks-Sake-Shochu-Japanese-Whisky-Beer-Wine-Cocktails-and-Other-Beverages

Maggie Campbell | Head Distiller, Privateer Rum, https://punchdrink.com/lookbook/maggie-campbell-head-distiller-privateer-rum/

Malczewski, Kate, *The big interview: Dwayne 'The Rock' Johnson, Teremana Tequila,* https://www.thespiritsbusiness.com/2022/01/the-big-interview-dwayne-the-rock-johnson-teremana-tequila/

Mays, Greg, *Meet Charles Tanqueray: History in a Bottle*, https://www.burn-blog.com/8554/meet-charles-tanqueray-history-in-a-bottle/

McCarthy, John, *Art, Love, And Mezcal: How Ron Cooper Sparked A Revolucion For Oaxaca's Smoky, Mysterious Spirit,* https://www.forbes.com/sites/johnmccarthy12/2018/04/16/art-love-and-mezcal-how-ron-cooper-sparked-a-revolucion-for-oaxacas-smoky-mysterious-spirit/

Meet Jerry Thomas, https://www.newyorkcity-eats.com/jerry-thomas

Meet The Distiller: Lesley Gracie, Hendricks Gin, https://www.theginguild.com/ginopedia/gin-distillers/lesley-gracie-hendricks-master-distiller/

Mee-yo, Kwon, *Soju is the most recognised Korean alcoholic drink, survey shows,* https://www.koreatimes.co.kr/www/culture/2024/07/135_374380.html

Mezcal History, https://www.pensadormezcal.com/blogs/journal/the-making-of-pensador-ensamble-batch-1

Mezcal Market Outlook from 2024 to 2034, https://www.futuremarketinsights.com/reports/mezcal-market

Mezcal Market Size, Share, and Industry Analysis, By Age (Mezcal Joven, Mezcal Reposado, and Mezcal Anejo), By Distribution Channel (On-premise and Off-premise), and Regional Forecast, 2024 – 2032, https://www.fortunebusinessinsights.com/mezcal-market-102652

Mezcal Story, https://mezcaldonavega.com/mezcal-story/

Minnick, Fred, *Bourbon: The Rise, Fall And Rebirth Of An American Whiskey* (Voyageur Press, 2016)

Morgan, Audrey, *What Is Bourbon? A Guide to America's Original Whiskey,* https://www.liquor.com/bourbon-whiskey-guide-7369244

Nieset, Lane, *Soju Explained: What Is It and How Do You Drink It?,* https://www.foodandwine.com/cocktails-spirits/korean-soju

O'Connell, Adam and Mountain, Jake, *How is Rum Made?,* https://www.masterofmalt.com/guides/rum-guides/how-is-rum-made/

Park, Hyunhee, *Soju: A Global History* (Cambridge University Press, 2021)

Pellegrini, Christopher, *The Shochu Handbook: An Introduction To Japan's Indigenous Distilled Drink* (Telemachus Press, 2020)

Pettid, J. Michael, *Korean Cuisine: An Illustrated History* (London: Reaktion Books, 2008)

Piercy, Joseph, *A Rum Tale: Spirit of The New World* (The History Press, 2019)

Pierini, Marco, *The Origins of Alcoholic Distillation in the West: 4. The Medical School of Salerno,* https://www.gotrum.com/the-rum-university/rum-in-history/the-origins-of-alcoholic-distillation-in-the-west-4-the-medical-school-of-solerno/

Quote Origin: Truth Is Stranger than Fiction, But It Is Because Fiction Is Obliged to Stick to Possibilities; Truth Isn't,

https://quoteinvestigator.com/2015/07/15/truth-stranger/

Ramsay, Stuart, *Booker Noe*, https://whiskymag.com/articles/booker-noe/

Reed, Patrick, *Vintage Ad Archive: Tequila For All!,* https://www.alcoholprofessor.com/blog-posts/blog/2014/08/22/vintage-ad-archive-tequila-for-all

Ren, Yuan, *5 Drunken Poems To Read While Drinking Chinese Liquor,* https://theculturetrip.com/asia/china/articles/5-drunken-poems-to-read-while-drinking-chinese-liquor

Reeves, Timothy, *Grant, Babcock and the Whiskey Ring,* https://www.archives.gov/publications/prologue/2000/fall/whiskey-ring-1

Russell, Ian, *Famous Whisky Drinkers: Mark Twain*, https://Scotchwhisky.com/magazine/famous-whisky-drinkers/6110/famous-whisky-drinkers-mark-twain/

Sake Kasu Shochu, https://honkakushochu-awamori.jp/english/professional/shochu-production-method/sake-kasu-shochu/

Sanders, Minnot, *Famous Bar Maids Who Worked at the Same Bar Twenty Years Without Speaking, Retire* https://www.coloradohistoricnewspapers.org/cgi-bin/colorado?a=d&d=adT19260216.2.2

Sandhaus, Derek, *Baijiu: The Essential Guide To Chinese Spirits* (Viking Australia, 2015)

Sandhaus, Derek, *The Panamanian connection*, https://300shots.wordpress.com/2012/01/31/the-panamanian-connection/

Satsuma Sweet Potatoes and the Man who Inadvertently Became a God, https://www.morethantokyo.com/satsuma-sweet-potatoes-man-became-god/

Shiltsev, Vladamir, *Dmitri Mendeleev and the science of vodka,* https://pubs.aip.org/physicstoday/online/5317/Dmitri-Mendeleev-and-the-science-of-vodka

Simpson, Scott, *History and Mythology of Polish Vodka: 1270–2007,* https://www.academia.edu/26879218/_History_and_Mythology_of_Polish_Vodka_1270_2007_Food_and_History_vol_8_no_1_2010_pp_121_148

Smith, D. Gavin, *Whisky Heroes: James Buchanan*, https://Scotchwhisky.com/magazine/whisky-heroes/10632/james-buchanan/

Smith, D. Gavin, *Whisky Heroes: Tommy Dewar*, https://Scotchwhisky.com/magazine/whisky-heroes/11735/tommy-dewar/

Smugglers' Britain: Guide-Book: South-East England, http://www.smuggling.co.uk/gazetteer_se_12.html

Songgi, Cho and Kimok, Yu, *A Study of the Establishment of the Identity of Soju's Alcohol Content* (Korea Alcohol Research Centre, 2010)

Stern, Abby, *Japanese Liquor Aren't Just A Splashy Cocktail Trend,* https://www.thezoereport.com/living/japanese-liquor

Stevenson, Steve, *The Cocktail Creationist,* https://nymag.com/nymetro/news/bizfinance/biz/features/10816/

Sutcliffe, Theodora, *Harry Craddock*, https://www.diffordsguide.com/encyclopedia/2345/people/harry-craddock

Sutcliffe, Theodora, '*The Only William' Schmidt,*
https://www.diffordsguide.com/encyclopedia/2964/people/the-only-william-schmidt

Sutcliffe, Theodora, *Jerry Thomas*, https://www.diffordsguide.com/encyclopedia/2882/people/jerry-thomas

Sutcliffe, Theodora, *Tom Bullock*, https://www.diffordsguide.com/encyclopedia/2953/people/tom-bullock

Sutcliffe, *Theodora, William T. Boothby, https://www.diffordsguide.com/encyclopedia/2963/people/william-t-boothby*

Taft, Howard William, *Decision on the Meaning of the Term 'Whisky' Under the Pure Food Act and the Proper Regulations for Branding Various Kinds of Whisky Under the Internal Revenue Act,* https://www.presidency.ucsb.edu/documents/decision-the-meaning-the-term-whisky-under-the-pure-food-act-and-the-proper-regulations

Tasci, Necat Ufuk, *Hayyan: the 9th-century polymath who brought scientific temper to alchemy,* https://www.trtworld.com/magazine/hayyan-the-9th-century-polymath-who-brought-scientific-temper-to-alchemy-12738769

Taylor, Elise, *How Yola Jimenez Is Making Mezcal With Women's Empowerment in Mind,* https://www.vogue.com/article/yola-jimenez-yola-mezcal

The Absolut Company (Destilleriet Nobbelov), https://www.diffordsguide.com/producers/214/the-absolut-company-destilleriet-nobbelov

The Big Four Distilling Companies, https://bourbonveach.com/2020/06/08/the-big-four-distilling-companies

The Captivating History of Smirnoff Vodka: From Russia to Global, https://junosliquor.com/f/the-captivating-history-of-smirnoff-vodka-from-russia-to-global

The Chinese Revolution of 1911, https://history.state.gov/milestones/1899-1913/chinese-rev

The fall of the Qing dynasty, https://www.bbc.co.uk/bitesize/articles

The Fascinating History of Amami Kokuto Shochu, https://amamikokutoshochu.jp/history

The Flowing Bowl By The Only William (1892), http://euvslibrary.com/?p=341

The Future of Sustainable Bourbon, https://www.wired.com/sponsored/story/the-future-of-sustainable-bourbon/

The History Of Grog, https://sailorjerry.com/en-gb/blog/post/the-storied-history-of-the-drink-we-call-grog

The History of Shochu, https://honkakushochu-awamori.jp/english/basic/history-of-shochu

The History of Tequila in North America Part 1: Pre-Hispanic Era – 1700, https://www.casamexicotequila.com/the-history-of-tequila-in-north-america-part-1

The History of Tequila in North America Part 2: 1700 – Present Day, https://www.casamexicotequila.com/the-history-of-tequila-in-north-america-part-2

The History of Vodka: From Rough Spirit To Refined Future, https://www.greygoose.com/en-gb/stories/vodka-essentials/history-of-vodka.html

The legend of tequila with worm, https://www.beverage-world.com/en/newsdetail/the-legend-of-tequila-with-worm

The making of ... Hoju Soju, https://hunterand.co/blog/the-making-of-hoju-soju

The Story of the Absolut bottle and brand, https://theabsolutgroup.com/legacy/post/lo-smith-english/the-story-of-the-absolut-bottle-and-brand/

Toasting a Korean-American Renaissance with Yobo Soju, https://www.linkedin.com/pulse/toasting-korean-american-renaissance-yobo-soju-/

To the mortal memory of Madam Geneva, https://www.britishmuseum.org/collection/object/P_1868-0808-3580

Veach, Michael, *The Future Of New Distillers,* https://bourbonveach.com/2024/05/13/the-future-of-new-distilleries/

Welcome to Smugglers' Town, https://www.yorkshire.com/inspiration/features/welcome-to-smugglers-town/

Whisky Making, https://www.Scotchwhiskyexperience.co.uk/about/about-whisky/whisky-making

Who shaved $250bn from Kweichow Moutai's market value? https://www.economist.com/business/2024/06/27/who-shaved-250bn-from-kweichow-moutais-market-value?giftId=86f576fe-126d-4b96-b122-31aee482c795

Who was Cleo Lythgoe?, https://lythgoebourbon.com/who-was-cleo/

Whymark, Bethany, *The gin-making siblings who built Sis4ers Distillery*, https://gin-mag.com/2021/03/25/sis4ers-distillery-founders-are-doing-it-for-themselves/

Wilkerson, Kevin, *How Prohibition Helped Tijuana Become A Nightlife Boomtown*, https://www.pubclub.com/destinations/mexico/tijuana/how-prohibition-helped-tijuana-become-a-nightlife-boomtown/

Wondrich, David, *IMBIBE!* (Penguin Group, 2007)

Wondrich, David, *Masters of Mixology: William Schmidt*, https://www.liquor.com/articles/masters-of-mixology-william-schmidt/

Wondrich, David, *Schmidt, William*, https://spiritsanddistilling.com/dictionary/id/acref-9780199311132-e-77/

Wondrich, David, *Tequila Daisy*, https://www.liquor.com/recipes/tequila-daisy/

Yeung, Gavin, *Why Is Shochu Suddenly Everywhere?*, https://www.tatlerasia.com/dining/drinks/the-new-age-of-shochu

Youngman, Angela, *The Weird & Wonderful Story Of Gin: From The seventeenth Century To The Present Day* (Pen And Sword History, 2022)

Zielinski, Tyler, *What Does Bottled-In-Bond Mean?*, https://www.foodandwine.com/cocktails-spirits/what-does-bottled-in-bond-mean